T0333965

Managing the Marketplace

This book charts the history of Australian retail developments as well as examining the social and cultural dimensions of shopping in Australia.

In the second half of the twentieth century, the shopping centre spread from America around the world. Australia was a very early adopter, and produced a unique shopping centre model. Situating Australian retail developments within a broader international and historical context, *Managing the Marketplace* demonstrates the ways that local conditions shape global retail forms. Knowledge transfer from Europe and America to Australia was a consistent feature of the Australian retail industry across the twentieth century. By critically examining the strengths and weaknesses of Australian retail firms' strategies across time, and drawing on the voices of both business elites and ordinary people, the book not only unearths the forgotten stories of Australian retail, it offers new insights into the opportunities and challenges that confront the sector today, both nationally and internationally.

This book will be of interest to all scholars and practitioners of retail, marketing, business history and economic geography, as well as social and cultural history.

Matthew Bailey is a lecturer in the Department of Modern History at Macquarie University with a research interest in urban, business and retail history.

Routledge Studies in the History of Marketing

Edited by Mark Tadajewski and Brian D. G. Jones

It is increasingly acknowledged that an awareness of marketing history and the history of marketing thought is relevant for all levels of marketing teaching and scholarship. Marketing history includes, but is not limited to, the histories of advertising, retailing, channels of distribution, product design and branding, pricing strategies, and consumption behaviour – all studied from the perspective of companies, industries, or even whole economies. The history of marketing thought examines marketing ideas, concepts, theories, and schools of marketing thought including the lives and times of marketing thinkers.

This series aims to be the central location for the publication of historical studies of marketing theory, thought and practice, and welcomes contributions from scholars from all disciplines that seek to explore some facet of marketing and consumer practice in a rigorous and scholarly fashion. It will also consider historical contributions that are conceptually and theoretically well-conceived, that engage with marketing theory and practice, in any time period, in any country.

3 Pioneering African-American Women in the Advertising Business
Biographies of MAD Black WOMEN
Judy Foster Davis

4 A History of American Consumption
Threads of Meaning, Gender, and Resistance
Terrence H. Witkowski

5 The Foundations of Marketing Thought
The Influence of the German Historical School
Mark Tadajewski and Brian D. G. Jones

6 Managing the Marketplace
Reinventing Shopping Centres in Post-War Australia
Matthew Bailey

For more information about this series, please visit: www.routledge.com/ Routledge-Studies-in-the-History-of-Marketing/book-series/RSHM

Managing the Marketplace

Reinventing Shopping Centres in
Post-War Australia

Matthew Bailey

LONDON AND NEW YORK

First published 2020
by Routledge
2 Park Square, Milton Park, Abingdon, Oxon OX14 4RN

and by Routledge
52 Vanderbilt Avenue, New York, NY 10017

Routledge is an imprint of the Taylor & Francis Group, an Informa business

British Library Cataloguing-in-Publication Data
A catalogue record for this book is available from the British Library

Library of Congress Cataloging-in-Publication Data
Names: Bailey, Matthew (Historian), author.
Title: Managing the marketplace: reinventing shopping
centres in post-war Australia / Matthew Bailey.
Description: Abingdon, Oxon; New York, NY: Routledge, 2020. |
Series: Routledge studies in the history of marketing; 6 |
Includes bibliographical references and index.
Identifiers: LCCN 2020003847 (print) | LCCN 2020003848 (ebook)
Subjects: LCSH: Shopping malls–Australia–History–20th century. |
Retail trade–Australia–History–20th century.
Classification: LCC HF5430.6.A8 B35 2020 (print) |
LCC HF5430.6.A8 (ebook) | DDC 381/.11099409045–dc23
LC record available at https://lccn.loc.gov/2020003847
LC ebook record available at https://lccn.loc.gov/2020003848

ISBN: 978-1-138-32302-5 (hbk)
ISBN: 978-0-367-50055-9 (pbk)
ISBN: 978-0-429-45165-2 (ebk)

Typeset in Bembo
by Newgen Publishing UK

For Jaymie

Contents

Figures

Tables

Acknowledgements

My first thanks, always and forever, are to Jaymie. Your ongoing love, support, jokes, smarts and affection are everything. The graphs and help with the title are the icing on the cake. Davor, Rasmus, Felix, thanks for the good times. I love you! To all my friends: hanging out makes life sweet. See you next weekend. I've had many great colleagues. Alison, Bridget and Hsu-Ming, your support and friendship over the years has been invaluable. Thank you! Robert, working and writing on cultural business history with you has taught me a great deal. Thanks for the collaboration and mentorship. It means a great deal to me. To all my students over the years. You make coming to work fun. I've learnt a lot from you all. A number of people who work in the retail property industry made the time to do interviews. I haven't quoted everyone in depth, but you all contributed to my understanding of the industry and its changes over time. I appreciate the time you took to discuss this history. I'm grateful for permission granted by *Urban History* to repurpose material from two articles (2015 and 2020 respectively) in Chapters 3 and 8. Coles and Myer both granted permission to reproduce images. Librarians in the state libraries around the country have been unfailingly helpful and knowledgeable. Particular thanks go to Lois McEvey and Greg Gerrand at the State Library of Victoria, and Bruce Carter at the State Library of New South Wales. My thanks also to everyone writing about retail history. Your work was vital for the development of this book. It's a privilege to make a small contribution to such a vibrant and fascinating field of research. Lastly, Bev Kingston, you read a lot of this over the years and especially in the last couple of months. I've benefited enormously from the time you invested and have loved all of our chats about this, that and the other.

Introduction

In the early 1950s, an American commentator declared that the "sudden mushrooming of suburban shopping centres" was one of the most fascinating developments in his country's post-war building boom. "Where," J. Ross McKeever asked, "did these come from and why?"[1] Retailers across the globe were equally intrigued, although less about the origins of this radical new retail form, than for the opportunities it might provide in their own countries. In Australia, there was both optimism and caution. Retail firms were keenly aware of shopping centre construction in both America and Europe, but plans to introduce the fomat remained speculative. This changed under the stress of demographic, economic and technological pressures. Australia's first shopping centre opened in the Brisbane suburb of Chermside in 1957 and was quickly followed by developments in the other state capital cities. Shopping centres were established nationally by the end of the 1960s, extended their reach in the 1970s and 1980s, and diversified through expansions from the late 1980s onwards. This book traces this history, describing the emergence and growth of a retail property industry that did not exist in Australia when McKeever posed his query.

Shopping centres changed the form of Australia's urban geographies and the everyday activities of its population. They evolved into important hubs in the built environment, acting as distribution points for retail firms, social centres for communities and sites of mass, conspicuous consumption. For consumers, shopping centres became places to visit, browse, purchase goods, socialise and congregate. Today they remain among the biggest buildings, most popularly visited sites, largest centres of employment, and most intensive sites of commercial activity in Australian cities, suburbs and regional towns. By 2018, more than 1,630 shopping centres had been built in Australia. They accounted for 46 per cent of retail space, garnering approximately $141 billion in retail sales — equivalent to 7.4 per cent of Australia's gross domestic product. Two-thirds of all retail employees now work within shopping centres, and the biggest attract more than 20 million customers a year.[2]

Australia also changed the shopping centre. The country's high level of urbanisation, class structure and demographic mix, as well as the needs of its big retail firms and the guiding constraints of planning regimes, produced a unique shopping centre form. A more comprehensive and effective "one-stop-shop" than its American progenitor, the Australian shopping centre was positioned to a very broad, price-conscious middle market. As such it was an early application to a planned retail environment of the retail strategies that came to characterise the mass market globally. In other countries these were applied through stand-alone retail formats like the supermarket, hypermarket and discount department store. In Australia, retail formats like these were absorbed into the shopping centre itself, allowing it to capture sales from a wide demographic spectrum, as well as catering to a very broad range of shopping needs. The highly productive and efficient Australian shopping centre model was later exported back to America and Europe by Australian firms like Westfield and Lend Lease.

As the first extensive history of Australian shopping centres, this book focuses on key features, notable examples and broad trends. It provides a map for more detailed work on retail property and retail firms, both small and large, as well as retailing in rural and regional areas of Australia. Here, attention is paid to the state capital cities where shopping centres rose and grew most strongly in response to population densities and spending power. The book begins by charting international predecessors of shopping centres – the market halls, arcades and department stores that emerged in Europe during the nineteenth century. Each of these retail formats responded to developments in productive and distribution technologies, changes in the spending capacity of populations, demographic movements and urbanism. Reflecting a growing sophistication in colonial consumption practices, Australia, too, developed arcades and department stores.

The scale of Australia's big city stores, their vertically integrated supply lines, administrative systems and marketing capabilities allowed them to dominate urban discretionary retailing, with many extending their reach into regional areas via mail order catalogues. Their power, though, rested on centralised urban geographies serviced by public transport networks that in the mid twentieth century experienced profound disruption with the widespread adoption of the automobile. As it did in other countries, the car broadened the geographic spread of urban populations, challenging the centralised structure of urban retailing. Difficulties accessing stores in central areas that became plagued by traffic and parking problems created an impetus for suburban retail development that first supplemented and then challenged city retailing.

In the United States, with supermarkets and discount stores flourishing and suburban retail growing apace, the great city department stores lost market share and faced stagnating sales. They turned to branch store decentralisation, including through the development of shopping centres. In Australia, as the car populated the urban fringe and suburban shopping strips expanded, city stores also began losing ground. Suburban retail, though, began to face its own problems. Traffic congestion and parking shortages constrained access to shops and reduced the amenity of shopping. How and where customers might park became a crucial consideration for any large retail store, creating a demand for architectural innovation. Observing the same problems being met in the

United States, Australian retailers borrowed the format for co-locating car and pedestrian traffic being developed there.

Shopping centres arrived in Australia heralded but untested. Many established retailers were reticent, cautious of incurring the unknown costs of moving first into such an expensive and transformative format. Australia's urban topology had not sprawled to nearly the same degree as in the United States. Populations were more heavily concentrated in state capital cities. Car ownership levels were lower. As a result, the early pattern of shopping centre construction in Australia became subject to specific circumstances and individual decision-making. Initial experiments proved successful, however, and development gained momentum by the early 1960s. The competitive matrix of Australian retailing also played a key role as retail property development became a means of expanding market share and an avenue for interstate growth. City department stores built the biggest shopping centres, while a host of small entrepreneurial developers were also highly active.

Australia's largest variety store chains, Coles and Woolworths (which was not associated with the American chain), horizontally expanded into food retailing in the late 1950s. They rolled out supermarket chains as shopping centres spread across the country during the 1960s. Developers needed these chains to drive customer traffic to their centres; the chains needed developers to acquire sites in good locations with attached parking facilities. The two have shared a symbiotic trajectory since The prominence of this private development, however, has tended to obscure the early role of public investment. Between the late 1950s and the mid 1960s, public housing authorities followed European trends, placing planned shopping precincts at the heart of their developments. In the process they contributed to the prevalence of the idea in Australia that shopping centres were important community hubs.

By the mid 1960s, shopping centres were sparsely distributed but firmly established in Australia, although they did not follow the latest American trends. Most centres still contained open-air sections and, aside from the Myer department store's massive Chadstone centre outside of Melbourne, the scale of construction remained relatively modest. By the second half of the decade, however, centres were more likely to be fully enclosed and the largest matched or surpassed Chadstone in size. This represented a transformation in shopping environments as well as the nature of shopping. Open or partially enclosed malls were contiguous to at least some degree with traditional shopping strips, were exposed to local conditions, and more readily evinced cultural variation. The newer shopping centres were promoted as self-contained worlds, separated from their external environs. This provided more control for developers, allowed less "spillage" of retail sales to the high street, and segregated shopping centres as spaces for distinct consumer communities. This is the model that, with refinements, became characteristic of retail for Australia's mass middle market. Only recently have shopping centres begun turning back towards the street, as they are remodelled to meet changing consumer tastes and to combat online retailing with a more open and experientially oriented architecture.

The largest enclosed shopping centres in the 1960s were promoted as cities in their own right, providing spaces for sociability, employment and an expansive retail offer. For many Australians, they were exciting, vibrant places in which to spend time. Teenagers were particularly enamoured with the social, and even romantic possibilities they facilitated. In one instance, a chance meeting inside a shopping centre led to a marriage reception inside the same centre a few months later. The bride was one of many young retail workers who found her first job inside the new cities of consumption. Local jobs were also embraced by women returning to the workforce after raising children, melding paid work with domestic roles. The latter included shopping, a labour-intensive chore that shopping centre marketers reimagined as a leisurely, pleasurable activity. Such marketing obscured the work involved in most shopping trips, but also reflected the utility of the new shopping centre format. As one-stop-shops with air-conditioning, toilets and baby change rooms, they were far more convenient for women shopping with children. A number of the large early centres included child-minding services that enabled women to shop and socialise without children in tow. Socially constructed roles, and the design of shopping centres to target them, thus resulted in largely feminised populations of customers and retail workers. Shopping centres today remain deeply gendered. Women are still the predominant shoppers and most likely floor staff, and are relatively poorly represented at the executive and board level of retail and retail property firms.

In the 1970s, Australian retailing underwent another evolution, again prompted by developments in the United States. There, variety and department stores had been losing market share to a new retail format since the early 1960s. The discount department store (DDS) used the supermarket innovation of self-service to sell merchandise sold in traditional department stores. Australia's three largest retailers – Coles, Myer and Woolworths – all introduced versions of the DDS format. They did this through formal and informal engagement with American firms, obtaining invaluable knowledge and operational expertise.[3] Local planning regimes, though, prevented the American approach of building stand-alone stores. This contributed to the creation of a unique Australian retail form, the sub-regional shopping centre, which deployed DDSs as customer-attracting anchor stores. The spread of these mid-tier centres across suburban areas and country towns solidified the gains made by big retail and retail property in the 1960s.

In the late 1980s, Australia's biggest shopping centres began to be repositioned as leisure destinations. Design aesthetics were refined, entertainment precincts featuring food courts and multiplex cinemas introduced.[4] This served the needs of cinema exhibition chains by providing suburban sites that had established infrastructure and car parking. For landlords cinemas broadened the function of centres, offering a new form of anchor and a tap into the growing leisure market. The provision of entertainment and eating facilities coincided with the deregulation of trading hours and rekindled the social dimensions of shopping.

This expanded role was one impetus for redevelopment strategies that expanded the footprint of established shopping centres. Another was the opportunity to include increasing numbers of specialty retail tenants. In the 1960s, specialty retail had a distinctly local flavour and there were a limited number of prospects that developers could pursue to fill out tenancy rosters. The specialty retail sector grew substantially through the 1970s and 1980s, partly as a result of the opportunities afforded by the shopping centre itself. Franchising fuelled further growth. The result was a vast palette of retailers from which leasing executives could curate tenancy mixes. This appealed to consumers, generated significant income for landlords, and broadened the mix of stakeholders in the industry. National chains had developed in a range of retail categories, but there were also many new small business people entering the field. Some of these had little retail experience. The major shopping centre firms, in contrast, had evolved into national enterprises and development was funded by large institutional investors. Power differentials between these groups resulted in tension, acrimony and allegations that market power was being abused. After numerous inquiries and attempts at industry self-regulation, retail tenancy legislation was enacted across Australia between the mid 1980s and the mid 1990s to protect the interests of smaller operators. This slowed but did not stop complaints. Government inquiries and amendments to legislation continue to this day because of misunderstandings about the business model of shopping centres, and because disparities in power are so difficult to address in a retail landscape where shopping centres have become so dominant.

This book explains this dominance by following the paths that led to it. Tracing these now, when the shopping centre's competitive advantages are being questioned for the first time, is instructive. The shopping centre succeeded and surpassed the department store as a format for retail distribution because it was a better fit for the private-transport city. Today, the shopping centre belongs to a mature industry facing another global evolution in distribution, online retailing. To date it has adapted successfully, while the retailers it houses have integrated e-commerce into their own operations. Further challenges loom, including to consumerism itself. However, while many malls in America are dying, Australian shopping centres largely enjoy continued success. Their history, and the local forces that shaped them, help us understand this situation as well as the format's future prospects. The context for this history, in turn, extends further back, to other countries and to earlier marketplace formats, including the market halls, arcades and department stores of nineteenth-century Europe.

Notes

1   McKeever, "Technical Bulletin No. 20," 145.
2   Figures exclude Homemaker/Large Format Retail centres. Shopping Centre Council of Australia, www.scca.org.au/industry-information/key-facts; Roy Morgan, Australia's Top 20 favourite Shopping Centres, 10 December 2015, www.roymorgan. com/findings/6598-top-20-shopping-centres-in-australia-2015-201512092342; *SMH*, 20 September 2016.
3   Bailey, "Absorptive Capacity"; Bailey, "Marketing to the Big Middle."
4   Bailey, "Shopping for Entertainment."

1 The prehistory of the shopping centre

The shopping centre, Victor Gruen and Larry Smith wrote evocatively in 1960, "is one of the few new building types created in our time." Gruen was an architect of Viennese origin, who had migrated to the United States in 1938; Smith, an economist and market researcher who worked with Gruen on shopping centre and urban development projects. Gruen is credited as one of the great innovators in retail architecture, and was the first to fully enclose an introverted, inward-facing shopping mall.[1] In promoting their vision of the urban future, Gruen and Smith situated the shopping mall within a long historical trajectory of commercial activity. In *Shopping Towns USA*, they mapped a brief history of retail responses to environmental and economic conditions, that began with the markets of the ancient world and ended with the modern shopping centre.[2] Their potted history included the Greek *stoa*, Roman forum, medieval market square, the town centre in Renaissance Europe, the congested jumble of industrial city markets, and the shopping strips that grew around European and North American suburban rail lines. "Buying and selling," they declared, "is as old as mankind."[3] The mall was new, but shared similarities with, and drew on features of, the arcades and marketplaces that preceded it.[4]

For Gruen, Smith and their contemporaries, the shopping centre was consciously developed in response to forces that characterised the post-war boom in America, Australia and other industrialised countries. In particular, it was built to accommodate the widespread adoption of the automobile, to service the rapidly expanding suburban populations that accompanied this, and to capture the spending potential of high-growth post-war consumer economies.[5] Early American industry literature defined modern shopping centres as architecturally unified structures containing groups of stores that were planned, developed, managed and marketed as single entities, and provided off-street parking for their customers.[6] These features were developed by entrepreneurs responding to market demand and business opportunities in a time of rapid and profound urban change. They also followed, as Gruen and Smith understood, from preceding retail structures and innovations.[7]

In premodern cities, "markets were the central nodes of the social metabolism, the link to the rural hinterland and the fundamental mechanism of food supply."[8] They provisioned the city, shaped its form and drove economic activity within and around it. By the eighteenth century, however, this system of distribution was coming under strain. Urban growth and an increasing demand for food and manufactured products produced congestion and overcrowding. Open-air markets became seen as disorderly, host to disreputable characters and "ungovernable street culture".[9] Towards the end of the century, a variety of architectural approaches were trialed to control commercial activity and separate it from the street. By the early nineteenth century these took the form of purpose built, large-scale, fully enclosed market halls. Beginning in the United Kingdom and France, the concept spread across Europe. Often vast in scale, they were a conscious design choice towards improving the efficiency of distribution, the rationalisation of public space, and the regulation of social behaviour. The first enclosed urban markets mostly sold food, but over time the larger halls evolved to sell a range of other goods, including crockery, hardware, books, and even bicycles.[10]

Schmiechen and Carls describe market halls as "the first large-scale, environmentally controlled general-merchandise retail" spaces.[11] Where suburban shopping centres in the mid twentieth century were positioned in contrast to the noise and chaos of the city, nineteenth-century market halls were designed in opposition to unruly, crowded and noisy street markets.[12] "Prohibition of street-selling, sanitary reforms and the erection of market halls often went hand in hand."[13] Undesirables were excluded, and middle-class codes of behaviour were enforced to provide a space that was considered respectable and safe.[14] Market halls attracted custom on the strength of retail agglomeration – the clustering together of multiple retail outlets to provide a wide range of goods and bustling commercial activity. They also offered protection from the weather and benefited from a unified management structure that monitored quality control and facilitated cohesion.[15] As with shopping centres later (and in markets for centuries previously), commerce intersected with social and cultural activity.[16] The vast Smithfield Market, constructed in Manchester in 1846, for example,

> was a feature of every worker's Saturday night out. A source of cheap food and free entertainment, it catered to a crowd that was as much in search of Sunday dinner as of a bit of a frolic on Saturday nights … amid a blaze of gaslights, thousands of families marched up and down the aisles and traversed the galleries, inspecting food and other goods, searching for bargains, and collecting a week's worth of news and sights.[17]

Other retail property innovations that generated competitive advantages from agglomeration and forms of regulation and control also emerged. Bazaars housed numerous stalls with open counters lining long passages on multiple floors. Stalls were rented from the building's owner, who set policies for the bazaar such as fixed pricing, cash purchases and commissions on sales.[18] Arcades were more elaborate constructions, providing a form of public space protected from traffic and the weather, and a distribution point for the expanding luxury goods industry.[19] The Galeries de Bois was a notable early example. Part of the Palais Royal built in Paris in 1786, its covered passageways were lined with shops and illuminated by skylights. More arcades, both modest and grand, followed in Paris, London, other European cities and the United States. By the second half of the nineteenth century they were prominent symbols of modernity in urban landscapes.[20] In 1852, the *Illustrated Guide to Paris* commented that:

> These arcades, a recent invention of industrial luxury, are glass-roofed, marble-paneled corridors extending through whole blocks of buildings, whose owners have joined together for such enterprises. Lining both sides of these corridors, which get their light from above, are the most elegant shops, so that the arcade is a city, a world in miniature, in which customers will find everything they need.[21]

The success and longevity of arcades was uneven and dependent on a range of local conditions. Broadly, as a retail format, however, some of their competitive advantages began to erode as conditions around them changed. Improvements in urban streetscapes reduced the need for clean, mud-and-traffic-free pedestrian thoroughfares. In this context, those in less favourable locations failed to generate sufficient custom. There was also a conflict between their different functions, "the shopkeepers' desire for regulation and respectability clashing with the status of the arcades as a place of entertainment open to everyone."[22] This tension remained an ongoing issue for modern retail environments. In response, attempts at regulation, security and surveillance became embedded operational logics to condition visitor compliance with the behaviours and norms considered conducive to commercial activity. In the second half of the nineteenth century, arcades also faced new forms of competition, including from department stores – a concentrated retail format that symbolised the commercial might of cities for almost a hundred years, until challenged by the suburban shopping mall in the 1950s.

Department stores

In terms of their retail function, twentieth-century American regional shopping centres resembled arcades with department stores attached to draw greater customer traffic.[23] The department store was thus a critical component of postwar, pre-planned retail property environments. Its historical evolution also contributed to innovations and systems that shaped most other forms of later retailing. Accounts of its history have tended to focus on iconic, large-scale urban stores that catered to a rising middle class. But department stores took a variety of forms, operated on a range of scales and appealed to different classes of customers. Many smaller firms played important roles in the commercial and social worlds of provincial and regional towns.[24] This was a similarly broad geographic and demographic landscape as that covered later by shopping centres in the American and Australian markets. For both retail formats, transportation technology and the spending power of the trade areas in which they were located were determinative of their form and function.

In the first half of the nineteenth century, the mobility of populations continued to dictate the scale and scope of urban retailing. The largest city stores rarely employed more than a hundred people. With the advent of horse-drawn buses and streetcar public transport, however, trading areas expanded and sales volumes increased. This attracted more retail investment in urban cores, leading to concentrations of volume-oriented firms, which in turn increased land values and rents. One response, by some firms, was to extend the depth and height of their selling space, usually by acquiring surrounding premises. This created larger enterprises selling on multiple floors.[25] "Monster shops" in England and *magasins de nouveautés* in France emerged as large-scale, dry-goods retail operations forming the genesis for the later evolution of department stores.[26]

Many of the large retailers that arose in this environment began as drapery stores – specialist cloth merchants that expanded to sell other textile products.[27] Drapers were uniquely positioned because they sold a product category that was the first to be transitioned into mass production during the Industrial Revolution. This encouraged specialisation, enabling retailers to focus their resources on distribution and marketing techniques. The larger drapers, particularly those that were centrally located, moved horizontally into new product categories. Product diversification began with other related goods such as furnishings, furniture and carpets but spread until the larger stores attained concentrated selling power across a broad range of product categories.[28] By the second half of the nineteenth century, large-scale, purpose-built stores that stocked goods meeting a full range of needs for the home as well as ready-made clothing, organised into separate departments, were being constructed in major cities across Europe, North America and Australasia.

While keeping in mind the gradual introduction of selling techniques across time, place and retail formats, large urban department stores coalesced a number of retail innovations and logics of scale. A new focus on turnover was critical.[29] This meant attracting more people into stores, encouraging return visitation, stimulating desire and leveraging the opportunities afforded by size. Entrance to stores did not oblige customers to make purchases. Advertising, once viewed with suspicion, was deployed to excite demand. Inside stores, display was enhanced to model combinations of goods. Provision of credit was eschewed in preference to cash sales. Fixed and marked prices limited the decisions staff had to make on the floor. This simplified transactions, which were also made more efficient by technologies such as pneumatic tubes that carried cash and receipts around stores. Staff training schemes reinforced service cultures and inculcated sales techniques. Policies of exchange or reimbursement promised satisfaction and generated return visits. An understanding developed about the relationship between turnover, margins and profits. This aligned with intensive production processes that were making goods cheaper and faster than previously possible. As the scope of merchandise grew, organisation by departments became entrenched and hierarchical systems were developed to manage them.[30] By 1900, the big urban department stores in a number of markets across the globe were complex organisations that had diversified significantly from their drapery backgrounds.[31]

The big city store should be understood not just as a retail type, but as a social arena. Department stores evolved in an environment where public space as a whole was under transformation. Buildings such as exhibition halls, arcades, museums and railway stations offered new sites for performative public display. The major city department stores similarly offered a public arena in which affluent and middle-class consumers could parade, and experience shopping as a leisurely and fashionable activity. Facilities like powder rooms, tea rooms, restaurants, auditoriums and art galleries were introduced, positioning stores as sites of indulgence and leisurely shopping.[32] The city stores provided exhibitions and entertainment, deployed sophisticated display techniques and offered comparison shopping of goods collated from around the globe.[33] In doing so they created immersive retail experiences that linked social aspiration with consumer goods. This elevated the retail experience in ways that were later incorporated into the biggest shopping malls in post-war consumer societies, including Australia, where retailing had always been characterised by judicious appropriation and adaptation of foreign retail models.

Retailing in the Australian public transport city

As was the case elsewhere, city markets were important retail and social sites in Australia during the nineteenth century. Graeme Davison argues that colonial Melbourne "was a city built around markets," beginning with the Western Market, which sold goods that had been cleared for importation at the nearby Customs House in Flinders Street. Other Melbourne markets, including the Eastern Market and Queen Victoria Market, were established later. Similarities with European markets are readily identifiable. Products were diverse, both second-hand and new, hand-made as well as manufactured, usually unpackaged. Prices were established by negotiation. The environment was noisy, chaotic, relatively unregulated and within walking distance of densely populated housing. These were sites of both commerce and entertainment as well as, at times, political unrest and protest.[34]

As in Britain, these sites of apparent disorder, which engendered a range of "nuisances" challenging respectability and the social order, attracted the attention of reformers.[35] The solution was, similarly, enclosure and regulation. Through the course of the nineteenth century, established markets were covered or closed in. By-laws and controls were introduced to regulate space and selling practices. New internalised markets were also developed. In Sydney, the Queen Victoria Building (QVB) replaced the city's central markets in the 1890s. While many market activities had already moved to other parts of the city, the new building was constructed after years of agitation about the noise, smell and unruly activity emanating from the heart of Sydney's commercial district. Although some market activities were retained in the basement of the QVB, its Romanesque design broke with the site's history, presenting the city with a lavish and ornately decorated three-story arcade.[36] Its construction formed part of a wave of arcade development in Australia, which had begun in Melbourne some forty years earlier. The Queens (1853) and The Royal (1869), like the QVB, were given appellations that the colonial imagination linked with class, taste and sophistication. Many others with similarly European titles were built during the 1870s and 1880s in both Melbourne and Sydney. This was a retail response to the economic activity and population growth generated by Australia's gold rushes, and the expansion of the wool, mining and agricultural industries. Before the end of the century, arcades had also been constructed in Adelaide and Brisbane.[37]

Arcades reflected changing shopping behaviours and tastes in the Australian colonies between the 1860s and 1920s. Sydney and Melbourne particularly, but also to a degree Hobart, Adelaide and Brisbane, moved from being outposts of the British Empire to prosperous towns in their own right. At the same time, shopping became a "feminine speciality." Wives of the local gentry as well as the middle classes elevated shopping as an art, emulating the style and taste associated with Europe. In this environment, social positions became linked to the conspicuous consumption of housing, clothing, carriages and other consumer goods.[38] Urban retailers catered to this clientele by improving store fit-outs and product ranges, flattering the sensibilities of the shopper, and training staff in deferential codes of service.[39]

The QVB was not the end of markets in central Sydney, but marked a separation of food and fashion precincts and provides a useful example of the ways in which public authorities sought to reshape the social order of the city by reconfiguring its built form. There were later continuities of such reformism in the ways that regulation, enclosure and control were viewed as positive assets, both commercially and in understandings of public utility, when shopping centres emerged in the mid twentieth century. More immediately, the QVB and other grand arcades set a standard of design for retail development at a time when large city shops were evolving into true department stores – again from drapery and general store foundations.[40] These were largely family concerns, branded with the name of an entrepreneurial founding figure (or that of her husband or sons), and grew over time in response to market demand and changing technologies of selling. Most never expanded beyond their home cities, although these were large enough to support the development of substantial enterprises.

In Brisbane, McDonnell & East, Finney Isles & Co. and Allan & Stark established the city's retail heart along Queen, Adelaide, Edward and George Streets, while large drapery stores such as McWhirters and T.C. Beirne opened in nearby Fortitude Valley.[41] Adelaide's CBD housed a number of large department stores, including Harris Scarfe, John Martin's, James Marshall and Charles Birks & Co. Boans department store dominated retailing in Perth. One of the few firms to expand nationally in the early twentieth century, Foy & Gibson began operations in Collingwood, Victoria, before moving into Brisbane, Perth and Adelaide after William Gibson had taken over the business from his partner

Figure 1.1 Allan and Stark drapery store, ca. 1910.

Francis Foy, who moved to Sydney to establish Mark Foy's department store there.[42]

Sydney was home to numerous other department stores, including Grace Bros., David Jones, Marcus Clark & Co., McDowells and Anthony Hordern & Sons, which opened the largest store in the city in 1906. In Melbourne, Foy & Gibson, Ball & Welch, Georges and Buckley & Nunn all served the metropolitan population from city stores. The city's dominant department store, Myer, was founded by Russian-Jewish immigrants Sidney and Elcon Myer, who acquired premises in Bourke Street in 1911 after running a successful operation in the Victorian regional city, Bendigo. They are just two early examples of the many Jewish immigrants who shaped Australian retailing in the twentieth century. The Myer Emporium subsequently expanded through both acquisition and development to become the country's largest department store chain.

With a flatter social hierarchy than the Old World, and a comparatively affluent working class, Australian retail formats were shaped for a broad middle market. This produced bustling, efficient department stores that were more utilitarian than those occupying the retail hearts of Europe's fashion capitals.[43] Sidney Myer, one of the most adept at reading his market, crafted the motto, "value and friendly service", positioning his store to "the thrifty, respectable, middle-class". He also instituted weekly bargain days, selling large volumes of popular stock at cut-rate prices to women from the working and lower-middle classes.[44] On the other side of the continent, Perth's Boans Ltd traded on a similar motto, "Boans for service," linking the attention and courtesy of sales assistants to a community-minded spirit.[45] In Sydney, Anthony Hordern was marketed as the "House of economy," Mark Foys the "House of good value."[46] These slogans were backed with practical comforts for shoppers. In the 1880s, Farmer's in Sydney provided a suite of refreshment and toiletry rooms adjacent to the ladies' department.[47] Sidney Myer later established areas within his store, such as a cafeteria and ladies' lounge, that were designed to make the store a meeting place and relaxing social centre for suburban house-wives on day trips to the city.[48] Such marketing strategies positioned the big stores as middle-class environments, but left the door open to working-class consumers, who might not spend as much, nor as frequently, but still provided valuable custom.[49]

Urban centres featuring markets, arcades, specialty shops, universal providers and evolving department stores dominated Australian retailing in the nine-teenth century. This reflected the concentration of urban populations, espe-cially in colonial capital cities, the close economic ties between these cities and their hinterlands, and the resulting underdevelopment of large country general merchandise stores that struggled to compete with the scale and reach of city providers. People living in rural areas made periodic trips to the city to stock up at the larger stores, sample fashions available in arcades, and purchase cloth from draperies that they turned into a variety of clothing and home furnishings upon their return.[50] Further, the extension of railways into hinterlands towards the end of the century allowed the big city stores to offer mail order services of their full merchandise range to country residents.[51] Those living in closer prox-imity, but outside of central city areas, still relied on city stores for their larger purchases and all but their day-to-day needs. And for much of the century, a large number of others were able to walk to the city centre from their homes in inner suburbs.[52]

Australian capital cities at the end of the nineteenth century, then, were the beating hearts of geographically centralised distribution systems. In a time of

Figure 1.2 Fabric display, Boans Department Store, ca. 1950.

expanding though still limited mobility, they were the most easily accessible locations from which scale operations could be run. And by building scale, city retailers could out-compete firms in other geographic locations, even in distant rural communities, that had much smaller market catchments. Increasing mobility for large segments of the population, however, laid a platform for the eventual decline of central city areas' locational advantage. In the late nineteenth century, the expansion of mass public transport systems branching into outlying areas provided a significant impetus to suburban retailing. Public transport systems had initially concentrated retail power in urban cores where routes converged, but as they expanded they opened up new areas for people to live, and new markets for businesses to service, slowly dismantling the big city stores' hold on discretionary expenditure.

Davison notes a common chronological ordering of shop types relating to needs and opportunities in emerging suburbs: real estate agents and sometimes a hotel in the frontier phase, followed by shops selling basic everyday goods – a grocer, fruiterer, butcher and hay and corn store. After these came newsagents, ironmongers, bootmakers and haberdashers. Suburbs grew further with the electrification of rail services in the early twentieth century, expanding catchment zones around railway stations and further consolidating the retail precincts attached to them. The introduction of feeder bus services after the First World

Figure 1.3 Men's hats department, Boans Department Store, ca. 1950.

War had an additional stimulatory effect on both population and retail.[53] Even with the development of public transport systems, though, walking remained intrinsic to Australian urban journeying in the early twentieth century. Local shops were built to capture the passing foot traffic of people making their way between homes and the junctions and stopping points of public transport networks.[54] Delivery services provided milk and bread daily, as well as weekly orders from butchers, fruiterers and grocers.

Trains generated small nuclear retail environments, clustered around stations.[55] Trams, which were slower and stopped more frequently, tended to create linear strip shopping precincts. Melbourne provides numerous examples, including former working-class strips such as Brunswick Street in Fitzroy, Chapel Street in Prahran and Smith Street in Collingwood, that are now iconic shopping destinations. By the early twentieth century, such districts housed not only a wide variety of shops catering to everyday needs, but two- and three-story department stores that acted as traffic generators for other stores. Shopping strips like these generated substantial trade and, like the big city markets, also operated as social meeting places, attracting large crowds to festivities and gatherings on Friday and Saturday evenings.[56] While patterns varied, and Melbourne's great shopping streets rivalled city retailing in a way not echoed elsewhere,[57] the tight interconnection between transport and retail pertains to development in other capital cities.

The rise of chains

Suburban population growth attracted larger-scale retailers, including chain stores, a retail business structure that had emerged in Britain and America in the second half of the nineteenth century. Chain stores, or multiple shops as they were known in Britain, were a group of stores under single ownership, trading in a number of locations, with centralised buying systems, usually selling similar merchandise in each store. Their scale allowed them to buy in bulk at a discount, and to bypass wholesalers by establishing their own purchasing departments that could negotiate directly with manufacturers.[58] Trading in cash removed the costs involved in providing credit, while efficiencies were generated by standardising operations across stores, refining stock control systems, and improving distribution speeds.[59]

In Australia, grocery chains began mass-market operations in the 1880s. The largest and most widespread in the late nineteenth and early twentieth century, Moran & Cato, employed the slogan "Food for the millions" and by 1906 had established 60 stores across metropolitan and country Victoria. The firm moved into Tasmania and New South Wales, did comparatively well during the Depression selling cheap goods in suburban locations, and by 1935 had around 160 stores.[60] Moran & Cato and other firms such as Derrin Bros, S. R. Buttle, McEwans, McIlraths and A. Thompson and Sons were the forerunners of the supermarket, paving the way for mass merchandising in Australia.

The efficiencies of chain store operation were not confined to groceries. Numerous firms developed scale operations selling general merchandise, apparel, drapery, furniture, musical instruments, footwear, tobacco and other consumables.[61] Variety stores, which were among the most successful chains, sold everyday necessities and simple luxuries. They were the first retail model to sell from open displays on flat counters, allowing customers to handle the goods on offer.[62] As they spread, independent merchants complained that the chains' growing market share came at a cost to the community, working conditions and product quality.[63] Consumers, though, appear to have been willing to trade these negatives for cheaper prices and convenience.[64]

Variety stores were spread extensively across suburbs and country towns, although ownership was concentrated in the capital cities. Chains included Coles and Gilpins based in Melbourne, Penneys in Brisbane, Woolworths and Selfridges in Sydney.[65] These were Australian firms, even where names were borrowed from chains in other countries. All leveraged the benefits of standardised operations, and employed high-turnover, low-margin approaches to out-compete independent retailers. Michael Kelly, who started in Woolworths' variety stores and later rose to the executive ranks of the company, remembers a "military" level of organisation, with every aspect of store operation recorded in voluminous manuals – right down to feeding the store cat.

> The manual says, "you will feed a cat one ounce of feed, usually meat, per pound weight of cat" ... so if you had a cat you knew exactly how to look

Figure 1.4 Woolworths variety store, Hamilton, Victoria, 1930s.

after this blasted cat … to keep it just living and hungry enough to chase any of the mice and rats that got loose in the place.[66]

Chains vigorously pursued "scientific' retailing" – observing and implementing international technologies, store designs and sales techniques. This was one example of the much broader adoption of scientific management across a range of industries at the time – in part to achieve efficiencies, but also to inculcate organisational cultures.[67] One feature of retailing's modernisation was the investment of company resources "to guide the flow of employee labour … to ensure reliable service and presentation in stores."[68] Bevan Bradbury, who became General Manager of Coles in 1974 and later the firm's Chairman, began his career in variety stores. He later recalled that:

There were systems to do everything. Nothing was left to chance at Coles. There was a way to receive merchandise, there was a way to order merchandise, there was a way to display merchandise. It was a highly systemised company and you were taught the system by people who themselves had been taught and … there was a handbook of course … there was a guy by the name of … Jimmy Galbraith [who] was quite a brain. He came from I think General Motors and he had a solid grounding in General Motors inventory systems – I think he was a key figure in building Coles inventory systems.[69]

Bradbury's account points to the cross-industry innovations that occurred in the business systems of consumer capitalism. Thousands of components were required to be manufactured, stored and assembled to build a car. Thousands of products needed to be sourced, stored and distributed to stock the shelves of the nation's chain stores. Experience in managing such a system in one industry was transferable to another. There were also less direct connections. Competitive advantages could be achieved across a wide range of industries through labour-saving innovations. In retailing, the introduction of self-service outsourced labour to customers. By transferring the work of selecting goods from shop assistants to customers, chains reduced their costs, could generate higher margins, lower their prices and undercut competitors. Attempts to introduce self-service began in Australia's smaller markets in the inter-war period. The Brisbane Cash and Carry (BCC) grocery chain was reportedly the first firm to implement it in Australia, while stores in Perth were also ahead of their counterparts in New South Wales and Victoria.[70] Self-service, though, initially proved too radical for customers and retailers. It relied on a packaging industry to produce goods ready for sale, and a marketing industry to brand and advertise them.[71] These industries were underdeveloped in Australia at the time. And with car ownership still nascent, the difficulty of transporting goods home without traditional delivery services was inconvenient and limiting. Adoption by firms was hesitant and it was not until the late 1950s that self-service grocery distribution was widely implemented.[72]

The variety chains were more successful introducing a self-selection model. "Open selling" became commonplace before World War Two. This enabled customers to browse items that were available for selection throughout stores, with sales assistance available if required.[73] Goods were plainly priced, displayed to their best advantage, sold for cash and carried home by the customer. Labour shortages and an associated decline in home delivery during the Second World War furthered the spread of self-selection.[74] This normalised it as a type of shopping trip and saw it transferred to retailers selling other categories of goods. A manager of Anthony Hordern's department store reported in the mid 1950s, that this development was occurring internationally:

> Customer self-selection is growing apace throughout the Western world in a great number of the exclusive, as well the middle-bracket and low-priced stores … Today only a very small percentage of shoppers desire to sit down and have merchandise brought from a safe deposit box to be inspected. The great majority of apparel, fancy, and household lines, as well as food, is on display for customers to handle and inspect. Salespeople are there to guide and assist where necessary and are no longer imprisoned in a chromium or mahogany island, separated from the customer by an ice-cold barrier of glass or wood.[75]

Figure 1.5 Interior of Coles variety store, Hay St, Perth, 1932.

Self-selection was conducive to scale operations selling high-turnover items backed with refund guarantees. The personal skills of staff became less important than an employee's ability to follow instructions and rules.[76] Staff could be trained to fit the system without having to undertake the higher time-cost activity of acquiring in-depth product knowledge – although this was still higher than it later became. The benefits accrued by standardisation, replication, efficiency and scale facilitated the expansion of Australia's two biggest variety chains, Coles and Woolworths. By the mid 1950s, each controlled a network of more than 200 stores.[77] They faced competition from a range of smaller chains in different states, but were spurred to greater growth at a national level by their own direct, and fierce, rivalry.[78] Friendly soccer (football) matches between the two had to be halted because of constant injuries to staff.

Despite their strength and national reach, both firms were also vulnerable. They were unlikely to be overtaken by other variety chains, but that format had arisen under historical circumstances that were now changing. As Coles' and Woolworths' variety store empires reached their zenith in the 1950s, pieces were already falling into place for the arrival of the quintessential modernist retail form, the supermarket. At the same time, retailing also shifted spatially with the vast majority of sales growth occurring in suburban locations; a result of demographic shifts driven by the twentieth century's great re-shaper of urban environments, the automobile.

Notes

1 Howard and Stobart, "Arcades, Shopping Centres," 197.
2 Gruen and Smith, *Shopping Towns USA*, 17–24.
3 Gruen and Smith, *Shopping Towns USA*, 17–24. See also Tedlow, "Fourth Phase," 10.
4 Sammartino and Van Ruth, "Westfield Group," 309.
5 Drew-Bear, *Mass Merchandising*, 13.
6 McKeever et al., *Shopping Center Development Handbook*, 1.
7 Stobart, *Spend, Spend, Spend*, 15.
8 Guàrdia, Oyón and Garriga, "Markets and Market Halls," 101–2.
9 Guàrdia, Oyón and Garriga, "Markets and Market Halls," 102; Alexander, *Retailing in England*, 1–11; Schmiechen and Carls, *British Market Hall*, 3; Burns, *British Shopping Centres*, 1.
10 Schmiechen and Carls, *British Market Hall*, x–xi.
11 Schmiechen and Carls, *British Market Hall*, x.
12 Lancaster, *Department Store*, 7–8; Harrison, *People and Shopping*, 120–1.
13 Trentmann, *Empire of Things*, 207.
14 Schmiechen and Carls, *British Market Hall*, 160–5, 77.
15 Stobart, *Spend, Spend, Spend*, 97–100; Lancaster, *Department Store*, 7–8; Harrison, *People and Shopping*, 120–1.
16 Stobart, *Spend, Spend, Spend*, 123–4.
17 Schmiechen and Carls, *British Market Hall*, 160.
18 Harrison, *People and Shopping*, 106–8; Shaw, "Evolution and Impact," 138; Stobart, *Spend, Spend, Spend*, 109.
19 Geist, *Arcades*, 12.
20 Howard and Stobart, "Arcades, Shopping Centres," 199.
21 Quoted in Benjamin, "Arcades Project," 120.
22 Howard and Stobart, "Arcades, Shopping Centres," 201.
23 Victor Gruen used the term "arcade" to describe the passageways lined with small stores in Southdale shopping centre. See Mennel, "Victor Gruen," 131.
24 Stobart, "Cathedrals of Consumption," 810–12.
25 Pasdermadjian, *Department Store*, 2–10.
26 Shaw, "Evolution and Impact," 138; Miller, *Bon Marché*, 21; Stobart, *Spend, Spend, Spend*, 105.
27 Shaw, "Large-scale Retailing in Germany," 173.
28 Lancaster, *Department Store*, 10–13.
29 Trentmann, *Empire of Things*, 192–3.
30 Davis, *History of Shopping*, 291–2; Miller, *Bon Marché*, 27–34; Alexander, *Retailing in England*, 136; MacPherson, "Introduction," 6.
31 Shaw, "Evolution and Impact," 146–51.
32 Elvins, "History of the Department Store," 139–41.
33 Henderson-Smith, "From Booth to Shop to Shopping Mall," 17–59.
34 Davison, "From the Market to the Mall," 3–4.
35 Brown-May, *Melbourne Street Life*, 64–89.
36 Ellmoos, "Queen Victoria Building."
37 Geist, *Arcades*, 65–70, 363–6, 554–6.
38 Davison, *The Rise and Fall of Marvellous Melbourne*, 190–228.
39 Kingston, *Basket, Bag and Trolley*, 25.
40 Miller, "Retailing in Australia and New Zealand," 415–16.

41 Warner, "Evolution of Brisbane Retailing," 4.
42 O'Neill, "Gibson, William."
43 Kingston, *Basket, Bag and Trolley*, 26.
44 Davison, "From the Market to the Mall," 12.
45 Hough, "From Clogs to Clogs," 199.
46 Wolfers, "Big Stores," 20.
47 Kingston, *Basket, Bag and Trolley*, 29.
48 Davison, "From the Market to the Mall," 12.
49 Reekie, *Temptations*, 28–9.
50 Kingston, *Basket, Bag and Trolley*, 28–9.
51 Wolfers, "Big Stores," 19.
52 Davison, "From the Market to the Mall," 7.
53 Davison, "From the Market to the Mall," 8–9.
54 Spearritt, *Sydney's Century*, 37–8; Davison, "From the Market to the Mall," 8–9.
55 Davison, "From the Market to the Mall," 8–9.
56 Davison, "From the Market to the Mall," 9–10.
57 Spearritt, "Suburban cathedrals," 91.
58 Thomas, "Service Sector," 115; Phillips, "Chain Store," 87.
59 Harrison, *People and Shopping*, 122.
60 Humphery, *Shelf Life*, 52; Anon., 'Cato, Frederick John'.
61 Industrial Commission of New South Wales, "Management, Control and Operations of Chain Stores," 4.
62 *RW*, 5 September 1979.
63 Kingston, *Basket, Bag and Trolley*, 49.
64 Coles Myer Archive (CMA), Box 4763, Stella Barber interview with Dave Davis, 13 November 1985.
65 Industrial Commission of New South Wales, "Management, Control and Operations of Chain Stores," 49.
66 State Library of NSW (SLNSW), MLOH 451, Nos. 58, 59 & 60, Jenny Hudson interview with Michael Kelly, 27 September 1996, transcript, 3.
67 Taksa, "Cultural Diffusion," 429.
68 Patterson, "Supermarket," 158.
69 CMA, Box 2927, Stella Barber interview with Bevan Bradbury, 18 December 1985, transcript, 2.
70 Ewing, "Marketing in Australia," 56.
71 De Grazia, *Irresistible Empire*, 385.
72 Kingston, *Basket, Bag and Trolley*, 86.
73 Kingston, *Basket, Bag and Trolley*, 58–9.
74 *RM*, January/ February 1960, 20.
75 *JRTANSW*, July 1957, 42.
76 Industrial Commission of New South Wales, "Management, Control and Operations of Chain Stores," 9–10.
77 Murray, *Woolworths Way*, 30–121; McLaughlin, *Nothing over Half a Crown*, 46–89.
78 CMA, Box 4763, Stella Barber interview with Sir Norman Coles, 5 July 1985.

2 Suburbanisation, supermarkets and shopping centres

Graeme Davison has written that should future archaeologists mine the debris of our civilization they "will surely find no more significant ruins than the highway flyovers and clover leafs, parking stations and drive-in shopping malls of a society whose most valued tool, and most powerful status symbol, is the automobile."[1] In 1940s Australia, any vision of such a society was more dream than reality. The car was welcomed as a harbinger of modernity, but remained beyond the reach of most.[2] In the 1950s, it became more affordable. A new Holden still cost more at the end of the decade than it had at the start, but the real price had dropped and average weekly male earnings more than quadrupled.[3] Between 1948 and 1962 motor vehicle registrations in Australia rose from less than 60,000 to more than 2,800,000.[4] In 1953, one Australian in every five owned a motorcar. By 1962, this had risen to one in every three. Car usage also increased as motoring shifted from a novelty to an accepted feature of contemporary life.[5] Public transport usage, which had so effectively transported customers to the big city stores, dropped significantly.[6]

Car ownership was distributed unevenly across economic and geographic landscapes: outer middle-class suburbs were more likely to contain car owners, while Adelaide, Brisbane and Melbourne had higher levels of car ownership than Sydney, which had greater housing densities and a stronger public transport system before the removal of its extensive tram network in the late 1950s. Driving, initially, was also gendered. It began largely as a male activity, particularly as a means to commute to work. Suburban women often remained confined to their immediate neighbourhood for much of their daily activity, although they might have access to a car for shopping or "special occasions."[7] It was not until the late 1960s that driving licences were being acquired equally by men and women, and the two-car household entered popular discourse as a marker of social evolution.[8] By 1980, 80 per cent of Australian households owned at least one car, and a third had two or more.[9]

The car changed the physical form of urban environments. At the end of the Second World War, Australia's state capital cities were densely crowded. During the 1930s Depression investment in housing stock had slumped. Building controls during the war slowed investment further.[10] At the war's conclusion, there was an enormous shortfall of as many as 480,000 dwellings.[11] Limited access to materials and resources continued to inhibit construction after the war. Australia's high marriage rate and accompanying baby boom added further demand.[12] Residential development at the time was focused around the urban core, with ribbons snaking outwards along public transport routes. Outside of these, cheaper land beckoned. Cars provided access and the opportunity to escape the clutches of the city, where in addition to undersupply, much of the existing housing stock was unsanitary and dilapidated.[13]

This breakdown of spatial constraints in a period of strong economic growth allowed Australians to invest more heavily in individual homeownership. Encouraged by both of Australia's major political parties, home ownership rates soared from 53.4 per cent in 1947, to 70.2 per cent in 1961.[14] Residential decentralisation was further fuelled by employment growth on the urban fringe, especially in Melbourne, Adelaide and Sydney, where cheap land, roads and trucks drew industries away from their traditional foundations near cities and ports. State governments added impetus to this shift through the construction of public housing estates that provided affordable accommodation for workers near places of employment.[15] Between 1947 and 1966, the fastest-growing suburban municipalities in Sydney and Melbourne more than tripled their populations.[16]

Suburbanisation opened up opportunities for retailers at a time when self-service was becoming more viable in Australia. There had been considerable advances in packaging as a result of technologies developed during the war, notably of plastics and plastic film, which retailers used in place of brown paper bags and cellophane.[17] Pre-packaged goods reduced labour costs at the retail level, helped rationalise the distribution process, and standardised goods at the point of sale. Self-service was also aided by a concentration of brand power, with a small number of brands dominating product categories nationally. One academic commentator at the time noted that "if the presence, voice, charm and intelligence of the human being can be replaced by capital equipment without detriment to the sale, then it will be."[18]

This was the underlying logic of the supermarket. The term was first used in the United States in the 1930s to describe large self-service food and grocery markets running high-volume, low-price, self-service operations.[19] The label proved adhesive and became widely adopted as early, ramshackle, warehouse-based outfits gave way to gleaming modern "machines" for selling. By 1950, the supermarket format had been standardised through "continual technical refinement and relentless rationalisation." As a retail technology, it applied systems to all aspects of selling, from store layouts to advertising, with the aim of increasing sales volumes and developing efficiencies of scale. Supermarkets were also dependent on a range of supporting technologies, including cash registers, shopping trolleys, refrigerators, freezers, new forms of shelving, pricing mechanisms and automobiles that expanded geographic trade areas and allowed customers to carry more goods home in single trips. In addition, they developed substantial logistics infrastructure to control and manage supply lines. Self-service, and then the supermarket, migrated to other countries, including in Europe and South America, in the late 1940s and 1950s.[20]

Australian observers were acutely aware of the competitive advantages supermarkets held over existing retail formats, including variety stores.[21] Bevan Bradbury noted in a 1985 interview that:

> It was quite evident through the fifties and especially the sixties that the variety chains had a limited future. Coles [variety stores] had been modeled on companies like Kresge in the United States ... on McCrory's, on F.W. Woolworths ... a whole lot of these companies, all of whom, with almost no exceptions have disappeared today ... One of the problems was that supermarkets were making substantial inroads into the traditional markets of the variety chains, things like stationary and toiletries ... and so it was evident ... that the variety stores as such had a limited future because of what was happening in America.[22]

In the mid 1950s, Coles dispatched General Manager Lance Robinson on a research trip to investigate developments. One of his key contacts was the American five-and-dime variety chain S. H. Kress, from which Coles had previously received advice. In this instance, however, Robinson learnt more from Kress' innovative new competitors than through his established contacts.

> I went round and saw in a self-service grocery store ... a big stack of toilet rolls and lunchwraps which were our two fastest lines in those days ... tremendous lines ... which they were selling cheaper than Kress ...Well that gave the thought ... these people are going to lose their buying power on these items ... Supermarkets [were] no dreamworld idea, I thought ... Now when I came back I gave a talk to the board about it and E.B. [Coles] went on a trip later and ... he sat at the foot of Benny Trujillo .... and he listened to Benny and he was hammering about the supermarkets. When E.B. got home he was like a crazed lion.[23]

Trujillo worked for the National Cash Register Corporation (NCR). He was an influential figure in the international spread of mass merchandising through his "conversionary" Modern Merchandising Methods (MMM) seminars, which drew attendees from across the globe.[24] Bevan Bradbury later described him as a dynamic presence who "could make facts stand up and talk," a visionary who predicted the future shape of the mass market.[25] Trujillo was a mentor to a number of senior Australian retail figures, persuading them that large-scale, self-service operations were the logical outcome of the available technology (manufactured by NCR) and would be embraced by consumers.

Woolworths had also decided that supermarkets were a necessary and opportune direction for growth. The issue had been debated in the early 1950s, but when Managing Director Theo Kelly returned from a tour of the United States in 1955, his report undercut opposition from the firm's board.[26] Kelly later recounted that:

Although at that stage it looked silly to have a shopping centre out of the town, it was obvious that was what was coming. It was equally obvious … that the variety store alone wasn't going to hold and that the big demand would come into food.[27]

For Kelly, these changes were entwined. Shopping centres would draw custom from the main street where most variety stores were located. They would provide parking where most variety stores could not. And their collation of stores would offer a range of merchandise beyond what could be handled in any one individual shop.

Both Coles and Woolworths entered food retailing from a position of strength, with stable leadership teams, a capacity to develop systems, and national branding. They built scale in their new ventures by obtaining buying power, management expertise and food retailing knowledge through the acquisition of established grocery chains.[28] Other supermarkets, such as Franklins, grew out of grocery chains. There was also direct foreign investment. Safeway was an expansionist American supermarket chain that moved into the United Kingdom, West Germany and Australia in the 1960s.[29] The Australian expansion began with the takeover of Bill Pratt's small Victorian supermarket operation in 1962. Safeway retained him as manager of the chain, which grew to 126 stores until it was eventually acquired by Woolworths in 1985.[30]

Figure 2.1 Coles New World Supermarket, Geelong, 1967.

Supermarkets were a radically different mode of selling.[31] Sir Thomas North, who became the Director of Coles Supermarket Division in 1963, later recalled that:

> A lot of the older people didn't take to the supermarkets, certainly for some time, there's no doubt. I think they resisted them a bit, but the younger people took to them fairly quickly and within a very, a relatively short period of time, I would say after two years perhaps, they were an accepted way of life.[32]

After decades of fairly local and sporadic experimentation with self-service, its widespread adoption in the late 1950s and the subsequent move into supermarketing occurred quickly.[33] During the 1960s, the number of grocery stores across Australia declined steadily while grocery sales overall increased, indicating the growth of scale operations.[34] In 1961/2 there were 33,000 small grocery retailers in Australia and only 200 supermarkets of any significant size. By 1968/9 there were 650 supermarkets, which garnered around a third of all grocery sales.[35] Coles and Woolworths soon developed dominant positions, leading some sections of the media to refer to them as "Colesworths." Each had recognised the American trend towards supermarkets and the threat this posed to their existing variety stores businesses if they did not innovate. Both did, opening supermarkets under their own brands in 1960.[36] This parallel choice to horizontally expand into mass-market grocery retailing was one of the most successful strategic innovations in Australian retail history.

Cities demagnetised

The majority of early supermarkets were located in suburban areas where the population was growing fastest and where suitably sized sites could be obtained, including, by the late 1950s, within pre-planned shopping centres. Although some local shops, particularly small grocers, could not directly compete with scale operations and closed down, large stores did not kill suburban retail. They encouraged modernisation and generated customer traffic. Suburban shopping precincts became increasingly viable for a range of specialty retailers. Clothing and footwear stores thrived, particularly on basic items like nightwear, school clothes and men's wear that did not require the city's stamp of class. Electrical retailers appeared selling radios, vacuum cleaners, refrigerators, washing machines and, after 1956, television sets. These complemented and supported established local businesses like butchers, bakers and chemists. In a sign of rising affluence, second-hand stores began closing or moving as the electrical and home-furnishing retailers moved in.[37]

Suburban stores benefited from the growth of branded merchandise, which had evolved significantly since the initial pre-war experiments with self-service. Manufacturers promoted brand names through extensive national advertising, set fixed prices for items, and invested in quality packaging.[38] This simplified the buying process and disrupted the merchandising power of city stores: if a shopper could purchase a certain brand locally, it made little sense to travel to the city to buy the same item for a similar price. In fashion there was also a movement towards standardisation of sizes, which diluted the hold of familiarity that individual stores held over customers. Many shoppers still preferred to visit the city because the concentration of retailers allowed for comparison shopping, although the growing scope of suburban retailing was also eroding this competitive advantage.[39] It was a problem traditional retailers faced in numerous other countries, including, most notably for Australian retailers, the United States.[40]

In 1955, the Victorian trade journal, *Retail Merchandiser*, suggested that "most retailers are primarily interested in the answer to the question: 'How has the central city shopping area progressed relative to the rest of the metropolitan area and the State?'"[41] Data from the Australian Bureau of Statistics (ABS) provided a definitive response, showing a steady decline in the share of metropolitan retail trade held by inner-city areas (Figure 2.2). It was not that city sales declined – at least not until the end of the decade, and then only marginally and in the more mature suburban markets of Sydney and Melbourne. Inner-city areas still recorded very large sales volumes and increased these through much of the 1950s. But growth was gradual compared to the rapid gains being made in suburban areas, which garnered ever-higher shares of retail revenue in a booming market. The larger cities led the way, but the trend was echoed in Adelaide, Brisbane and Perth. Between 1947/8 and 1962/3 the value of city sales in Sydney grew by 54 per cent, while suburban sales grew by 320 per cent. In Melbourne, the respective figures were 73 per cent and 285 per cent; in Adelaide 112 per cent and 279 per cent.[42] Seeking to identify the exact nature of the retail shift, Farmer's department store commissioned a study that found sales of department-store-type merchandise increased by 71.1 per cent in Sydney's suburbs, and by just 3.4 per cent in the city. The report, like others at the time, suggested this was a trend highly likely to continue and that while city retailing would retain significant volume, growth in urban cores, particularly in Sydney and Melbourne, would be largely stagnant.[43]

"A retail location," the *Retail Merchandiser* noted, "is only as good as the amount of buying foot traffic delivered to it."[44] In the age of mass public transport, the concentration of retail in central business districts had been a competitive advantage for stores that could draw customers from across entire metropolitan areas. These firms included large-scale, full-line department stores as well as specialty stores dealing in comparison goods such as apparel, jewellery, home furnishings and furniture.[45] With the rise of the automobile, this centralised distribution system was disrupted by traffic congestion and parking problems, which were blamed for "slowly strangling trade."[46] Sir Norman Nock, the President of the Australian Council for Retailers, which represented the interests of large-scale operators, declared that the "almost complete absence of any constructive attempt to overcome the problem is a cause for the most serious alarm" and urged retailers and their associations to "convince government of the vital urgency of this matter."[47]

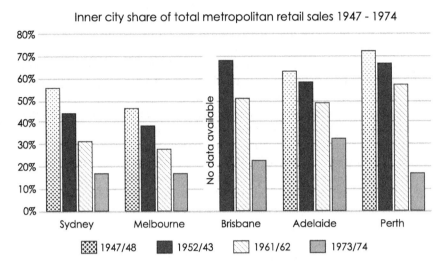

Figure 2.2 Inner-city share of total metropolitan retail sales, 1947–74.

While there may well have been "fumbling and inadequate traffic and transport arrangements" as the big stores claimed, the general problems were not
unique to Australian cities.[48] In the United States, the Urban Land Institute
noted a number of improvements required to support city retail as technological change undermined the logistical certainties that had once sustained it.
These included:

> freedom from congestion, provision for off street parking spaces in
> ample number, convenient access, better and faster mass transit, attractive
> modernized buildings, and attention to amenities including elimination of
> garishness, unnecessary noise and impediments to easy circulation.[49]

Attempts were made along these lines in Australia – for example, city car parking
stations began to be built, and some city stores undertook refurbishments[50] –
but such investments were insufficient to deal with the disruption caused by a
society-wide transition to a new mode of transport.

Consumers also reported a range of other disadvantages with shopping "in
town." It was more formal, requiring time, effort and expense to dress up for
the trip; it was viewed as "less friendly" than shopping at local suburban stores;
shopping trips to the city took longer and were more expensive as communities
sprawled further away from it; and there were no easy solutions to arranging
child care covering the duration of the shop.[51] Weather conditions could also
have a deleterious impact on city sales. Discussing a particularly bad sales season
in 1963, the managing director of Farmer's department store, E. L. Byrne, wrote
to Larry Smith in America:

> One of the reasons for the substantial lift in the suburbs [sales, has been] … continuous heavy rain right throughout the winter. The City reminded me of a forsaken battlefield on many of these cold, wet days. We feel sure that many people who normally shopped in the city found they could shop more comfortably in the suburbs during this unpleasant weather cycle … All in all it has been a testing time.[52]

Byrne positioned the weather as a significant deterrent. Rain, though, fell on a field in which consumers had been scattered. For women living in the outer suburbs, tasked with caring for children in one-car families, the city was almost inaccessible. Local shops offered credit, delivery services, exchange systems and personal service.[53] Numerous small department stores grew up locally and were followed by branches of the city stores.[54] In combination with supermarkets, variety stores and specialty stores, they anchored busy, productive shopping precincts. An excerpt from the *Retail Merchandiser* in 1955 describes a hive of activity and development that was characteristic of busy suburban centres at the time:

> Box Hill shopping area [in Melbourne's eastern suburbs] … is a thriving and progressive district of 37,000 people, with ideas of civic development advancing as fast as the population. There is a constant whirr of engines, laying pavements, raising steel structures and delivering goods to the existing shops. The constant movement of feeder bus services, coming from as many as five other suburbs, converging on this pulsing shopping [area] … is evidence of its growing importance.[55]

Suburban centres like these, filled with bustle and enterprise, made a trip to the city ever more unnecessary. As car ownership and usage climbed, however, the parking and traffic congestion that plagued inner-city retailing spread outwards. Roads, that were often no wider than they had been before the war, now carried much greater volumes of both local and through traffic.[56] Many established suburban shopping precincts did not contain sufficient parking. Often the only way to provide it was to demolish existing commercial or residential buildings, and little of this occurred in the 1950s. Land was expensive and there was competition for suitable sites, including from oil companies bidding for petrol station locations.[57]

Regulated shopping hours also served to concentrate traffic. Retail trading hours had been unrestricted in the nineteenth century, but the onerous conditions of retail employees, their increasing numbers as large shops grew more prevalent, and the concerns of religious groups about church attendance saw legislation to limit opening hours imposed in all states during the 1880s and 1890s. Further restrictions followed and by the 1950s, retailing generally shared with other industries the eight-hour weekday and half-day Saturday working week, with the addition of at least one night of late trading. Restricted trading hours meant shorter windows for shopping around paid work commitments, which were also growing with women's workforce participation.[58] As traffic increased, the utility and attractiveness of strip shopping precincts declined.[59] Commentary in one retail trade journal at the time noted that "the last justification for this kind of shopping centre goes when the volume of traffic makes easy, free customer-parking in front of the shops impossible."[60]

The suburban market

The growth of the suburban middle-income market, however presented a compelling opportunity for retailers.[61] GDP growth rates from 1945 to 1973 were the highest in Australia's history to that point. Employment levels were also strong. Manufacturing had expanded considerably during the war, not only in size but in capacity and sophistication. It became an increasingly important component of the economy as the 1950s progressed. It also drove job creation in spin-off industries, as did the suburban housing boom. Unemployment was exceptionally low in the first half of the 1950s, and for much of the 1960s averaged around 1.2 per cent. This occurred as the labour force was dramatically expanding with an increase in women's participation and the absorption of millions of migrants.[62] The latter resulted from a dedicated federal government program of assisted migration, sparked by fears of Asian invasion from the north. There was also natural increase. In the 1950s, couples got married younger, fewer people remained unmarried, and married women's fertility rates rose, resulting in a baby boom that resisted a longer-term trend towards smaller family sizes.[63] Australia's population grew from 7.1 million in 1940 to 12.75 million in 1971.[64]

This growing population experienced markedly improved purchasing power. Between 1890 and the start of the Second World War, the Australian economy had ebbed and flowed with little overall growth. "Thrift was a daily discipline." Adults and children in the middle class possessed few clothes, and mended shoes rather than replacing them. Household furniture was a lifetime purchase. Restaurants were scarce and few people ate out.[65] Michael Lloyd, who emigrated from Britain in the 1970s, before joining Lend Lease and rising to senior executive and board positions in the firm's property division, describes comparable conditions in England, even after World War Two:

> half a percent of the population had a few bob. Most of the people spent about a quarter to a third of their income on their home ... Food came next. And, clothing came next, but they didn't have any. I mean, people had one pair of shoes. And, you had another pair in the cupboard, which you only wore on Sunday. When the shoes you were wearing everyday weren't wearable anymore, because they'd been repaired so many times they were falling off, you took the Sunday shoes and they became your day shoes and you got a new pair and they were for Sunday. That's what you had ... There was no disposable income.[66]

In Australia, in the immediate aftermath of the war, shortages of goods and the hangover of rationing on clothes and food had restricted retail sales. The lag in home building and the delays caused by manufacturers regearing to the production of consumer durables meant that retail was primarily focused on consumables, which were subject to federal government price controls. In 1948, rationing on clothes was discontinued, and a Federal referendum determined that price control should be returned to the states. Manufacturing of consumer durables was also gaining momentum.[67] Between 1939 and 1974, Australians increased their consumption expenditure by some 126 per cent. This reflected growing purchasing power: real household disposable income growth averaged 3.5 per cent a year between 1953/4 and 1961/2, and 5.3 per cent annually between 1961/2 and 1975/6. Poverty remained a consistent reality for marginalised segments of the population, but retailers benefited from the good fortune of most households. Consumers proved "both willing and able to spend their increasing discretionary income on an abundance of consumer durables."[68] Purchases of motorcars offer a prime example of this development, but the expansion of home ownership also generated greater demand for hardware, electrical appliances, white goods, furniture and other household items.[69]

The strength of this market created a strong incentive to remove bottlenecks in distribution. In America, the advantages of car-friendly distribution formats and the appeal of modern retailing were being proven. Australia's large city retailers and developers looked there for a "retail cure-all" for what was now being described as "the chaos created by suburban sprawl and inner-city congestion."[70] Planners, influenced by both European town planning and American retail development, became convinced that segregating shoppers and car traffic was both an aesthetic and logistical necessity.[71] By the mid 1950s, a belief was taking hold (albeit gradually and inconsistently), that the rise of the automobile rendered the distribution sector unsustainable in its current form. The golden age of city retailing had passed, the suburbs were the future, and different retail forms would be required to service them. In the United States, entrepreneurs and architects had already developed a solution: the pre-planned, privately owned and managed shopping centre.

Developing the modern shopping centre

The changes to urban environments wrought by the automobile in Australia occurred earlier and more dramatically in the United States. Between 1925 and 1940 the number of automobiles there increased from 20 to 32 million.[72] Growing suburban populations and difficulties accessing the city created the impetus for outlying retail development that first supplemented and then challenged city retailing. Around cities like Los Angeles where car usage was comparatively high, numerous commercial precincts containing between 40 and 80 shops had been established outside the city limits by the early 1920s.[73] Such precincts began with freestanding stores, established by general merchandising firms, supermarkets and other chains.[74] These included branches of city stores, which found a compelling case for locating outlets selling limited selections of their stock in far cheaper locations close to their decentralising customer base.[75] The drawing power of these firms attracted other retailers, both small and large, creating active retail precincts, which encouraged further investment and increased surrounding property values.[76] As occurred later in Australia, the growth of suburban shopping eroded city trade: to continue with the example of Los Angeles, the share of retail sales held by the central city area dropped from 34 percent of the county total in 1929 to less than 20 percent by 1939.[77] Such shifts further impelled branch store decentralisation as retailers sought to retain and grow market share.[78]

In response to demand for sites, entrepreneurial developers began constructing uniform rows of stores, with accessible car parking and display windows fronting streets.[79] The first recognised example of this format opened in Baltimore in 1907. The Roland Park Shopping Centre contained only six stores set back from the street, but as a pre-planned centre under unified management with set policies guiding retail activity, it lays a claim to being the first modern shopping centre.[80] Other developments followed as entrepreneurs experimented with cohesively designed and managed retail environments that could comfortably accommodate cars, people and shops. To compete against the drawing power of the city, they also sought to expand their offer of comparison and fashion goods.[81] Curating tenancy mixes to serve surrounding populations created magnetic retail environments that could compete with the city, but which were also more compelling than heterogeneous suburban shopping strips that had no capacity for organisational unity.[82]

By the 1920s the principles that had been founded in Roland Park were being applied to larger, more sophisticated developments generating further innovation. In 1923, four miles south of Kansas City, the J. C. Nichols Country Club Plaza opened to service a planned community. The Plaza comprised a series of separate buildings occupied by a diverse collection of retailers and services. In addition to higher-end fashion stores it included mid-range retailers, a grocer, bowling alley and theatre. The design was also consciously social. Greenery and open space for community activities were plentiful, as were park benches, tiled fountains and public art. The Country Club targeted an affluent demographic. Its aesthetics and layout appealed to civic pride and provided an important underpinning for the commercial side of the enterprise.[83] Nichols insisted, however, that the Club's success derived from its extensive and free car parking facilities.[84]

Other large-scale shopping centres that opened during the 1930s were similarly located in high-status, high-income areas – the "cream of the all-American market," as one contemporary described them.[85] Catering to white middle-class families migrating from downtown areas,[86] they included the River Oaks Center in Houston and the Highland Park Center in Dallas. The latter introduced the innovation of inward-facing shops, turning them away from the street, and providing off-street parking.[87] Such developments spread the idea of the shopping centre, which became acknowledged as an efficient means of serving growing suburban markets of mobile consumers.[88] The Depression and Second World War, however, slowed development: there were only eight shopping centres of significant size in the United States in 1946.[89]

Despite these modest foundations, the industry was sufficiently established to expand rapidly in what became favourable post-war conditions. There existed a concept of pre-planned complexes under unified ownership and management; a body of planners and architects with the expertise to build them; developers prepared to finance and organise construction; retailers willing to occupy tenancies; and suburban consumers well versed in the language and culture of mass consumption.[90] Further, the "long festering parking problem" loomed ever larger in national debates and was described as the major problem facing downtown shopping.[91] The Chairman of Sears, Roebuck and Co., reportedly declared that "expecting people to shop by car where there are no ample parking facilities is as silly as expecting them to buy radio sets in a country where there are no radio stations."[92]

Planned suburban shopping centres offered a ready solution, particularly after 1954 when tax laws were altered to accelerate depreciation and virtually guarantee developers a return on retail property investments. Further incentives were provided through economic development grants, infrastructure provision and the easing of local taxes.[93] Moreover, between 1950 and 1955, suburban populations grew seven times faster and were far more affluent than inner-city populations.[94] This hastened the growth of suburban department store branches, including in shopping centres, which began including department store anchors in the late 1940s.[95]

One of the most significant American centres of the early post-war period, Northgate, opened in Seattle where, between 1940 and the centre's opening in 1950, the suburban population had grown by more than 90 percent. Adjacent to a highway, Northgate provided surround, flat tarmac parking for 4,000 cars. Within this sea of automobiles, its architect John Graham created a covered pedestrian mall 1,500 feet in length, flanked by rows of stores facing each other.[96] Delivery access ran beneath the mall, improving aesthetics and segregating the distributive and purchasing functions of shopping. Northgate was developed by Allied Stores, the parent company of the Bon Marché department store, which was one of two department stores anchoring the complex. These, along with a variety store and supermarket, were strategically located to increase custom for specialty shops flanking the mall.[97] This innovation became critical to the profitability of shopping centres because it increased specialty tenant rents. Shopping centre layouts varied widely depending on architect, developer, the particularities of trade areas and the physical geography of sites, but the core principle of using traffic-generating anchor stores to move customers past specialty stores and improve their productivity remained a core tenet of shopping centre design across the post-war period.

Building on earlier developments such as Northgate, the man commonly credited as the great innovator in mall design, Victor Gruen, established an international profile in 1954 with his design of Northland in Detroit – then the world's largest mall and the first to have central heating and air-conditioning.[98] Northland was the first and largest of four planned centres of similar design built for the J. L. Hudson department store firm, which in the 1950s dominated Detroit retailing from its six-story city store. Each new suburban mall, named by the compass points, was spaced equidistant from the others and approximately 10–12 miles from downtown.[99] While it took some time to complete, the plan was to encircle the city and thus dominate its entire retail geography. Hudson's formula soon influenced the thinking of Australian capital city department stores.

Northland was formed from a cluster of single-story buildings grouped around the central focus of Hudson's three-story department store, which at 485,000 square feet set a new scale for a suburban branch.[100] The surrounding car park for 10,000 cars was distinctly American, but the retail architecture hinted at European influences. The buildings were separated with landscaped garden courts where shoppers could relax on benches amidst sculptures, fountains, colonnades and flowerbeds.[101] Mature trees softened the centre's exterior and provided shade in summer, while pedestrian malls and covered walkways connected the different structures and unified the design. Northland became one of the most popular and commercially successful malls in America, described by *Architectural Forum* as a "classic in shopping center planning."[102] By the mid 1970s, it would attract more retail trade than Detroit's entire central business district.[103]

Gruen was strongly influenced by European modernist architects like Gropius, van der Rohe, Behrens, Loos, Sitte and Le Corbusier. He also held powerful and nostalgic memories of his childhood in early-century Vienna, recalling an urbane cultural and intellectual life where a broad cross-section of the population came to discuss politics, culture and daily affairs in outdoor cafes and public spaces. When he arrived in the United States, Gruen was left aghast by suburban sprawl. Northland, and his next great project, Southdale, were attempts to emulate European urban public space in modern commercial terms. He argued that

> by affording opportunities for social life and recreation in a protected pedestrian environment, by incorporating civic and educational facilities, shopping centers can fill an existing void. They can provide the needed place and opportunity for participation in modern community life.[104]

Southdale cemented Gruen's place in American architectural and retail history.[105] America's first completely internalised, large-scale shopping centre, it provided parking for 5,200 cars, contained a wide range of specialty shops spread over two levels, and was anchored by two department stores.[106] Its standout visual feature was a monumental, naturally lit central court. Trees fifty feet high towered above fountains, ponds, cafes, a giant birdcage and children's zoo. Magnolia trees, orchids and eucalypts were planted alongside native Californian flora and modernist sculptures.[107] The central court solved a long-term problem faced by multi-story shops: how to attract customers upwards to higher floors. Lifts and escalators had improved customer traffic flow, but restrictions on sight lines remained an issue. Southdale's central court opened through two levels, revealing shopping activity, public art and attractively displayed shop windows above.[108] Parking lots also had entrances into both levels. Gruen's design rendered the historical dominance of ground floors obsolete, increasing overall rental returns by improving the productivity of upper floors.

The central court at Southdale was designed to fill the same function as the outdoor gardens at Northland. Gruen's intention was to create non-commercial space – a place for people to take a break from shopping, relax and be entertained. Its attractions were positioned in the centre of the court so that people watching them would turn their backs to the stores. The "Gruen Transfer" – a strategy to encourage impulse purchases by deliberately discombobulating shoppers through over-stimulation – is thus misattributed: Gruen fought a running and ultimately unsuccessful battle to limit wall-to-wall commercialism at Southdale. By the late 1960s, he had become deeply disillusioned with the overt commercialism of shopping centres, even as their spread was accelerating.[109] In 1956 when Southdale opened, there were 1,100 planned shopping centres operating in suburban areas across the United States.[110] This climbed to 4,500 in 1960, and then 8,600 by 1965.[111]

These shopping centres were categorised into a tripartite hierarchy, ranging from smallest to largest: neighbourhood, community and regional shopping centres.[112] Neighbourhood centres were positioned to provide for the daily needs of an immediate local trade area, supplying food and convenience goods with 10–15 shops anchored by a supermarket. They offered a range of basic services through stores such as beauty parlours, shoe repairers, barbers, laundries and dry cleaners. Community centres sold a greater depth and breadth of merchandise, including apparel. They included junior (small-scale) department or variety store anchors and sometimes a supermarket. Banking, professional services and a post office might also be provided, while the specialty offer extended to stores such as florists, milliners and haberdashers, as well as lingerie, footwear, children's wear and toy stores. Regional centres attempted to duplicate the city retail offer, providing one-stop shopping for a complete range of merchandise, as well as a variety of services and recreational facilities. They were anchored by at least one full-line department store, although even in the 1950s it was being argued that two or more should be included to encourage competition, enable comparison shopping and draw greater customer traffic. Regionals included most of the retail housed in smaller centre types, and added fashion goods, home furnishings and household equipment. They covered at least 30 acres, offering parking for up to 10,000 cars.[113]

The demarcation of centre types was not precise. Retail mix and the characteristics of the leading tenant were the key defining features, but centres of all types ranged in size and character. Some shopping centre formats, such as fashion centres in which collections of apparel merchants and sometimes a department store would group together, did not fit neatly into a type. Definitions also evolved as the market matured. The three basic types, however, are useful for thinking about the scope, positioning and reach of shopping centres. Moving up the hierarchy, trade areas got bigger, the mix of sociability with commerce became more important, the time spent on shopping trips increased, and expenditure became more discretionary.

By the 1950s, department stores in the United States were heavily engaged in out-of-town regional shopping centre development, either as developers or tenants. Within existing suburban shopping precincts, it was difficult to find suitable sites, land prices were high, traffic congestion already a problem, and parking expensive to provide even if there was space to do so. Stand-alone stores outside of established areas were cheap but were open to unfettered competition and dependent on their own drawing power.[114] Regional shopping centres on greenfield sites, in contrast, allowed department stores to control tenancy mixes, set the character and tone of the development, benefit from the drawing power of other merchants, subsidise costs through rents from those same merchants, pre-empt competitors' entry into trade areas already serviced by their city stores, and build on cheap sites beside highways that enabled easy car access with space for parking.[115] Department stores taking a lease in out-of-town shopping centres accrued the same benefits of agglomeration, accessibility and parking, with less financial upside, but also lower costs and risk.[116]

The utility of the shopping centre format saw it imported and adapted to a broad array of urban markets globally in the second half of the twentieth century. Gosseye and Avermaete note that "in Europe, shopping centres emerged and became an everyday phenomenon roughly between the early-1950s and the mid-1970s." Sweden had developed a consumerist society before the Second World War and embraced the shopping centre early.[117] One of its first developments, simply named Shopping, located in Luleå in northern Sweden, opened a year earlier than Southdale. Arguably the first fully internalised shopping centre in the world, it offered year-round protection from the often-harsh weather as well as social space and entertainment facilities. Shopping in Luleå followed the development of Vallingby Centrum, which opened in 1954 as the commercial and civic heart of Vallingby, a new town on the outskirts of Stockholm. This presaged a planning movement in which shopping centres were used to provide social and commercial infrastructure for new towns being built during Europe's post-war reconstruction. England, France, Finland, Belgium, Germany and a number of other European countries embraced open-air shopping centres as mixed-use solutions to urban renewal, congestion and crowding during the 1950s. From the mid 1960s onwards, enclosed, multi-level retail centres began appearing in inner-city areas. Often built through public–private partnerships, they were designed to revitalise urban cores suffering decline as a result of middle-class flight to suburban areas.[118]

Out-of-town enclosed shopping centres along the American model were slower arriving and faced considerable opposition from land-use planners observing the plight of American downtowns. Numerous study tours to the United States by public delegates, entrepreneurs and retail executives softened resistance.[119] Main Taunus Zentrum opened near Frankfurt in 1964, and by 1972, 16 out-of-town centres had been constructed in Germany.[120] In 1969, Parly 2 opened on the outskirts of Paris. Built over two levels and surrounded by a huge parking lot, it included branches of the city department stores Printemps and BHV as well as more than 100 boutique stores, a supermarket, cinema, bars and restaurant. It was promoted as an interiorised city in its own right. Other shopping centres of similar design were built around Paris and across Europe during the early 1970s.[121] Britain's first American-style centre, Brent Cross, opened in 1976. It rapidly became one of the country's most successful retail sites and set a precedent for a number of fully enclosed, air-conditioned centres that followed.[122]

Brent Cross was built by the Hammerson Property and Investment Trust. Like another prominent British retail development firm, Arndale, Hammerson gained experience constructing shopping centres in Australia where the experiment with American-style shopping centres began earlier and more intensively. Australian urban planners and retailers were influenced by European developments in the 1950s, but also faced a different set of problems. Australia was not rebuilding a shattered urban landscape but experiencing profound local migration from urban cores to periphery suburbs. America thus offered a more directly transferable model.[123] Australia was one of the first countries to import variations of the tripartite hierarchy of American shopping centres. This indicated not only the presence of shared preconditions, but the eagerness of Australian retailers to continue their practice of borrowing retail systems and formats from peers in the United States. In this way, it was an antipodean example of the global knowledge transfers that have long been a feature of retail history internationally.[124] By the mid 1950s, even before the triumph of Southdale echoed across the retail world, developers and large retailers were setting plans to introduce shopping centres to the Australian market.

Notes

1 Davison, *Car Wars*, ix.
2 Spearritt, "Cars for the People," 119.
3 Davison, *Car Wars*, 15.
4 Australian Bureau of Statistics (ABS), *Australian Year Book*, 1951; ABS, *Census of Motor Vehicles*, 1955, 1962.
5 *RM*, October 1960, 12.
6 CMA, Box 142, Larry Smith & Company, Market Analysis of the Sydney Metropolitan Area, 21 May 1963, 3.
7 Davison, *Car Wars*, 15–24.
8 Forster, *Australian Cities*, 17.

9 Spearritt, "Cars for the People," 128.
10 Connell and Irving, *Class Structure in Australian History*, 280; O'Hanlon, "Modernism and Prefabrication," 108, 111.
11 Frost and O'Hanlon, "Urban History," 9. Note, estimates on this vary considerably depending on the measures used.
12 Hutchings and Garnaut, "Private Development Company," 98; Frost and O'Hanlon, "Urban history," 9.
13 Davison, *Car Wars*, 23–4.
14 Hall, "Trends in Home Ownership."
15 Frost and Dingle, "Sustaining Suburbia," 33.
16 Census of the Commonwealth of Australia, 1947, 1954, 1961.
17 Kingston, *Basket, Bag and Trolley*, 89.
18 *RM*, June 1957, 10–12; *RM*, April 1966, 23.
19 Liebs, *Main Street*, 123–7.
20 Patterson, "The Supermarket," 156–8; Alexander, Nell, Bailey and Shaw, "Co-Creation of a Retail Innovation," 536; De Grazia, *Irresistible Empire*, 377–85; Alexander and Phillips, "Retail Innovation and Shopping Practices," 2209; Trentmann, *Empire of Things*, 348.
21 Merrett, "Making of Australia's Supermarket Duopoly," 7; CMA, Box 1505, Stella Barber interview with Lance Robinson, 29 November 1985.
22 CMA, Box 2927, Stella Barber interview with Bevan Bradbury, 18 December 1985, transcript, 10.
23 CMA, Box 4764, Stella Barber interview with Lance Robinson, 29 November 1985.
24 Gosseye, "Janus-Faced Shopping Center," 863; De Grazia, *Irresistible Empire*, 399.
25 CMA, Box 2927, Stella Barber interview with Bevan Bradbury, 18 December 1985, transcript, 5.
26 SLNSW, MLOH 451, Nos. 23 and 24, Jenny Hudson interview with Fraser Coss, ca. 1995, transcript, 11.
27 SLNSW, MLOH 451, No. 61, Jenny Hudson interview with Sir Theo Kelly, ca. 1996, transcript, 4–5.
28 Merrett, "Making of Australia's Supermarket Duopoly," 5–14.
29 Humphery, *Shelf Life*, 75.
30 Pratt, *My Safeway Story*, 63–138.
31 Alexander, Nell, Bailey and Shaw, "Co-Creation of a Retail Innovation."
32 CMA, Box 4763, Stella Barber interview with Sir Thomas North, 11 October 1985.
33 Humphery, *Shelf Life*, 84–7.
34 Hutchings, "Battle for Consumer Power," 67.
35 Miller, "Retailing in Australia and New Zealand," 421.
36 Fleming, Merrett and Ville, *Big End of Town*, 88.
37 Kingston, *Basket, Bag and Trolley*, 85–6.
38 Humphery, *Shelf Life*, 40–67.
39 *RM*, March 1962, 23; CMA, Box 142, Letter from J. G. Clarke, Director, Holeproof NSW Limited to E. L. Byrne, Managing Director, Farmer & Co. Ltd, 17 June 1963.
40 Howard, *From Main Street to Mall*, 133.
41 *RM*, August 1955, 8.
42 Calculated from ABS, Census of Retail Establishments, 1947/8, 1952/3, 1956/7, 1962/3.
43 CMA, Box 142, Peter Hyde, Suburban Opportunities in Sydney Metropolitan Area – Sydney Survey, May 1965, 2; CMA, Box 142, Larry Smith & Company, Market Analysis of the Sydney Metropolitan Area, 21 May 1963, 5, 7.

44 *RT*, March 1958, 44–5.
45 *RM*, May 1956, 7–10.
46 *RT*, July 1960, 17; June 1962, 5; *RM*, July 1956, 18. For the American experience, see Howard, *From Main Street to Mall*, 134.
47 *RM*, July 1956, 18.
48 *SMH*, 8 January 1961, 31; Elvins, "History of the Department Store," 148–9; *RT*, January 1960, 32.
49 Architectural Record, *Design for Modern Merchandising*, 145.
50 *RM*, October 1956, 27; *RM*, February 1961, 15; Myer Emporium Annual Report, 1955.
51 Modern Merchandising Methods, *Australian Shopping Centres*, 3.
52 CMA, Box 143, Letter from E. L. Byrne to Keith Kelly, Larry Smith & Company, 29 October 1963.
53 Kingston, *Basket, Bag and Trolley*, 45–6.
54 Beed, "Growth of Suburban Retailing," 88–91.
55 *RM*, May 1955, 18.
56 *AR*, April 1969, 6; *RT*, March 1964, 13.
57 Spearritt, "Suburban Cathedrals," 94.
58 Kingston, *Basket, Bag and Trolley*, 111–13; *AB*, 16 July 1981, 74.
59 *RT*, July 1959, 14; *BLE*, 24 April 1958, 44.
60 *RT*, July 1959, 14; *AR*, September 1967, 29.
61 *RM*, May 1955, 21–5. Reprinted from The Department Store Economist.
62 Whitwell, *Making the Market*, 16–25.
63 Forster, *Australian Cities*, 15.
64 ABS, *Year Book Australia*, 1971, 124; ABS, *Census of Population and Housing*, 1971, 1.
65 McCalman, "Private Life," 53.
66 Author interview with Michael Lloyd, 11 June 2014.
67 *RM*, January/February 1960, 20.
68 McLeod, *Abundance*, 27.
69 Whitwell, *Making the Market*, 18–31.
70 *RT*, August 1962, 44; Harris and Harper, *Urbs*, 71–3.
71 Spearritt, "Suburban Cathedrals," 94.
72 Baker and Funaro, *Shopping Centers*, 6.
73 Longstreth, *City Center to Regional Mall*, 57–8.
74 Smith, *Shopping Centers*, 14.
75 Hoyt, *One Hundred Years*, 226.
76 Longstreth, *City Center to Regional Mall*, 73.
77 Cassady and Bowden, "Shifting Retail Trade," 398.
78 Gruen and Smith, *Shopping Towns USA*, 37.
79 Dawson, *Shopping Centre Development*, 4.
80 Smith, *Shopping Centers*, 15–16; Liebs, *Main Street*, 130.
81 Hutson, "I Dream of Jeannie," 20.
82 Cohen, *Diffusion*, 27.
83 Farrell, *One Nation*, 6–7.
84 Crawford, "World in a Shopping Mall," 20.
85 Smith, *Shopping Centers*, 3.
86 Elvins, "History of the Department Store," 148.
87 Dawson, *Shopping Centre Development*, 5–6; Liebs, *Main Street*, 130.
88 Cohen, *Diffusion*, 28.

89 Jackson, "All the World's a Mall," 1113; Dawson, *Shopping Centre Development*, 5–6; Farrell, *One Nation*, 6–7.
90 Dawson, *Shopping Centre Development*, 6–7.
91 *RM*, April 1956, 8; *RM*, June 1956, 22.
92 *RM*, September 1956, 24.
93 Hayden, *Building Suburbia*, 168; Jackson, "All the World's a Mall," 1115.
94 Howard, *From Main Street to Mall*, 133–4; Smith, *Shopping Centers*, 21; Howard and Stobart, "Arcades, Shopping Centres," 203.
95 Smith, *Shopping Centers*, 7, 22.
96 Baker and Funaro, *Shopping Centers*, 212–20.
97 Jackson, "All the World's a Mall," 1114; Clausen, "Northgate."
98 Farrell, *One Nation*, 7–8.
99 McKeever et al., *Shopping Center Development Handbook*, 233.
100 Smith, *Shopping Centers*, 15.
101 Howard and Stobart, "Arcades, Shopping Centres," 205.
102 Hardwick, *Mall Maker*, 142.
103 McKeever et al., *Shopping Center Development Handbook*, 233.
104 Victor Gruen quoted in Farrell, *One Nation*, 9–10.
105 Farrell, *One Nation*, 7–8.
106 Jackson, "All the World's a Mall," 1114; Gosseye and Avermaete, "Shopping Towns Europe," 4.
107 Gruen and Smith, *Shopping Towns USA*, 153; Liebs, *Main Street*, 131.
108 Hardwick, *Mall Maker*, 148–9.
109 Gosseye and Avermaete, "Shopping Towns Europe," 5.
110 Smith, *Shopping Centers*, 3, 19.
111 Modern Merchandising Methods, *Australian Shopping Centres*, 7.
112 Cohen, *Diffusion*, 27.
113 McKeever et al., *Shopping Center Development Handbook*, 4–7; Smith, *Shopping Centers*, 17–18; Cohen, *Diffusion*, 29–30; Baker and Funaro, *Shopping Centers*, 10–11.
114 Guernsey, "Suburban branches," 42.
115 Smith, *Shopping Centers*, 31–8; *RM*, April 1956, 22–5.
116 Smith, *Shopping Centers*, 41.
117 Gosseye, "Janus-Faced Shopping Center," 866–7.
118 Gosseye and Avermaete, "Shopping Towns Europe," 5–18.
119 Gosseye, "Janus-Faced Shopping Center," 862–4.
120 Gosseye and Avermaete, "Shopping Towns Europe," 15–17.
121 Cupers, "Shopping à l'américaine," 25–6.
122 Jackson, "Consumption and Identity," 30; Scott, *Property Masters*, 203.
123 *RM*, September 1956, 24.
124 See, for example, Stobart, *Spend, Spend, Spend*, 19.

3 Importing shopping centres

Shopping centres arrived in Australia heralded, but untested.[1] The utility of their design had been demonstrated by their acceptance in the United States, although even there, department store firms had equivocated about the best approach to the challenges posed by suburban sprawl.[2] Australia was a different, smaller market. There were fewer greenfield sites available. Suburban retail sales were growing rapidly, but considerable capital remained invested in city retail property. Senior retail managers retained a strong cultural connection to the urban core that had dominated retailing for their entire careers. These factors, as well as the expense of development and the risks inherent in moving first, surround the initial forays into shopping centre construction in Australia. Early development was thus sporadic and uneven. But there was a recognition that conditions might be similar enough in Australia for shopping centres to be transplanted. One early spruiker and developer, Peter Yeomans, declared that:

> We are in a wonderful business. Everything is on our side as far as the future is concerned. The rush to the suburbs is continuing, and that type of rush is the right type of rush for us. The people who are going to the suburbs are young people, people with children, people in the better income groups – and I do not mean high – who are perfect for the shopping centre market. Expressways will be built; they will reach out further to bring people from greater distances. There are more and better automobiles, there is the coming trend towards two-car families, and this is a fact tremendously favourable to shopping centres.[3]

Retail concentration and the push for growth

The first regional shopping centre to open in Australia was built by Brisbane department store firm, Allan & Stark. Chermside Drive-In Shopping Centre opened in May 1957, seven miles north of Brisbane. Its categorisation as "regional" reflected the adoption of the American tripartite typology. This was not widely used in Europe where there was a more informal hierarchy,[4] but in Australia it was copied fairly precisely, albeit scaled down for the smaller market.[5] The merchandise function of each type was largely the same, ranging from convenience at the neighbourhood level through to comprehensive retail provision in regional centres. The scale of Chermside was modest. There were only 25 specialty shops and 700 car parking spaces. But it was well located for both public and private transport, situated adjacent to a tram terminus, and on the intersection of two roads, one of which channelled four lanes of traffic through a growing residential belt. It was estimated that 100,000 people lived within a three-mile radius. Chermside employed an open-air mall design and devoted almost half of the total retail area to Allan & Stark's 40,000 square foot department store.[6]

Peter Scott has noted that the ease with which retail companies can construct or move into new premises can have a major influence on the pace of diffusion of technological innovations.[7] The inclusion of a Woolworths/BCC supermarket at Chermside is instructive in this regard. The store had previously been located across the road, but had faced problems with customer parking. The new shopping centre provided parking, gave Allan & Stark a second anchor for the centre, and marked the beginning of Woolworths' strategy to use shopping centres as a vehicle for national expansion. Both Coles and Woolworths had faced relatively few problems gaining approvals for high street variety store developments, but supermarkets of around 20,000 square feet with parking facilities required sites of up to four acres. These were difficult to find.[8] Shopping centre developers seeking anchor tenants provided them and were prepared to undertake the onerous task of gaining rezoning and development approvals. Supermarkets thus became a standard feature of Australian shopping centres from the beginning. Michael Lloyd describes this as a fundamental distinction between American and Australian regional shopping centres:

> The first American malls were developed as these freeways intersected outside the major cities. The land around them was cheap … So they build a shopping mall there, which was primarily luxury: luxury and leisure orientated. Major department stores, which were fashion orientated, beauticians, hairdressers, specialty shops, jewelers, personal grooming, cafes, restaurants. That was it. No supermarkets or food. No nothing, just luxury items.[9]

Some early regional shopping centres in the United States did contain supermarkets. They were also included in European shopping centres.[10] But the American industry formed a view fairly quickly that food was incompatible with general merchandise and apparel.[11] Department stores influenced this policy, preferring to position regional centres as discretionary shopping environments. The size of the American market, and the limited restrictions that planning placed on development, also allowed for a wider variety of centre types to be developed, and more specialisation at the regional level as the industry matured. The smaller Australian market resulted in more utilitarian shopping centres that catered to a broad cross-section of the population. Tony

Dimasi, who has been conducting economic research for the Australian retail property sector since the early 1980s, argues that:

> Australia is a pretty small place. It's not a mass-market or a huge market ... so one of the things the centres have had to be is almost a jack-of-all-trades. You haven't had this layer of specialisation that you can have with 300 million people. In the US a centre can kind of be one thing, it's a power centre or a food centre. If it's a regional centre it's got five department stores and only apparel. We haven't had the luxury of doing that ... all of our centres have had to appeal to all layers ...[12]

As Australia's first regional, Chermside drew considerable interest from other retail firms and public authorities across the country.[13] Retail press noted, however, that the venture had "an experimental quality" and that other retailers were reserving "judgement on imitative action until they see the results."[14] Myer, in particular were watching closely. The Melbourne firm had plans of its own to develop shopping centres and was also aggressively expansionist. Indeed, Chermside was a form of forward defence for the Brisbane firm, which harboured a prescient concern that it would be taken over by one of the big southern department stores. Sydney's David Jones had acquired Brisbane's Finney Isles & Co. department store in 1955.[15] Myer had begun interstate acquisitions in the 1920s, had necessarily curtailed expansion during the war years, and then absorbed a number of smaller department stores in the 1950s.[16] In 1955 it declared that it was "constantly alert ... and very strongly placed both financially and in terms of personnel to take advantages of any opportunities" for takeovers that presented. The same year it acquired McWhirters, Brisbane's largest retail store.[17] Allan & Stark's general manager and director, T. J. Weedman, declared that "today in business you have to be either very large or remain small."[18] Commentators at the time concurred, questioning the viability of single department stores in a future of chains.[19] So while Chermside was an attempt by Allan & Stark to grow their own market share, it made the firm even more attractive to Myer because of its own desire for growth and its assessment of the opportunities shopping centres held in the Australian market. Myer acquired Allan & Stark and with it, Chermside, in 1959.[20]

Stand-alone or shopping centre?

Sydney was the next Australian city to house a regional shopping centre. The country's biggest retail market (Figure 3.1) had given rise to more large department store firms than any other state capital city. Collectively, these city retailers faced the question their American peers had been grappling with as early as the 1920s, and acutely since the end of the war.[21] How best to meet the suburban market? Looking out to the blossoming suburbs from a sluggish urban core, most Sydney department stores chose to follow their customers, although their approaches varied in scale and form. Pre-planned shopping centres were a recognisable mechanism, but they would not fit neatly into the city's established suburban landscape. In America, freeways provided access to cheap land that could be developed. In Sydney, vacant land accessible to population centres was harder to find. A swamp, a drowned quarry and a former golf course sit beneath three of Sydney's earliest and most recognisable regional shopping centres: Warringah Mall, Miranda Fair and Roselands. Others were built over dozens of smaller parcels of land that were acquired piecemeal through the purchase of existing buildings that were razed.

The difficulty of finding sites initially pushed the city's department stores to construct stand-alone suburban branches, but the value of overcoming this obstacle also incentivised the pursuit of more comprehensive developments by entrepreneurs. Sydney recorded more suburban sales than Melbourne, but was proportionally more dependent on city retailing (Figures 2.2 and 3.1). Melbourne actually had more suburban stores in many key product categories, including men's and women's wear, but the stores on average produced lower sales volumes than in Sydney. Sydney had more big department stores than

Figure 3.1 Australian metropolitan retail sales, 1956/7.

Melbourne, which was dominated by Myer. In 1962, Myer's massive city operation accounted for more than 27 per cent of all Melbourne's inner-city retail trade.[22] In contrast, Sydney's largest stores, David Jones and Grace Bros., respectively garnered 13 and 9 per cent of CBD retail sales.[23] In Melbourne this resulted in lower levels of suburban investment by decentralising city firms in both stand-alone stores and, later, shopping centres.

By the mid sixties, every one of Sydney's 11 full-line inner-city department stores had opened a suburban store, with a total of 69 such stores in operation.[24] Market research suggested that this "oversupply" of stores, combined with those then in development, would "more than adequately service the present population," and that there were "no large unexploited areas remaining" in the metropolitan area.[25] This steady opening of individual department stores combined with the difficulty of finding suitable sites for large-scale centres, explains to some degree why it was not Sydney's largest stores that led the initial foray into suburban shopping centre development. Individuals also made a difference: in Melbourne the Myer board was the reluctant recipient of earnest entreaties by Kenneth Myer to embrace shopping centre construction. The board, however, shared the reserve of Sydney's largest stores, which also, at least initially, appear to have preferred less ambitious developments.

City branch store decentralisation activated shopping strips, attracting broad retail mixes responding to customer needs. As car usage grew and these precincts experienced more traffic congestion, pre-planned shopping centres became more appealing. But in the 1950s, many district high streets were strong enough to inhibit investment by the major department stores in shopping centre development.[26] Balancing this decision was all the more important in Sydney because of the high costs of land compared with other capitals.[27] The two big Sydney retailers that were later most prominent in developing shopping centres, David Jones and Grace Bros., began decentralisation more circumspectly through stand-alone stores. Some other Sydney firms experimented with hybrid developments, in which a few large stores co-located to reduce costs and leverage off one another's drawing power. But mostly the other big city stores also opted for stand-alone developments.

Grace Bros. had opened branches in Parramatta (Sydney's second city) and Bondi Junction (the major tramway junction in the eastern suburbs) in the 1930s. This became necessary when the Sydney harbour bridge and a new underground railway channelled customer traffic away from its Broadway store at the inland mouth of the city. These two sites left Grace Bros. well geared for suburban growth early in the post-war boom. It conducted substantial renovations on both stores in the late 1950s and early 1960s, and then built a 200,000 square foot suburban store to the north of the city at Chatswood.[28] Commentators at the time argued that the success of these stores indicated that branch decentralisation could be achieved without planned shopping centres.[29] David Jones also believed this to be true, and started its suburban foray on the outer fringe of Parramatta's shopping precinct in Sydney's west. The store was eventually abandoned, unable to compete with a massive shopping centre that

Westfield built in the middle of Parramatta in 1975, and which David Jones would itself eventually join in the mid 1990s.

With these dynamics in play, it was smaller developers and lesser department stores that set the pace of early suburban shopping centre development in Sydney. Sydney's first shopping centre, Top Ryde, opened shortly after Chermside in November 1957. The project originated in the offices of the Ryde Municipal Council. Showing considerable foresight, as early as 1943 and well before Australia's major retailers had begun their entry into the field, the council identified a need for a commercial centre in the municipality and, after some delays, set about acquiring properties behind the existing shopping strip. Unable to secure finance from higher levels of government, though, they eventually sold the land to a suburban department store, A. J. Benjamin.[30] The Council then approved construction of a commercial centre that brought investment, retail infrastructure and parking to the municipality. This private–public compact became a feature of the industry in Australia, pre-empting the privatisation ethos that characterised infrastructure projects more broadly later in the century.

A. J. Benjamin was a small but ambitious firm that had begun expanding by acquiring subsidiaries in southern Sydney and Broken Hill. It also established a separate hardware and gardening store in Chatswood called Benjamin's Building Centre, which formed the origins of the nationwide BBC hardware chain still in operation today.[31] Top Ryde represented a new phase of growth, the seeds of which were planted when the proprietor's son, Peter Benjamin, visited around twenty American centres in 1953, meeting up with his friend Peter Yeoman who was undertaking postgraduate studies on American shopping centres in Detroit. The two men worked together developing Top Ryde, which Peter Spearritt has described as "one of the most sordid examples of late 1950s architecture in Australia, worse even than the high schools built in that era."[32] Contemporary commentary was more positive, extolling the virtues of an American format adapted to Australian conditions. Newspaper coverage emphasised Top Ryde's modern design, noting that the centre was "entirely for the pedestrian, but the pedestrian who shops by car is given the easiest possible access."[33] This, according to one of the early spruikers of shopping centre development in Australia, Denis Winston, head of Sydney University's Department of Town and Country Planning, was an essential requirement for retailing in the private transport city:

> There is a vital need to separate the heavy, fast [car] traffic from the pedestrians, working and visiting the stores … there must be easy access to the shops for vehicles carrying the shoppers, at the same time as the centre provides peace, quiet and safety. Moreover, delivery vehicles must have good entry to the centre without clashing with the shoppers. This problem has now been satisfactorily solved, and the Americans, not for the first time, have got in first … The new regional shopping centres are the first example of the return to the amenities of the pre-industrial city.[34]

Chermside and Top Ryde were significant for providing a proof of concept for the shopping centre form in Australia, but they did not provide lasting success for their founders.[35] Neither firm grew to the scale identified by T. J. Weedman as necessary to survive in a rapidly changing industry. Not long after Myer acquired Allan & Stark, A. J. Benjamin's was bankrupt, a result of Grace Bros.' expansion which destroyed sales in the former's original suburban store at Chatswood. Grace Bros subsequently took over the Benjamin's store in Top Ryde. As one of the department managers, Gwen Jackson, later recalled: "All the managers were called into the store at 8am on a Sunday. We knew that meant that the store had been sold, but we didn't know if we were going to be a Myer, Walton's or Grace Bros. store."[36] Jackson, like Weedman, was aware that medium-size retail firms with stores in desirable locations, including shopping centre anchor tenancies, were ripe pickings for acquisitive larger department store chains.[37]

A retail property industry in Australia

The shopping centre introduced a new industry to Australia. The retail formats that evolved internationally in the nineteenth century, as well as the earlier shopping environments identified by Gruen and Smith, thrived on the appeal of traders grouped together in one location. Shopping centres also traded on the strength of retail agglomeration. Further, they captured its value in a way that individual landlords in high streets could not. High streets offered customers a wide retail offer, but individual landlords could not materially improve the overall precinct. Shopping centre landlords could. And the improvements they made could be monetised. When tenants rented space in a shopping centre, they purchased customer traffic. The landlord created this traffic by convincing anchor stores to locate in a centre, adding a mix of retailers attractive to the surrounding market, building in an accessible location, providing sufficient parking and air-conditioning, and generally investing in the overall amenity of the environment. Retailers could initiate, drive and manage this process, as Allan & Stark and A. J. Benjamin's had done. So, too, could entrepreneurial developers − if they could convince major retailers to anchor their projects and sign up enough specialty stores to round out the tenancy mix.

> The developers said: "what do you want?" And, the department store gave them the specification. The supermarkets gave them the specification. But there were hardly any supermarkets. I mean supermarkets only came in the 60s. So they [also] went out onto the street and they saw the local greengrocer. They saw he had a shop for about 80 square meters and they put a shop [in the shopping centre] of about 80 square meters and said, "do you want it?" And they did the same with the local butcher, and the baker, and the deli.[38]

The demise of A. J. Benjamin's provided an entry point for a firm that would become one of the country's most significant shopping centre developers. Lend Lease, which acquired Top Ryde in 1961, arose out of the Dutch firm, Bredero's Construction Company. Seeking large-scale construction expertise, an Australian government mission was sent abroad in the late 1940s to canvas expressions of interest for the Snowy Mountains Hydro-Electric scheme and other development projects. Bredero's assigned the task of scoping these opportunities in Australia to a thirty-year-old engineer who headed their construction department, G. J. Dusseldorp.[39]

Dusseldorp compiled a favourable report and travelled to Australia with his family to run the Bredero operation, Civil and Civic. Dusseldorp's ambitions, as well as frustration with inefficient tendering and building practices, encouraged him to expand from his initial construction remit. In the process he gained control over all phases of development projects. Arguing that architects were incentivised to increase expenditure, leaving builders to carry the cost of changes and delays, he set up a Design Services Group, "which included architectural, structural, electrical, mechanical and plumbing design services, and quantity surveying."[40] This single design and construct product disrupted the market, intervening in the relationship between client, builder and architect. Dusseldorp then began offering finance to growing companies that required larger premises but wanted to lease or purchase them over time rather than pay upfront development costs. By adding finance to his package, Dusseldorp provided his firm with entrepreneurial control over projects. In 1958, Civil and Civic established Lend Lease as a public company to provide finance for projects through share issues. It was soon generating projects for Civil and Civic, buying sites, planning, designing and constructing residential, office and commercial buildings. In 1961, Lend Lease took over Civil & Civic, forming a fully integrated group. By 1963, the firm employed more than 3,000 people across the country.[41] It subsequently became one of the country's largest and most influential shopping centre developers, building a number of landmark centres and training a generation of executives working across the retail property industry both in Australia and internationally.

In the late 1950s and early 1960s, though, it was small, energetic start-up firms driving neighbourhood and community shopping centre construction across the country. Tony Dimasi argues that it was these firms that were "the innovators. They didn't necessarily have big balance sheets, they made a lot of mistakes … [but they were] pioneering developers … up and comers who were just blue-sky visionaries."[42] When these entrepreneurs offered retail space in desirable locations, they facilitated the expansionist strategies of big retail. The supermarkets, in particular, needed sites that provided good parking near growing populations. Fraser Cross, responsible for finding sites for Woolworths' supermarkets in the 1960s, later recalled that:

> individual developers came on the scene and they came to us and asked us
> if we would be willing to put a supermarket into a small shopping centre

at such and such a place and I said I didn't see any reason why we wouldn't because I knew the area fairly well and I knew it had a fairly decent population. So, we went in with those people and we took the lease of their supermarket.[43]

Many of these firms were operated by men who had recently arrived in Australia from Europe. Ervin Graf, a Hungarian immigrant and qualified architect who began his post-war life in Australia as a bricklayer, moved into residential development in 1952, and then into retail property with community centres at Wollongong (1961) and Maroubra (1963), and a neighbourhood centre in Toongabbie (1963). Such firms presaged the corporate multinationals that dominate the industry's more recent history. Many have disappeared. Some, such as Graf's Stocks and Holdings (later Stockland), grew into national firms with footprints indelibly imprinted in communities across Australia. The most successful was Westfield, which from the humblest of beginnings evolved into the largest retail property company in the world.[44]

The Westfield retail property story has its Australian roots in 1950s Blacktown, a suburb 25 miles to the west of Sydney's CBD. Blacktown almost quadrupled its population between 1946/7 and 1961/2, by which time 86,295 people lived in the municipality. It was identified as an ideal location to open a delicatessen by two recent migrants, Frank Lowy and Jeno Schwarcz (later John Saunders). Lowy had arrived in Australia, a penniless Holocaust survivor. Born in Czechoslovakia in 1930, his family experienced the deprivations of the Great Depression, foreign occupation, the Second World War and the Nazis' genocidal regime. Germany's annexation of the Czech Sudetenland border region under the Munich agreement in 1938 encouraged land grabs of Czechoslovakia by Poland and Hungary, the latter occupying the region where Lowy's family lived. Amidst growing anti-semitism, his mother's family, living in what had become Slovakia, were rounded up, deported and disappeared. Lowy's immediate family moved to Budapest seeking anonymity in numbers. Despite these efforts, his brother was placed in a labour group and lost touch with the family. In 1944, Lowy's father was interned in a Hungarian concentration camp, Kistarcsa, before being transferred to Auschwitz where he was murdered by the Nazis.[45]

To improve their chances of survival the family split up. Frank remained with his mother and the two were soon moved to a ghetto under curfew. Aged 14 he operated on the streets gathering food and information to protect his family through the final precarious, terrifying months of the war. At its cessation the family moved back to their hometown of Filakovo before Frank and his brother John travelled to Palestine, across heavy seas, with little food or water, in a dilapidated boat with 400 other refugees. Around the same time, his sister Edith emigrated to Australia with her husband. Following the partition of Palestine in November 1947, Lowy fought in its civil war, including house-to-house urban street fighting in Tiberias before being assigned to the Golani brigade, which undertook countless night-time raids into enemy territory during the Arab-Israeli war. After the war, he studied accountancy and joined a bank in a junior position, but with his mother, sister and one brother now in Australia, elected to join them, arriving together with his brother John on Australia Day 1952. With no money, Frank worked in a factory, then in a sandwich shop, and then as a delivery driver for a Hungarian small goods trader. He built a progressively larger customer base (and commissions) through an almost obsessive approach to the job. One of his regular customers was Jeno Schwarcz, a Hungarian Jew who ran a delicatessen at Sydney's Town Hall Station.

Schwarcz, too, had a traumatic history. In 1933, at the age of ten, he lost his father to leukemia. He left school three years later to help run the family's small leather shop in Satoraljaujhely in north-eastern Hungary. He made a success of the business, exhibiting innate people skills and a capacity to make advantageous business deals, but was operating in an environment in which "the Jewish question" loomed ever larger. Jews were scapegoated for Hungary's economic problems, and when war broke out, violent, systemic persecution escalated. In 1943, aged 21, Schwarcz was arrested, interrogated and sent to the Garany administrative detention camp for Jews, located some 18 miles from his home town. Following the Nazi occupation, he was sent to Auschwitz, surviving by the mere chance that he was sent on again to a work camp. Personal courage and enterprise kept him and a number of his close comrades alive. He returned home, to be greeted by his two sisters and the devastating news that the Nazis had murdered the remainder of his family.[46]

In the immediate aftermath of the war Schwarcz returned to business, wheeling and dealing to locate and add value to scarce resources. Although turning a profit, the political situation in Eastern Europe encouraged him to leave Hungary, via Slovakia and Vienna. He married while in Austria, and with long waiting periods for emigration to the United States and Canada, settled on Australia as the country in which he would start a new life. In Sydney he began working as an upholsterer, moved to a position in Anthony Hordern's department store, and then set up a small shop in the underpass of the Town Hall railway station selling small goods. When Lowy began deliveries, Schwarcz was struck by his efficiency, competency and honesty. Shared backgrounds, ambition and a mutual respect led to a partnership.

Schwarcz and Lowy opened a delicatessen in Blacktown in 1955, providing fresh bread and small goods unavailable elsewhere to the large immigrant population. The logic behind their business strategy is encapsulated in a quote attributed to Saunders: "In the city delicatessens, Australians buy devon by the slice; in Blacktown immigrants buy salami by the yard."[47] The store thrived and ten months later the pair converted a vacant nearby shop into an espresso bar that found favour with local Italians. They then moved into residential development and formed a company named after their activities subdividing paddocks in Sydney's western suburbs. Westfield soon moved into retail development. Ervin Graf was a regular visitor to the delicatessen, later recalling: "I suggested to Jeno that, instead of selling salami in Blacktown, they might do better building a few shops."[48] After building a number of individual stores, they bought a large block of land, again in Blacktown, and built a shopping centre.

Westfield Place opened on 2 July 1959.[49] The design was an open U-shaped mall, with a junior department store at the apex, parking provision for around 80–90 cars, and a pharmacy, appliance store, delicatessen, butcher, fruit market, small supermarket, restaurant and shoe store.[50] It was the first foothold of an enterprise that would change the built form of Australian cities and act as an exemplar of the contribution that immigrant entrepreneurs made to post-war Australian society.

Public shopping centre development

The late 1950s shopping centres thus far described were built by private enterprise pursuing solutions and opportunities during a period of intense urban disruption. For designs they largely looked to America. Public housing authorities also developed shopping centres as commercial community centres for housing estates.[51] They were influenced by European ideas. The most substantial public shopping centres were built in South Australia under the auspices of the South Australian Housing Trust (SAHT). The SAHT differed from authorities in other states in that, more than just providing low-cost housing, it was tasked with facilitating the industrialisation of South Australia. Its estates were not built for "the slum dweller," but for the working family. The SAHT's largest and most influential project, Elizabeth, was located 19 miles north of Adelaide. It shared many similarities with the British 'Mark 1' New Town, which utilised "spacious garden city lines with distinct neighbourhoods served by local shops and a school, together with a town centre and single industrial areas."[52] To these the SAHT added leisure facilities such as theatres and churches. European-inspired, it was a working-class parallel to the upper-middle-class J. C. Nichols Country Club in America.

Initially, houses preceded infrastructure, leaving incoming residents wondering where they had arrived. Amelia Redmond, an early resident, later remembered:

> we were offered a house in Elizabeth Downs … It was a lovely spanking new place but at the end of civilisation. Houses were put up so quickly there were no roads, lights, paths or driveways. You stepped from a sea of red mud into the lounge … At night it looked like we were on the edge of nowhere.[53]

Development after this, including of shopping centres, was relatively rapid. In all, nine neighbourhood shopping centres were constructed in Elizabeth between 1957 and 1965. Each was intended to serve around 5,000 to 6,000 people, catering to "the housewife's day-by-day needs, but [were not] … sufficiently comprehensive to make it unnecessary for her to visit the Town Centre."[54] The latter was situated close to the geographic heart of Elizabeth and opened in November 1960. It was comprised of a number of shopping blocks connected by partially covered pedestrian malls. There was parking for more than 3,000 cars, with an average walking distance to the shops of 300 feet. Service and delivery access points were screened to improve amenity.[55] The SAHT built some buildings, and sold other sites to individual retailers for private construction. Elizabeth was projected to become by far the largest population centre in South Australia outside of the capital, Adelaide. This was an appealing market to retailers. The city's biggest department store firm, John Martin & Co., built a 120,000 square foot department store in Elizabeth Town Centre.[56] Woolworths built the town's largest supermarket. Coles opened a hybrid variety store supermarket in a building built by the SAHT.[57]

The rapid construction of infrastructure transformed what had been an almost desolate landscape. Continuing her account of these early years, Amelia Redmond remembers: the "city was taking shape, we had a new shopping centre, a swimming pool and two theatres. We were made a city. We've got Johnny Martins."[58] Her comment reveals the importance of retail infrastructure to residents in outlying suburban areas: similar enthusiasm greeted the arrival of city department store branches in western Sydney in the 1970s. More than just sites of distribution, such developments transformed understandings of place, making accessible a lifestyle taken for granted in established areas to people who keenly felt its absence on the urban fringe.

Before the collapse of the post-war boom in the 1970s, when the manufacturing industries for which Elizabeth was built began declining, the town was lauded as a successful example of modernist urban planning. One retail trade journal noted that the Elizabeth shopping centres "must be of interest to all Australian retailers, who will recognise that planned shopping will be the rule, not the exception, in the future."[59] While this prediction proved accurate, the involvement of public authorities as owners and developers never surpassed the efforts of the SAHT at Elizabeth. Indeed, the town has been described as the "last gasp" of Ebenezer Howard's Garden City ideal. While a small number of shopping centres were developed by public authorities in the eastern states and Canberra in the 1960s and 1970s, fealty to the notion of publicly developed retail sites faded in the post-war years. Retailers were also not always enthusiastic about public designs. While the large immediate population of working-class residents proved to be a strong customer base, Elizabeth's architects and planners lacked retail experience and the size and layout of shops did not always suit the requirements of the larger operators.[60]

Over time, the early centres built by public authorities were transferred into private hands. In 1982, Elizabeth Town Centre was acquired under a 99-year lease by a joint venture between Myer Shopping Centres and Jennings Industries.[61] Like other centres transferred to the private sector, it became largely indistinguishable from the privately developed centres that overwhelmingly characterise the history of Australian shopping centre development. The most prominent early example of these opened in Melbourne just six weeks before Elizabeth Town Centre. It remains, today, one of the largest and most productive centres in the country. Through a number of redevelopments, it has set new benchmarks through innovations that changed the shape of the industry. After considerable internal debate, the Myer board had decided to move into shopping centre construction and approved planning for the largest, most expensive centre yet constructed in Australia: Chadstone.

Notes

1 For an analysis of the introduction of shopping centres to Australia, see Bailey, "Urban Disruption."
2 Howard, *From Main Street to Mall*, 134–5.
3 Peter Yeomans quoted in *RT*, February 1961, 46.
4 Howard and Stobart, "Arcades, Shopping Centres," 203.
5 Modern Merchandising Methods, *Australian Shopping Centres*, 3–4.
6 CMA, Box 2012, Chermside and Coorparoo Stores.
7 Scott, *Property Masters*, 1–2.
8 CMA, Box 4097, Stella Barber interview with Arthur Coles, 24 February 1988; Scott, *Property Masters*, 203.
9 Author interview with Michael Lloyd, 11 June 2014.
10 Jackson, "Consumption and Identity," 30; Gosseye, "Janus-Faced Shopping Center," 871–3.
11 *RM*, February 1958, 11; *RM*, July 1959, 4; Baker and Funaro, *Shopping Centers*, 177; McKeever et al., *Shopping Center Development Handbook*, 72.
12 Author interview with Tony Dimasi, 3 November 2014.
13 Bailey, "Urban Disruption."
14 *RM*, July 1957, 25–6.
15 Beed, "Growth of Suburban Retailing," 158.
16 Barber, *Your Store Myer*, 42–102.
17 Myer Emporium Annual Report, 1955.
18 *CM*, 29 May 1970, 22.
19 *RM*, June 1957, 15.
20 Barber, *Your Store Myer*, 89.
21 Howard, *From Main Street to Mall*, 134–9.
22 CMA, Box 142, Memorandum, The drift from the cities, 29 July 1963.
23 CMA, Box 142, Larry Smith & Company, Market Analysis of the Sydney Metropolitan Area, 21 May 1963, 3; ABS, *Census of Retail Establishments*, 1961/2.
24 Modern Merchandising Methods, *Australian Shopping Centres*, 2.
25 CMA, Box 142, Peter Hyde, Suburban Opportunities in Sydney Metropolitan Area – Sydney Survey, May 1965, 3.
26 Cumberland County Council, "Effects of Urban Decentralization."
27 CMA, Box 4765, Stella Barber interview with Geoff Tate, 28 June 1986.
28 Brash, *Model Store*, 270–6.
29 *RM*, January 1961, 9.
30 Beed, "Growth of Suburban Retailing," 265–9.
31 *DT*, 13 November 1957, 19.
32 Spearritt, "Suburban Cathedrals," 97.
33 *SMH*, 12 November 1957, 19.
34 *SMH*, 12 November 1957, 21.
35 *DT*, 13 November 1957, 20.
36 CMA, Box 75, *G. B. News* 26(5), May 1985, 1.

37 *RM*, June 1957, 10–11.
38 Author interview with Michael Lloyd, 11 June 2014.
39 Murphy, *Challenges of Change*, 1–10.
40 Murphy, *Challenges of Change*, 29–35.
41 *CT*, 5 March 1963, 1.
42 Author interview with Tony Dimasi, 3 November 2014.
43 SLNSW, MLOH 451, Nos. 23 and 24, Jenny Hudson interview with Fraser Coss, ca. 1995, transcript, 12.
44 Sammartino and Van Ruth, "Westfield Group," 308.
45 The information about Frank Lowy and Westfield in this and subsequent paragraphs is largely drawn from Margo, *Frank Lowy*, 1–79.
46 John Saunders' personal history here and in subsequent paragraphs is largely drawn from Kune, *Nothing Is Impossible*, 1–73.
47 Westfield Holdings Ltd, *Westfield Story*, 9.
48 Kune, *Nothing Is Impossible*, 79.
49 Sammartino and Van Ruth, "Westfield Group," 309–10.
50 *Blacktown Advocate*, 25 June 1959, 13.
51 *RM*, September 1959, 14.
52 Kemeny, "South Australian Housing Trust," 109; Peel, "Planning the Good City," 10; Marsden, 'The South Australian Housing Trust', 50–5.
53 Marsden, "South Australian Housing Trust," 52.
54 SAHT, "Proposed Shopping Facilities," 2.
55 Smith, "Town Planning in Elizabeth," 19–23.
56 Peel, *Good Times*, 80–1.
57 Modern Merchandising Methods, *Australian Shopping Centres* (1971 edn).
58 Marsden, "South Australian Housing Trust," 52.
59 *RM*, January 1957, 10.
60 CMA, Box 4766, Stella Barber interview with Brian Quinn, 10 July 1987.
61 Peel, *Good Times*, 193.

4 Scale, enclosure and proliferation

When it acquired Allan & Stark in 1959, Myer gained Chermside shopping centre, which was undergoing expansion, as well as land at Coorparoo, southeast of the city, that the Brisbane firm had purchased to build a second regional shopping centre. These projects had placed Allan & Stark at the forefront of shopping centre development in Australia – a strategy now recognisably farsighted – but they were not enough to overcome the advantages that history had bequeathed Myer. The Melbourne firm dominated its large home city market like no other store in the country and had begun acquisitive expansion earlier and more aggressively than any of its peers nationally. The acquisition of Allan & Stark gave Myer a foothold in both central and suburban Brisbane as well as ownership of the then largest shopping centre in the country, which had generated sales 15 per cent higher than projected in its first year.[1] These represented gains for Myer's business strategy at the time: as well as moving towards greater scale and scope via geographical expansion through acquisitions, it was also building new capabilities as a retail property firm.

This strategy had been developed over almost a decade of planning and internal firm debate. On a business trip to the United States in 1949, Director Kenneth Myer, the eldest son of founder Sidney Myer, met a number of developers engaged in the construction of regional shopping centres. In Los Angeles he visited the Broadway-Crenshaw Center, and Gruen Associates' first major project, Milliron's Department Store in downtown Westchester.[2] The Broadway-Crenshaw Center was the first shopping mall on the west coast. Anchored by a May department store, a Woolworths variety store and a Von's supermarket, it demonstrated to Kenneth Myer the possibilities of agglomerated retail. Milliron's was a modernist masterpiece, with both surround and rooftop parking, that included a restaurant, beauty parlor and auditorium. Like the later Grace Bros. suburban department stores in Sydney, it was an example of the evolution of department stores towards the shopping centre concept – a horizontal expansion of their offering to become a more comprehensive one-stop-shop.[3]

Kenneth Myer returned to Australia convinced that he had seen the future of retailing. However, his firm was deeply invested in downtown department stores and he was unable to persuade the board, under the chairmanship of his older cousin Norman Myer, to pursue suburban shopping centre construction.[4]

Norman, 24 years Kenneth's senior, had demonstrated strategic nous and a commitment to store development in driving the expansion of Myer since the death of Sidney Myer in 1934. His retail outlook, though, had been conditioned by a career during which the power of central-city retailing had never been challenged. For a man that one favourable obituary described as "no reckless experimenter," it was too soon to emulate the few untested American examples at the time.[5] Norman was insistent that the future of the company lay in further expansion through the acquisition of urban, suburban and regional stores, and through continued investment in CBD retailing, not through the decentralisation strategy of suburban shopping centre development being suggested by Kenneth Myer.[6]

Later in the decade, Coles' NSW merchandise manager, A. R. Bracher, suggested to a retail conference that over the previous 15–20 years the average age of business managers had "trended downwards," producing an "accelerative factor" as fresh ideas and enthusiasm were injected into management practice. He claimed that the phrase "we always did it that way" was being replaced by "sounds feasible and practical, let's give it a try."[7] Generalised arguments such as Bracher's can mask more complex processes, but it is useful for considering the appeal of modernisation for a younger generation of retailers. When Coles purchased the Matthews Thompson chain in 1960, its elderly Chairman, F. L. Thompson, reportedly declared that "these supermarkets will never succeed in Australia."[8] His claim seems short-sighted now, but demonstrates the difficulty of changing tack towards the end of a long and largely profitable journey.

Frustrated and convinced that Australia must inevitably follow the American trend, Kenneth and his brother Sidney Baillieu ("Bails") Myer, who had recently returned from Cambridge with an economics degree, were determined to set a new path forward. They engaged economic consultant George Connor to scope for suitable sites in Melbourne's suburbs. Connor was the first serious economic researcher for retail property development in the country. He had informal relationships with Larry Smith and other economists in the United States, and had decided to set up a similar line of business in Australia. Reg Jebb, who had just completed a commerce degree with a thesis on shopping centre development, joined Connor in the mid 1960s. Jebb became Connor's first associate, and subsequently one of the key researchers for the retail property industry in Australia. He recounts that during the war, Connor

> was seconded by the Australian Navy to be an intelligence officer, a liaison intelligence officer with MacArthur, and the US fleet and so forth. So, he went all around ... island hopping with MacArthur, and when he came back to Australia after the war, he went on a couple of trade delegations to Japan and that sort of stuff. And Melbourne was about to prepare a new planning scheme, which became the 1954 planning scheme for Melbourne, and George got the task of being a chief economist writing that plan ... [providing] all the economic input, the operation growth and demography, such as it was in those days. He was sort of pioneering in that sort of stuff.

And that was finished in 1954, and he went off and sold himself as a consultant. He sold himself to Myers and he knew them, Ken and Bails Myer
who were then directors, more or less, of the company … And he basically
went to them and said, "Look, I have done all the planning, the economics
side of it for Melbourne, and I can tell you where population growth is
going to go…" So … they gave George the job of doing it, which he did,
and he organised for them to buy a large parcel of land on the corner of the
Burwood Highway where the Kmart development is now, and also at Bass
Hill in Sydney and others, but the way that things worked out planning
wise, it was not necessarily those sites that were later developed.[9]

On return tours to the United States in 1953, 1955 and 1958, Kenneth Myer
made further studies of shopping centre development and began meeting
with industry professionals, including Gruen, Smith and the architects at
Welton Becket & Associates.[10] The latter had been responsible for the design
of Stonestown Shopping Center in San Francisco, which drew on Northgate's
model of an open-air central pedestrian spine, a segregated parking lot, and an
underground delivery tunnel to maintain the relaxed amenity of the shopping
environment.[11] A department store anchored one end of the mall, a supermarket the other. The department store was accessible on two levels from both
the parking lot and the mall.[12] This design formed the template for Chadstone.[13]

Through personal advocacy and networking, Kenneth Myer thus assembled
a formidable team. The death of Norman Myer in December 1956 reduced
board opposition to his decentralisation strategy, and by 1957 solid plans were
being formulated for the firm's first shopping centre development. Larry Smith
& Co. were appointed as consultants, Welton Becket & Associates the design
architects. Melbourne firm, Tompkins & Shaw Architects, which had designed
Myer's Bourke and Lonsdale Street city stores, were assigned the role of production architects. Myer senior board member, George McMahon, was given project management duties.[14] Myer publicly announced that it was seeking a site
of at least 30 acres for a suburban shopping centre development, and combed
the city for suitable locations.[15] Analysis was undertaken on population growth,
spending patterns, transportation networks and the relative intensity of Myer
customers in given areas. Melbourne's south-eastern suburbs, then experiencing substantial growth, were identified as the preferred area for development.[16]

Good fortune arrived through an unexpected offer from the sisters at the
Convent of the Good Shepherd for 28 acres in East Malvern, 8 miles south-
east of Melbourne, enabling Myer to build its own cathedral of consumption
on ground consecrated by demographic and economic research. The site was
situated on the corner of Chadstone Road and a new four-lane highway that
led to the expanding industrial suburbs of Dandenong. An evaluation showed
that 216,000 people lived within a 15-minute drive, with most of these within 3
miles of the site. While many local women did not own or drive cars, there was
a strong public transport network of buses connecting to nearby train stations.[17]
As it shaped a vision for the trade area, Myer became dissatisfied with the

American architects who were supposed to realise it. There were suggestions that Welton Becket were paying scant attention to the distant project, as well as cryptic comments about the American firm's failure to grasp "Australian thinking" and an "Australian approach" to development. What this meant is not explicitly articulated in surviving records, but Welton Becket's role was soon curtailed. Tompkins & Shaw were given primary responsibility for Chadstone's design.

Myer were conscious of the need to align the shopping centre to Australian conditions, although in practice modifications were modest. At the time, open-mall designs were being superseded in America – Gruen having just completed the fully internalised Southdale – but the Stonestown model was cheaper, proven, probably considered more suitable to Melbourne's climate, and bore a closer resemblance to the traditional shopping street familiar to Australian shoppers. The site's bow-tie shape presented difficulties, necessitating a design with a clear front and back that contrasted with the latest American designs that (with larger, cheaper sites) tended to place shopping centres in the middle of surrounding car parks. The clear frontage at Chadstone, though, was used advantageously by incorporating a landscaped plaza opening onto the car park, reducing the length of the mall area and creating a welcoming entrance to the shops. Another major difference from American designs arose from the insistence by S. E. Dickens that their supermarket open primarily into the car park rather than the mall, reducing its effectiveness as an anchor.[18]

These modifications aside, the American influence was as clear at Chadstone as it was in Australia's other early shopping centres: the entire complex was architecturally cohesive and designed as a single operating unit; parking was fundamental to its form (with parking bays large enough to accommodate American cars); anchor stores were utilised as branded draw cards; the centre housed city stores seeking to capture suburban custom; modernist imagery was employed because it was "intrinsically associated with … commercially successful shopping developments"; and tenant rentals were tied to turnover. This leasing system holds significance extending far beyond Chadstone. It became widely adopted across the industry because it was highly useful for landlords: the reporting of individual stores' sales figures provided a data set on retail operations that could be used to drive efficiencies and assess rental levels. Turnover rents later became a key issue of contention between tenants and landlords, although in the early days at Chadstone they were promoted as a clever appropriation of American methods.[19]

Chadstone offered Australian consumers a unique proposition, elevating the scale of suburban retail development to a new level (Figure 4.1). Myer's 150,000 square foot store was the country's first full-line, shopping centre department store, far larger than the junior department stores anchoring centres like Chermside, Top Ryde and Westfield Place.[20] It included a three-hundred-seat cafeteria, beauty parlours, a ladies' lounge, glass-sided escalators and modernist fittings. A food parcel pick-up system allowed customers to browse other shops before collecting their purchases and heading home.[21] Such a substantial store,

Figure 4.1 Aerial photo of Chadstone, ca. 1960.

and the move to the suburbs by the country's largest department store firm, were an unmistakable signal of the city's retail recession and the structural shift in Australia's retail geography.

Myer also convinced other major retailers to embrace retail agglomeration. Where Chermside and Top Ryde offered a single department store, Chadstone incorporated branches of a number of city-based competitors and general merchandise chains. In all, the £6 million centre – the largest project ever undertaken by an Australian retail firm at the time[22] – housed 80 shops, including branches of the Melbourne department store firms Buckley & Nunn and Foy & Gibson. These stores had long competed with Myer's massive CBD store: Buckley & Nunn adjoined Myer in both the city and Chadstone.[23] This echoed the experience in America where the disadvantages of competing from separate stand-alone sites were recognised, and as many as five department stores shared space in some early regional centres.[24] While Chadstone's other department store outlets, at a tenth the size of the centre's Myer store, were more "twigs" than "branches" of city parent stores, their presence demonstrated the value of co-location in the Australian context.

Co-location followed the same logic that drew big city stores into close proximity in central business districts: their combined presence amplified retail drawing power. As had long been the case in the city, people were prepared to travel further to visit the concentration of shops housed in a shopping centre than they were to visit a single store – however large, well-stocked or cheap – in a stand-alone suburban location. One-stop-shopping, where everything could be purchased in a single trip, with the opportunity to comparison shop for the best value and most suitable item, proved a compelling proposition. Stand-alone store development was also expensive: it was cheaper and easier for Buckley & Nunn and Foy & Gibson to join Myer's development at Chadstone than it was to organise, finance, gain approval and build their own suburban stores or shopping centres. Other specialty chains at Chadstone, including Portman's, Rockmans, Sussan and Sportsgirl, similarly benefited from joining a development that generated mass customer traffic.

Chadstone's scale and innovation drew voluminous attention. A few weeks prior to opening, readers of *The Sun* were advised that a "giant is stirring in suburban Melbourne." They were asked "to imagine all the best known city shops and offices squeezed under one airfield size roof."[25] On 3 October 1960, 10,000 people attended Chadstone's opening ceremony and watched the Premier of Victoria, Henry Bolte, cut the ceremonial ribbon. Bolte described the centre as an example of the forward-looking approach his government was fostering in the state. Chadstone, he said, "was such a radical departure from traditional retailing that it had a significance of its own."[26] One retail journal declared that the atmosphere at the opening ceremony was "faintly reminiscent of Flemington on Cup Day. There were the crowds pleasantly jostling to inspect all the entrants, well-dressed ladies, free literature of all kinds, and a roped-off centre square which gave a hint of the theatrical focal point. ..."[27]

The smaller formal opening for dignitaries was a more exclusive, invitation-only affair. Major retail, business and political figures attended but there was no place for newcomers to the industry like Frank Lowy and John Saunders. Determined to see the new venture and to harvest knowledge from the wealth of experience in attendance, Saunders flew to Melbourne, took a taxi to Chadstone, climbed under the fence surrounding the freshly built centre (keeping his suit in good repair), and spent the morning mingling, observing and mentally recording its innovations. He left by the official entrance and returned to Sydney in the afternoon.[28]

Chadstone heralded Myer's entrance into regional shopping centre planning and construction – a field it would dominate in the 1960s, and which helped maintain its pre-eminence in Australia's retail hierarchy across the second half of the twentieth century. A fortnight after opening, nearly 500,000 people had visited and around 50,000 cars had snaked their way through the car park.[29] Chadstone also raised questions. Within a week the *Retail Merchandiser* voiced a concern that has surrounded Australian retail property development since. How many shopping centres were enough? Or too many?

> Already the apparent success of Chadstone – and it can hardly be a prema-
> ture judgement – has sparked off enquiries about the potential number of
> Chadstones that Melbourne can sustain ... while we have no information

[on which to base a judgment] … we can be sure that some day, not far off, other centres will appear. Imitation is the sincerest form of flattery.[30]

Two-and-a-half years later, the same journal reported that the "success of the Chadstone Shopping Centre was so spectacular that it was obvious that a progressive organisation such as the Myer Emporium would be looking for another such attractive venture." If anything, this underplayed the firm's vision. It had opened the Allan & Stark Coorparoo centre in Queensland shortly after Chadstone, and was engaged in the construction of Miranda Fair in Sydney's southern suburbs – a project inherited when it acquired the Farmer and Co. department store in 1960. NSW Labor Premier, Bob Heffron, who opened Miranda Fair in March 1964, described it as private enterprises' response to the growing pains and traffic issues arising from Sydney's rapid suburbanisation.[31] His comments reflected concern that facilities and infrastructure had not kept pace with suburban population growth. One newspaper at the time reported that

> dozens of streets have no footpaths. In their place are rough tracks over which housewives must push strollers and prams when they go out to shop … on either side the water run off cascades down loose dirt shoulders into rocky crevices …[32]

In this environment, Miranda Fair was welcomed as a harbinger of modernity, described by its marketers as a "shopping paradise," "as modern as tomorrow" and the equal of any shopping facility in the world.[33]

The role of specialist developers

To Sydney's north, Warringah Mall (1963) offered similar conveniences and provided branch stores for the city's biggest retailers, David Jones and Grace Bros. It was developed by the British firm, the Hammerson Group of Companies. Hammerson had entered the residential real estate market in Britain during World War Two. By the mid 1950s, it held one of the largest real estate portfolios in the United Kingdom. It built its first shopping centre at the end of the decade in Bradford, Yorkshire. In the 1960s, Hammerson expanded into other countries, including Australia, New Zealand and the United States.[34] These markets offered more opportunities for growth than the United Kingdom, and provided an opportunity to develop further commercial development capabilities. In addition to Warringah Mall, Hammerson built the Floreat Forum in Perth, Western Australia, which opened in 1965. These projects accumulated expertise that was taken back to Britain and used in the development of Brent Cross in the mid 1970s.[35]

Another United Kingdom firm, the Arndale Property Trust, was also active in Australia. Arndale was founded in 1960 by Arnold Hagenbach and Sam Chippindale and was the first British firm to build shopping centres in the UK. In cooperation with local councils, it constructed more than 20 by acquiring and demolishing older shops in town centres such as Armley, Headingley, Bradford, Sunderland, Lancaster, Bolton and Doncaster.[36] The form and pattern of these developments reflected a British concern with the protection of town centres, even if it meant knocking them down for new construction that in time would itself become considered an eyesore.[37] Shopping centres were seen as a means of modernising and further activating unplanned town centres, but a threat to established retail precincts if allowed to develop in out-of-town locations.[38] Australia offered conditions part way between those in America and Britain. It did not have the freeways and greenfield sites available in America, but nor were its suburbs as densely developed as British towns. Australia's far younger urban geographies encouraged suburban development, even if planning sought to control its location and usage, and sites were difficult to find. In this environment, Arndale Developments (Australia) Pty Ltd built centres that were more American in style, on larger sites than were available in Britain. The firm opened small regional centres at Kilkenny, South Australia in 1963 and French's Forest in NSW in 1964. It built a neighbourhood centre in Croydon, Victoria in 1964, and a large regional centre at Marion, South Australia in 1968.

The American design orientation, and the scope of Arndale's ambitions, were reflected in their engagement of John Graham as a consultant for their Australian operations.[39] Since designing Northgate in Seattle, Graham's firm had designed more than 70 shopping centres and he had become an influential and internationally recognised leader in the field. Graham's influence informed Arndale's decision to pursue introverted designs, a strategy also undertaken by Lend Lease when building Monaro Mall in Canberra.[40] Arndale claimed that Kilkenny, opening eight months after Monaro Mall, was the first fully enclosed, completely air-conditioned shopping centre in the country. As with many claims about innovations emanating from the industry, this "first" depended on one's definitions; in this case about what constituted "completely air-conditioned."[41] Nuances aside, both Arndale Kilkenny and Monaro Mall were important for piloting fully enclosed designs, with each bringing a new form of retail property to their respective cities.

Canberra was a unique city in the Australian context because of the degree of planning control exerted over it by the National Capital Development Commission (NCDC) and Walter Burley Griffen's master plan on which Canberra was based. The NCDC, formed in 1958, sought to implement Griffen's plan under the guidance of its first Chief Planner, Peter Harrison. Harrison believed strongly in cooperative development between public authorities and private enterprise. In his view, the role of planning was not to create hurdles for developers, but to "set up the right opportunities for development of the right kind in the right locations and at the right time." In 1959, he secured the site on which Monaro Mall would later be built and argued the case for introducing a pre-planned shopping centre rather than the string of individual shops that others at the time were suggesting.[42] This recognised, the *Canberra Times* noted, "the trend in Australia to the new age in retailing."[43]

Lend Lease, which had already contributed heavily to the construction of the nation's capital,[44] purchased the lease for the site at auction in 1961, and spent approximately 20 months building the centre within the parameters designated by the NCDC. The press favourably compared this time frame to construction in America where it was suggested the same build might take three to five years.[45] The speed of construction reflected Lend Lease's approach to industrial relations, in which it engaged proactively with unions to improve working conditions in return for productivity gains. This reduced industrial action, incentivised efficiency and brought benefits to both workers and the firm. It also bolstered Lend Lease's public image as an efficient and highly productive builder. Similarly, while the decision to fully enclose Monaro Mall in "year round comfort for shoppers" was a response to Canberra's wide variations in temperature, it also allowed Lend Lease to position itself as an innovative firm. It received positive coverage in the press for its foresight and ambition, which it leveraged to generate further work.[46]

Westfield, which went public in 1960, also benefited from enthusiastic reportage about Westfield Place. It responded to numerous resulting requests to build stores in Sydney, and also purchased sites for its own shopping centre developments. While building a centre at Hornsby, 18 miles north-west of Sydney's CBD, an opportunity emerged that elevated Westfield to the next level as a developer. The Matthews Thompson grocery chain was contracted as an anchor for the centre when it was acquired by Coles. Westfield persuaded Coles to anchor the centre instead, and also suggested other prospective sites for the Victorian firm in Sydney.[47] Prior to the Matthews Thompson purchase, Coles had struggled to gain a foothold in NSW. This caused considerable consternation within the firm because Woolworths was well advanced developing a complete grocery network around Sydney.[48]

The purchase of Matthews Thompson gave Coles a presence and buying power in New South Wales, but its stores were small and built for old retail technologies. Coles needed large modern retail stores. The Hornsby development provided an introduction to Westfield and the firm's capabilities, which resulted in a number of building contracts. The process of site selection was not overly scientific: Lowy was reportedly driven around Sydney in Sir Edgar Coles' chauffeur-driven Rolls Royce as he pointed to locations pronouncing: "Get me a site here. Get me a site there." By the mid 1960s, Westfield had built 17 supermarkets for Coles. Westfield's self-published company history regards the affiliation as "a mutually beneficial relationship," noting that "Westfield played a major role in getting Coles established in New South Wales, and Coles contributed greatly to getting Westfield launched in Australia."[49]

Sir Edgar's intuitive approach to site selection was not uncommon at the time. Alan Briggs, who became chief operating office for Westfield Australia in the 1980s and head of their American operations in the 1990s, notes that when Lowy and Saunders were starting out:

> The opportunities were there, everywhere, and in terms of trying to determine how much retail floor space there was around, it was not necessary

... Sydney was blowing out like crazy ... you could put a dog box in the middle of a paddock somewhere and you'd attract somebody. That's how John and Frank started ... from the conversations that I had with John Saunders ... that's how it was, and I said to him one day, "what sort of research do you do with a shopping centre?" He said, "Al, I get in the cab, I drive around a little while. I come back and I say to Frank, 'what about we have a shopping centre here, maybe with three department stores, four supermarkets?'. Frank would say, 'ok, maybe we can have one department store, one supermarket and so on'", and almost essentially build it. I think some of the rationale was essentially build it around the railway ... and it didn't work out exactly that way, but that's the kind of really rough and tumble thinking that was pervasive ...[50]

Such large-scale visions were still in the future, and the mention of train station locations reveals far more strategic nous than is suggested by Saunders' conversational outline, but the dialogue recalled by Briggs is instructive of both the opportunities available in the Sydney market at the time, and the intuitive approach of many firms during the emergent phase of the industry in Australia. As the industry matured, market research became far more sophisticated, but in the halcyon days of mass suburban expansion and a booming economy, development was based more on observation and opportunity. Fraser Coss, who bought sites all around Australia for Woolworths, later noted that:

There was no established material that you could rely on that would help in selecting a site. There is a certain feeling about it, you get a feeling when you walk in an area, this is a good area and we should have a store here and so on. But if you asked me to say in so many words in black and white, why, I probably couldn't tell you. But I know it's good. You can say you are flying by the seat of your pants if you like, and I was on a number of occasions, but they all turned out well. Where there are houses, there are people and they've all got to eat.[51]

Again, Coss's recollection is informative of the opportunities available but also belies the value of his experience, his understanding of property and his capacity to assess the value of particular locations. The best property buyers, even when research was limited and they were "flying by the seat of their pants," were able to assess accessibility, convenience and the market potential of prospective sites. As the car changed the parameters of convenience, they needed to adapt their criteria. Where once high-visibility main street frontage was all-important, now road access and space for parking needed to be considered. Coss recalls that:

On one occasion in Victoria the Property Manager rang me up and said "I've got a wonderful site in Dandenong" ... I said, "All right, I'll come down and have a look at it." So I went down to have a look at it and I said, "This is not right. This is the site that you want us to take?" He said, "Yes, a beautiful site right in the centre of main street." I said, "What's that land across the road there?" There was enough land there to build a supermarket and car parking and everything else ... "buy it [I said] because that's the place to be ... you're going to choke to death here [in the first site], really you are." Anyway ... we bought the vacant land ... and we built a very fine supermarket with car parking and small shops and what have you.[52]

Operating in this new environment, understanding the need to cater for the car, but also aware of the ongoing value of sites adjacent to major public transport hubs, Westfield very quickly built an in-house team capable of planning, designing and developing retail stores and shopping centres.[53] It acted as a consultant to retailers and, as with Lend Lease, its in-house development model drove efficiencies and ensured high levels of quality control. The Coles' construction deals provided Lowy and Saunders with experience and capital. They became investor builders, holding and managing the centres they built to retain cash flow, security for finance and 'live' assets that could be upgraded through active expansion and redevelopment. Table 4.1 lists selected shopping centres constructed by Westfield during the 1960s.[54] It shows that the firm established a strong base in NSW before expanding interstate. It developed capabilities and capital by building neighbourhood centres before moving into larger construction and more ambitious projects later in the decade. It maintained a consistent relationship with Coles and demonstrated an early ability to attract mid-size retail firms as general merchandise anchors, before eventually cementing a relationship with Myer at the end of the decade.

Coles' deal with Westfield was neither exclusive nor unique. The major retail chains, especially the supermarkets, had their own property managers scouring the country for high-traffic sites, buying pubs, picture theatres, shops and residential properties that were demolished to make way for modern stores.[55] Relationships were also localised. Coles' growth in South Australia was aided to a significant degree by another developer, Jack Weinert. One Coles executive later described Weinert as "a very progressive and energetic developer who had a lot of clout in South Australia. He knew the right people and he knew how to get around. A real go-getter."[56] The capacity to identify sites, gain approval and build extremely efficiently made him an ideal partner in the development of Coles in South Australia, and enabled Weinert to develop "a very deep relationship" with the two most powerful men in the Coles organisation, Joint Managing Directors Lance Robinson and Sir Edgar Coles. Shortly after the firm's purchase of the Dickins chain in 1958, Coles' executives attended the opening of a Dickins supermarket in Adelaide that Weinert had built. Robinson later recalled that:

We were introduced and we said to him "How much did it cost to build this store?" and he told us. [Sir Edgar Coles] said "How can you possibly build it for that price?" "I'll show you" [Weinert responded]. We walked outside ... and there's a ring [of plaster] about as big as this table and

Table 4.1 Selected Westfield shopping centres, 1959–70

Year	Location	State	Type	Style	Rentable area (sq. ft.)	Parking spaces	Stores	Supermarket	Other anchors
1959	Blacktown	NSW	N	Open	Unavailable	87	15	Gavan's Grocery	Winns, Snows, Illawarra Appliance Store, G.T. Greenaway hardware
1961	Hornsby	NSW	C/R	Closed mall	65,000 (gross)	300	23	Coles	McDowells, Best & Less, Nock & Kirby hardware, David Glover drug store
1964	Baulkam Hills	NSW	N	Open	26,500 (gross)	100	12	Coles	
1965	West Merrylands	NSW	N	Open	22,000 (gross)	100	7	Coles	
1965	Figtree	NSW	N	Enclosed	57,000	640	26	Coles	Coles Variety
1965	Eastwood	NSW	C	Open	72,000 (gross)	500	18	Coles	Mark Foy's, Coles Variety
1966	Lane Cove	NSW	N	Split level	22,000 (gross)	80	6	Coles	
1966	Penrith	NSW	N	Semi-enclosed	28,500	Council parking	11	Coles	
1966	Burwood	NSW	R	Enclosed	278,000	1,000	60	Coles	Farmers, Winns, Coles Variety
1967	Toombul	Qld	R	Enclosed	191,000	1,650	60	Coles	Barry & Roberts, Bayards, Royal Art Furnishings
1969	Doncaster	Vic	R	Enclosed	444,996	3 100	83	Dickins	Myer, Coles Variety, Waltons homemaker store, McEwans hardware store
1970	Indooroopilly	Qld	R	Enclosed	490,000	2,300	69	Woolworths Family Centre	Myer, Target, Royal Art Furnishings, Bretts hardware store

Source: Modern Merchandising Methods, Australian Shopping Centres, 1971.

Notes:

★ N = Neighbourhood, C = Community, R = Regional

★★ Gross floor area (where leased retail area is not available) there's one broken brick in it and a piece of wood about that long and he said: "That's how I make my profit. That's my total waste on this building. I order exactly the right number of bricks, ordered everything right to end." He used to build them so cheap it was remarkable.[57]

While Weinert often canvassed site selections, sometimes even he had to be persuaded. Robinson remembers visiting Unley in suburban Adelaide in the early sixties:

> It was a dead suburb, a dead suburb. We had a little variety store there that did all right and I saw this picture theatre empty … then a row of shops and our little shop and a few more shops and then another picture theatre and I thought, gee whiz, if we could get that theatre and put a supermarket there, how wonderful it would be.
>
> So I got Tommy North out and Tommy looked up and down the street and said "Crikey this is … a crummy place. This town's dead." I said "Now we've all got to eat Tom, everybody's got to eat" … "Oh," Tommy said, "you've got to put them in the big suburbs where they're spenders." I said "No way pal, where the hungriest are we've got to put the supermarkets … I'll get Jack Weinert out here."
>
> He came out and I said "Jack have a look at this theatre, can you imagine putting a supermarket here. In Unley", he said, "this is a dead place, not on your life … I wouldn't have a bar of it, crazy." … Then somewhere around 1 o'clock in the morning I had a telephone call [from Weinert]. "Hey listen, I want to go out to Unley in the morning."
>
> So he picked me up in the morning around 6 o'clock and out we go to Unley. "Now listen, I've been thinking of this dream of yours all night," he said. "What we should do is buy both theatres and push all that junk out and I'll build a shopping centre there." And I thought here we go, going from what I thought was courageous to this was terrifying. [The shopping centre was built, opening on 3 March 1966, and] it just lifted the whole suburb. It lifted everything.
>
> So we did the same thing again. We would buy the land. He would use that then to get the money from the bank, a loan, and then he'd say we'll open another shopping centre here … we'll pay this one off and buy that one so that we've got that off our books. And E. B. and I thought the world of him … I think he was just so far ahead of us all.[58]

Like Lowy and Saunders in New South Wales, Weinert recognised the long-term benefits of capital appreciation and had ambitions to own shopping centres rather than just develop them. He entered into 40/60 ownership agreements with Coles for a number of centres he constructed. This gave both parties the benefits of ownership, allowed Weinert to obtain finance through Coles, and meant that Coles could outsource development to a man who could procure sites in desired locations. Coles paid rent into the jointly owned company for its stores, but effectively retained 60 per cent of this because of its ownership stake. A former executive later recalled that Weinert developed a number of very, very good shopping centres that certainly put us in a very dominating position in South Australia, with variety stores and supermarkets as they progressed ... the sites were good and they were good centres and therefore our retailing powers were enhanced in the State ... The other thing that we gained [was] ... the capital appreciation of those shopping centres ... We were in a far better and happier position owning 60% than say had we been paying rent to a shopping centre company ... So I think it was a very prosperous [relationship, which] ... helped the company ... to establish itself as the leading retailer in South Australia.[59]

Coles tended to develop community centres, banking on the complementary drawing power of its supermarkets and junior department stores. Many included services such as Baby Health Centres, Post Office branches, banks, doctors and dentists. There was a trend across the decade to larger supermarkets, albeit with variations depending on respective trade areas and site constraints. A fruit and vegetable shop, butcher, delicatessen and often a fish shop complemented the offer of grocery-focused supermarkets. Such tenants catered to the high demand for food in the suburbs and were almost ubiquitous, highlighting the convenience function that extended through all levels of shopping centres from their beginnings in Australia.[60]

The Coles centres, though, were very much a vehicle for the supermarket chain, and their layouts indicate a relatively crude approach to customer traffic management. At Unley, for example, the supermarket and variety stores were positioned at either end of the centre but they were inefficient anchors. From within the centre no avenue to the supermarket was provided, and access to the variety store was limited. While both acted as customer traffic generators, they did not channel this traffic effectively to the specialty stores. To access the public toilets, customers had to walk away from most of the shops, out of the centre proper and around a corner. Unley was a late example of partially enclosed mall designs that were being overtaken by fully internalised centres. Indeed, improving on earlier designs and enclosing shopping centres to more effectively manage the flow of customers was becoming a defining characteristic of the industry. At the same time, larger, regional shopping centres were being imagined in ever-grander terms. Fully introverted, they were increasingly promoted as cities in their own right, delineated from their surrounds, and defined against the grit, congestion and inconvenience of the urban core.[61]

Shopping cities

When J. C. Nichols designed his Country Club Plaza early in the twentieth century, he envisaged "a more profitable, more beautiful, and more convenient type of downtown shopping center." To do this he would need to provide "a well-balanced group of stores giving complete and slightly competitive shopping."[62] When American shopping centre construction resumed in the 1950s, it was suggested that the regional suburban mall should aspire to be a "miniature 'downtown'"; to "duplicate the downtown area with all of its variety of merchandise"; to reproduce the "shopping facilities and customer attraction once available only in central business districts."[63] These ideas travelled with the shopping centre to Europe and Australia.[64] In the latter, the use of the term "shopping city" was instituted at Chadstone, where marketers argued that transformations in urban demography had created an imperative for the city to "be brought to the suburbs … [where] the volume and variety of a city market [could be] combined with convenience and accessibility."[65] As the decade progressed, and large-scale centres became more numerous and more likely to be enclosed, descriptions of them as cities in their own right became more common.

Of all the developments in the 1960s, Roselands, 12 miles south-west of Sydney's CBD, was the centre that emphasised its role as a minor city most emphatically (Figure 4.2). It was Sydney's first great regional shopping centre, arriving in 1965 on a site first located by aerial reconnaissance almost ten years earlier. Looking down from a Tiger Moth during peak hour in 1956, architect Jim Whitehead identified a small sea of green amidst a maze of "traffic-choked" roads. The *Sydney Morning Herald* later recounted the escapade, reporting that Whitehead and a photographer

> watched the columns of city-bound traffic along two highways that hemmed the area in; they watched the frustrated efforts of local cars to muscle-in to one of the streams. For what? To reach a traffic-choked city, and scour its streets for a spot to park.[66]

The green oasis was the Roselands golf course, situated in the populous and rapidly growing Canterbury Shire. Its owner, Stan Evan Parry, was a powerful and controversial figure who had been the Mayor of Canterbury from 1932 to 1947. He had bought the land in 1943, running it first as a market garden and then as a golf course. In 1947 he was forced to flee abroad from a Royal Commission into land speculation.[67] He returned ten years later and sold the estate, at a substantial profit, to Grace Bros.

Roselands, the shopping centre, was designed by Whitehead and Payne and built by E. A. Watts. The former had already designed Grace Bros.' Chatswood store and would later design Macquarie Centre for the retail firm, as well as Northgate at Hornsby and Erina Fair on the central coast, north of Sydney. The builder, Ernest Alfred Watts, had started a residential development firm shortly after World War One when he was just 24 years of age. In the mid 1920s he moved into larger-scale projects, including a variety store for G. J. Coles & Co. in Melbourne's CBD. In the 1930s he expanded further, building hotels, as well as the southern stand of the Melbourne cricket ground. He obtained defence contracts during the war, re-established his commercial practice in the 1950s and prospered in the early 1960s building some of the country's most significant shopping centres, including Chadstone, Miranda Fair and Roselands.[68]

Figure 4.2 The trend-setting city in the suburbs, Roselands, ca. 1965.

The latter was the biggest shopping centre built in Australia during the 1960s (Figure 4.2). The Grace Bros. department store anchor was almost twice the size of the Myer and David Jones stores in the next largest centres. It was also bigger than any of the stand-alone suburban branches built by city retailers at the time. Advertisements declared that Sydneysiders had "never seen anything like ROSELANDS." It was touted as "the biggest thing of its kind in the southern hemisphere [and] – in some important ways more advanced than anything in the United States."[69] Critical of sprawling single-level American centres, although drawing strongly on Gruen's Southdale design, the architects sought to minimise walking distance, compacting the shopping centre form into "a three-level, weatherproof, air-conditioned town."[70] They claimed that the decked car park, which held almost 2,000 cars (on top of another 1,000 spaces provided in tarmac parking), was the largest directly linked to a regional shopping centre in the world.[71] Ending "the days of the 'long hike'" from car to shop, it was part of a design strategy that sought to maximise convenience. It also reflected a new sophistication in merchandising and customer traffic management with categories of goods grouped together, floor by floor. According to the architects:

> The clustering of individual shops around the centre court so that each contributes a liveliness and personality to the whole shopping establishment has abolished the "hot" and "cold" spots which exist in conventional regional centres where trade areas are usually dominated by the "magnet" stores at each end of elongated plazas … [In Roselands this] allows the happy, harmonious grouping of merchandise so that each floor of the department store is completed by the independent shops each selling a similar, yet competitive range of merchandise.[72]

When opening Roselands in October 1965, the recently elected Premier of NSW, Robin (later Robert) Askin, echoed industry phraseology, declaring that Roselands' "million dollar spread of merchandise … brings the city to the suburbs in a glittering way that must rival even the fabled Persian Bazaars."[73] Roselands, marketers boasted of the country's largest public-address system, its 26,600 light bulbs, and its private electrical substation that was powerful enough "to supply the needs of an average sized country town."[74] They pointed to its huge range of shops, and the interest it was said to have generated in America. One newspaper claimed that "the visitor's first reaction is to wonder … at the sort of courage that was needed to sink £six million into a spot by-passed by commerce."[75] "Bringing the city to the suburbs" carried weight in such areas: centres like Chadstone, Warringah Mall, Miranda Fair, Arndale Kilkenny and Roselands were stark and monumental markers of the dramatic shift of retailing underway in Australia's metropolitan markets. During the second half of the 1960s they were joined by more "shopping cities," which pegged out new sites, encircling the city proper.

A year after the launch of Roselands, Lend Lease opened Sydney's next great regional centre, Bankstown Square. The Bankstown municipality was the most populous in Sydney with a retail precinct that had not kept pace with population growth.[76] This provided a significant opportunity, but with no suitable greenfield site available, the challenges to realise it were significant. Unpacking the process by which Bankstown Square was developed offers an insight into the problems developers faced locating sites in Sydney, the difficulties involved in building large-scale retail facilities in established and populous suburbs, and the complexities of negotiating this process with local government authorities. It began with Lend Lease taking a "punt," purchasing more than 80 small properties within walking distance of Bankstown train station. Some buyers held out, forcing the firm to invest more than £1 million acquiring land in what became a 26-acre block. The firm then applied to have the site rezoned for commercial development.[77]

Rezoning is frequently contentious. It changes designated land-use patterns relied upon by other stakeholders and may interfere with their investments. It shifts the ground beneath existing and planned public infrastructure, which can bring public costs. By changing the value of sites, it may bestow benefits on some private landholders. And regardless of the level of consultation, the potential advantages and disadvantages are decided by a relatively small group of public officials. Occasionally, the value this power generates entices corruption. In 1963, Lend Lease was offered cash bribes in return for guaranteed approval of Bankstown Square. The firm responded by contacting the police who put a sting operation in place. Meetings between Lend Lease officials and a conspirator took place and were recorded with a wiretap at a city restaurant and Rosehill Racetrack.[78] These documented an arrangement for cash to be deposited behind a pot plant outside the office of Bankstown alderman Charles Little. Police later found the money hidden at the back of Little's office premises.[79] The operation resulted in five aldermen and an accomplice being charged with criminal offences. Three went to jail and the Bankstown Municipal Council was dismissed.[80]

As this was occurring, the merits of the project were subject to public debate. The Town Planner noted that as the "largest single retail development yet proposed in any suburban area in Australia" (with Roselands still in the planning stages), the Square would consolidate Bankstown as a district centre and align with broader regional planning objectives. He noted, however, that it was "essential that the development be treated as an extension of the Bankstown shopping centre both visually and functionally and that there should be a connecting link between the two."[81] The Bankstown Chamber of Commerce equivocated, but eventually opposed the development, arguing that while the existing shopping precinct was not "ultra modern," it was still "one of the best" outside of Sydney's CBD and council should not undermine it by spending ratepayers' money "constructing roads leading to the Square."[82] It expressed concern that declining trade caused by Bankstown Square would force high street retailers "to open businesses in the new centre – at higher rentals – in order to hold their customers."[83] Lend Lease, in response, argued that its development would increase trade in the area, preventing expenditure leakage to other locales by attracting customers into Bankstown.[84] Such claims and counter claims would become more common as shopping centres spread across the country in proceeding decades, although they rarely halted development. The Bankstown Square "shopping metropolis," self-contained and largely segregated from existing retail facilities, was opened to lavish praise in September 1966.[85] This meant that "shopping cities" were now located within 17 miles to the north, south and west of Sydney's CBD, although dense residential development and geographical constraints continued to limit construction possibilities to the east.

While in Sydney this process of encirclement was shared, in Melbourne, Myer sought retail supremacy over the entire metropolitan landscape. As Miranda Fair was being built in southern Sydney, Myer sought more sites in its home city, hoping to replicate Hudson's approach of circling Detroit with shopping centres named by the compass points and anchored by its own branch stores.[86]

At East Preston, to the city's north, Myer acquired 51 acres of vacant industrial land from the Victorian Housing Trust.[87] After getting the land rezoned, it built Northland, described as "a complete shopping town … an entire heart-of-a-city"; "a city within a city."[88] The Buckley & Nunn and Foy & Gibson department stores again joined Myer in the centre, although the latter was again vastly larger.[89] In total the centre housed around 75 stores, as well as 35 stall-holders in a permanent market, a variety store, supermarket, furniture and hardware store.[90]

Hardware businesses were sought-after tenants for shopping centres catering to home-owning and building suburban consumers.[91] This was a response to the market at the time: department stores also included hardware sections, and even house design services for owner builders.[92] By 1969, 48 per cent of regional shopping centres, and 38 per cent of all centres in Australia, contained a hardware store.[93] They were predominantly local or state-based concerns. In Victoria, McEwans opened in a number of the Myer and Westfield centres, as well as in numerous smaller community centres. In NSW, BBC and Nock & Kirby both opened in community and regional centres, a strategy that helped Nock & Kirby expand prolifically across Sydney during the 1960s. Bunnings, today the largest hardware chain in Australia, began life as a West Australian sawmill, moved into retail through acquisitions (including McEwans in 1993), and opened shopping centre branches in community shopping centres during the 1970s.[94] By the 1980s and 1990s, however, hardware stores were moving out of shopping centres. Facing prohibitive rentals, the need for more retail floor-space because of their expanding range of merchandise, and the upwards positioning of regional shopping centres, the major hardware chains instead began relocating to stand-alone, big-box formats.

Northland built on the experience Myer had gained at Chadstone and Miranda Fair through its acquisition of Farmers. It consolidated the firm's in-house capabilities in retail property planning, development, finance, management and leasing. It also continued Myer's relationship with the architectural firm Tompkins, Shaw & Evans. After taking the opportunity presented by the perceived shortcomings of the original American architects at Chadstone, Tompkins, Shaw & Evans had gone on to design Miranda Fair. After Northland they would also design Eastland (1967) and Southland (1968).[95] These centres cemented Myer's hold over Melbourne: its city store still overwhelmingly dominated sales in the CBD, and looking out in all directions, the firm owned and operated the city's biggest suburban regional shopping centres in which it operated the largest anchor stores. This almost unique retail power base was in addition to the strong footholds Myer had already established in Queensland, and the inroads it would make into South Australia in the late 1960s. There it opened a store in Arndale's Marion centre in 1968 and built Tea Tree Plaza to the north of the city in 1970. The former was Adelaide's first privately built regional shopping centre, and the first Australian centre to include two major department stores of equivalent size – John Martin's and Myer – competing against one another.[96] Indeed Myer's entry into South Australia was a major competitive challenge to John Martin's, the state's largest retail firm, most famous outside of the state for sponsoring the Beatles tour stop in Adelaide in 1964. Eschewing shopping centre construction, John Martin's joined centres built by the SAHT and Arndale to establish a suburban presence.[97]

Myer's push into South Australia continued its national expansion. In Perth, Boans department store was acutely aware of the danger this posed as well as the transformations underway in retail property development. Following a tour of the United States by Frank Boan, his firm built centres at Medina (1960), Morley Park (1961), Peppermint Grove (1964), Melville (1967) and Innaloo (1967) in or around Perth. In addition to its own developments, Boans also took up tenancies in regional centres such as Garden City (1972), Carousel (1972) and Karrinyup (1973) to further entrench its place at the top of Western Australia's retail hierarchy.[98] These stores and centres were considerably smaller than those in the eastern states, reflecting comparative population sizes: Lend Lease, claimed that Bankstown Square's trade area included more people than the entire Perth metropolitan market Boans' regional shopping centres in Perth were closer in size to large community centres in Sydney and Melbourne.

Boans' development programme came the closest to matching Myer's strategy of encircling its home city. This reflected its dominance of the Perth market, its capacity to innovate and identify avenues of consolidation in Western Australia (such as instituting friendly takeovers and joining buying groups), as well as the protection offered by geographic distance.[99] With Myer and David Jones consolidating on Australia's east coast, Boans, operating around 3,500 kilometres to the west, had more time than Brisbane's Allan & Stark to develop a network of suburban stores and regional shopping centres. This confluence of factors helped protect the Western Australian firm until the mid 1980s when Myer's quest for growth finally brought it west.

By the end of the 1960s, Australian capital cities were serviced from most sides by regional shopping centres. An assortment of community and neighbourhood centres filled the gaps between. From the beginning, these developments had been driven by the needs of retailers, including, most conspicuously, the country's three largest retail firms. This was directly related to their desire to capture larger market share during an economic boom in a landscape opened up by the car. For Myer, shopping centres established a suburban presence and were a vehicle for entering new metropolitan markets on ground not yet occupied by existing firms. Coles, Woolworths and other chains such as Safeway and Franklins, required accessible sites with parking for their new supermarkets. This often ruled out construction within the built fabric of high streets, where there was little space to build parking stations, and traffic congestion was becoming a major issue. As a retail technology conceived to accommodate the motorcar, shopping centres thus served the supermarkets well. The needs of these large firms refracted against a host of smaller retailers, which experimented with development and took space in centres in response to opportunities available. As demand for retail space in suburban areas grew, developers increased the floor space of their projects accordingly. Completely enclosing these centres created interiorised shopping worlds that imitated a sanitised version of the city and set the blueprint for shopping centre design in Australia for the remainder of the twentieth century.

It was Australia's largest retailers, then, that most fully embraced shopping centre development during the 1960s. This strategy was facilitated by their scale, which provided them with the capital to innovate via development, building and taking long-term tenancies in shopping centres of all types. By 1969, Woolworths and Coles respectively operated a supermarket in 43 per cent and 24 per cent of all Australian shopping centres. Franklins, with supermarkets in 9 per cent of all centres, and Safeway with 7 per cent, tended to operate smaller stores, frequently as second, complementary stores to the larger chains. Woolworths also moved into large-scale general merchandise retailing. In 1969, it opened six mid-sized department stores in community or regional shopping centres in NSW and Queensland. Boans had four department stores in regional shopping centres in Perth. David Jones, John Martin and Grace Bros. each had three in other cities.

Myer was the most prolific early developer of large-scale shopping centres. The Melbourne firm had ten shopping centre department stores, including stores operating under the Allan & Stark and Farmers brands. This gave it a presence in 37 per cent of all regional shopping centres in the country. Myer owned seven of these centres, of which it had designed and built six. In 1970, it added stores in two more shopping centres: Tea Tree Plaza, which it developed in South Australia; and Indooroopilly in Queensland, Westfield's largest centre at the time, and the third with a Myer store. This relationship provides yet another indication of the rise of Westfield in the ten years since Jeno Schwarcz had snuck under a fence to watch Myer dignitaries launch Chadstone. Over virtually the same period, a retail property industry non-existent in the mid 1950s had been firmly established in Australia.

Notes

1 *RM*, October 1958, 19.
2 Vernon, "Shopping Towns Australia," 108.
3 http://gruenassociates.com/project/millirons-department-store, accessed 5 November 2019.
4 Author interview with Reg Jebb, 23 February 2015.
5 *RM*, January 1957, 9.
6 Ebury, *Many Lives*, 236–7, 263–4.
7 CMA, Box 1505, A. R. Bracher, The changing patterns of buying, merchandising & promotion, March 1969, 2.
8 CMA, Box 4763, Stella Barber interview with Sir Thomas North, 11 October 1985.
9 Author interview with Reg Jebb, 23 February 2015.
10 Ebury, *Many Lives*, 236–7, 263–4.
11 CMA, Box 1800, Australia's Largest Regional Shopping Centre: Chadstone Victoria, ca. 1960.

12 Hutson, "I Dream of Jeannie," 21.
13 *RM*, May 1960, 8–10.
14 CMA, Box 1429, Letter from Larry Smith & Company to George McMahon, 22 December 1958; Hutson, "I Dream of Jeannie," 23–4.
15 CMA, Box 1941, Jean Carter, First one-stop-shop revolutionizes Australian's shopping habits, 3 September 1980.
16 *RM*, May 1960, 8–10.
17 Ebury, *Many Lives*, 265.
18 Hutson, "I Dream of Jeannie," 25–6.
19 Hutson, "I Dream of Jeannie," 27.
20 CMA, Box 1800, Chadstone News, No. 2, ca. 1960.
21 *RM*, May 1960, 8–10.
22 CMA, Box 1941, Press Release, Chadstone Shopping Centre, 19 February 1959.
23 CMA, Box 1941, Press Release, Chadstone Shopping Centre Participants, 15 May 1959.
24 *RM*, February 1958, 13.
25 *The Sun*, 4 August 1960, 26–7.
26 *RM*, October 1960, 8.
27 *RM*, October 1960, 7–9.
28 Westfield Holdings Ltd, *Westfield Story*, 30.
29 Ebury, *Many Lives*, 267.
30 *RM*, October 1960, 7–9. In its first full year of operation, Chadstone exceeded planned turnover and profits. See CMA, Box 2877, The Myer Emporium (Chadstone) Ltd, Reports and Accounts, 1962.
31 *SGSSL*, 18 March 1964, 5.
32 Quoted in Ashton, Cornwall and Salt, *Sutherland Shire*, 157.
33 *SGSSL*, 5 February 1964, 9.
34 Anon., "Hammerson PLC," 165–6; Scott, *Property Masters*, 105.
35 *RT*, October 1962, 4–5.
36 McIntosh, *Towns and Cities*, 61; *The Times*, 8 April 2005, 69; Scott, *Property Masters*, 126.
37 Scott, *Shopping Centre Design*, 14.
38 Guy, "Whatever Happened," 299.
39 Tulloh, "Australia's First," 82.
40 Modern Merchandising Methods, *Australian Shopping Centres*, 6.
41 Tulloh, "Australia's First," 79; *CT*, 5 March 1963, 26.
42 *CT*, 4 November 1990, 21.
43 *CT*, 4 March 1963, 11.
44 *CT*, 4 March 1963, 10.
45 *CT*, 5 March 1963, 20.
46 *CT*, 4 March 1963, 13; 5 March 1963, 26.
47 Westfield Holdings Ltd, *Westfield Story*, 33.
48 CMA, Box 2927, Stella Barber interview with Bevan Bradbury, 18 December 1985, transcript, 5.
49 Westfield Holdings Ltd, *Westfield Story*, 33.
50 Author interview with Alan Briggs, 26 June 2014.
51 SLNSW, MLOH 451, Nos. 23 and 24, Jenny Hudson interview with Fraser Coss, ca. 1995, transcript, 25.

52 SLNSW, MLOH 451, Nos. 23 and 24, Jenny Hudson interview with Fraser Coss, ca. 1995, transcript, 27.
53 Sammartino and Van Ruth, "Westfield Group," 309–10.
54 Westfield also built centres at Dee Why and Yagoona in Sydney, but details such as retail floor space and tenancy mix are unavailable.
55 SLNSW, MLOH 451, Nos. 23 and 24, Jenny Hudson interview with Fraser Coss, ca. 1995, transcript, 24.
56 CMA, Box 4767, Stella Barber interview with Jim Thomas, 22 January 1988.
57 CMA, Box 1505, Stella Barber interview with Lance Robinson, 29 November 1985, transcript,
58 CMA, Box 1505, Stella Barber interview with Lance Robinson, 22 November 1985, transcript, 8.
59 CMA, Box 4767, Stella Barber interview with Jim Thomas, 22 January 1988.
60 *RM*, May 1960, 8–10.
61 Gosseye and Vernon, "Shopping Towns Australia," 219; Modern Merchandising Methods, *Australian Shopping Centres* (1971 edn), 149.64.
62 Baker and Funaro, *Shopping Centers*, 81.
63 Hoyt, "Current Trend," 4; McKeever et al., *Shopping Centre Development Handbook*, 7; Welch, "Regional Shopping Centres."
64 Cupers, "Shopping à l'américaine," 25.
65 *RM*, May 1960, 8. CMA, Box 1725, Chadstone Shopping Centre Pty Ltd, Promotional brochure, ca. 1960.
66 *SMH*, 12 October 1965, 33.
67 Larcombe, *Change and Challenge*, 176; Lawrence, Madden and Muir, *Pictorial History*, 87.
68 Strahan, "Watts, Ernest Alfred."
69 *SMH*, 12 October 1965, 33.
70 *SMH*, 12 October 1965, 33.
71 *SMH*, 12 October 1965, 39.
72 *SMH*, Roselands Feature, 12 October 1965, 10.
73 Robert Askin quoted in Barrett, "Roselands," 124.
74 *SMH*, Roselands Feature, 12 October 1965, 9; *SMH*, 21 September 1966, Special Feature, 6.
75 Barrett, "Roselands," 126.
76 *SMH*, 21 September 1966, Special Feature, 1.
77 Murphy, *Challenges*, 109; *BO*, 26 June 1963, 1.
78 Bailey, "Power, Politics."
79 Murphy, *Challenges*, 110.
80 Murphy, *Challenges*, 110.
81 J. Gilmour quoted in *BO*, 14 August 1963, 1, 3.
82 *BO*, 11 September 1963, 2; 18 September 1963, 2.
83 *BO*, 18 September 1963, 2.
84 *SMH*, 21 September 1966, Special Feature, 1; *RT*, August 1962, 50; Murphy, *Challenges*, 108.
85 *ST*, 18 September 1966; *SMH*, 20 September 1966, 4, 22; *SMH*, 21 September 1966, Special Feature, 6; *BO*, 21 September 1966.
86 CMA, Box 1946, J. L. Hudson, Northland complete suburban shopping town.
87 *RM*, April 1963, 23.

88 CMA, Box 1800, Northland promotional brochure, c1966.

89 *RM*, July 1964, 21.

90 *RM*, February 1966, 34.

91 *RT*, February 1961, 42.

92 Bailey, "Retailing and the Home."

93 Calculated from Modern Merchandising Methods, *Shopping Centre Directory* (1971 edn).

94 BOMA, *Directory of Australian Shopping Centres.*

95 *RM*, February 1966, 17; Modern Merchandising Methods, *Shopping Centre Directory* (1971 edn); retailplan, https://retailplan.com.au/our-story, accessed 14 November 2019.

96 *AR*, June 1967, 4–5.

97 *AR*, April 1968, 7; Sloan, "Marion."

98 Hough, *Boans*, 199–226.

99 Hough, *Boans*, 199–226.

5 The social world of shopping

As a business innovation, the primary purpose of Australian shopping centres in the 1960s was to foster retail sales in suburban environments. Increasingly constructed and envisaged as self-contained environments, they also operated as enclosed social worlds. This was particularly the case for regional centres. When marketers positioned the largest of these as "shopping cities," scale was a substantial plank of their argument: they were among the largest building projects undertaken in Australia's history and their range of retail merchandise, stores and services echoed the traditional city in concentrated form. They were also abundantly populated – at least during shopping hours. Outside of these they were largely dormant, save for night-time workers. In a further contrast with the city proper, their enclosure enabled tighter regulation of a space in which public and private were increasingly being conflated.

Positioned as self-contained cities and community hubs, shopping centres provided an early post-war model of spatial privatisation in which social space was monetised by entwining it with commercial infrastructure. This is now a familiar logic of urbanism, found in settings as diverse as sporting arenas, airports and waterside redevelopment projects. Firms controlled access to "shopping cities" and regulated the activities of visitors to them. But this did not intrude enough to prevent visitation by most consumers. Indeed, many derived considerable logistical and social goods from suburban shopping centre construction. Many also identified strongly with the normative framework that shopping centres represented and promoted. Shopping centres thus helped naturalise a public–private development compact, and educated publics towards the acceptance of its spread.

They did this as a new form of national self-understanding emerged in Australia. Richard White argues that a nationalistic, rural, white and masculine Australian type began to fade in the post-war years (although its ghostly trails lingered). In its place emerged an American import adapted to local conditions: the "Australian way of life." Vaguely defined, it operated as a unifying ideology in the Cold War climate and "was closely related to the image of Australia as a sophisticated, urban, industrialised, consumer society." It was also a whitewashed national identity, with little acknowledgement of Indigenous Australians or non-white immigrants. In this monocultural ideal, the suburban family loomed large, identified by home ownership, their car (or cars), consumer durables and, by the late 1950s, a television.[1] Seamus O'Hanlon argues that the "suburban ideal was, and to an extent remains, the social bedrock upon which Australian cities are based."[2]

Shopping centres were pitched as the retail "Mecca" and social space for these suburban families that occupied a very wide middle section of Australia's socioeconomic spectrum.[3] In America, regional shopping centres had been the protected preserve of affluent, white suburbanites; built on greenfield sites adjacent to freeways, they often sat beyond the public-transport reach of urban poor, coloured and ethnic populations. Australia's early shopping centres, in contrast, were built in accessible areas of capital cities within reach of public transport routes, in areas of high population growth that was frequently fuelled by immigration. If a trade area was affluent, that was seen positively, but it was not essential for success.[4] Demographic diversity was also largely ignored: just like the 'Australian' in the 'Australian way of life,' retail promotional material whitewashed and homogenised consumers.[5] Architectural sketches or artist's mock-ups of prospective centres were also invariably populated by the ideal Anglo family shopping type (Figure 5.1).[6]

For these customers, and for many other Australians who didn't look like them but also visited shopping centres, the retail offer was the biggest drawcard. But shopping centres became embedded in their locales in a variety of other ways. The "shopping cities" built during the 1960s expanded on the facilities provided in smaller centres by including auditoriums, function rooms, libraries and child-minding services. They were also an important generator of employment, largely for men during construction, and predominantly for women once retail operations commenced. Shopping centres thus became far more than just sites of retail distribution. To call them "cities" was marketing spin: they were privately owned, instituted their own regulatory regimes, closed at night and most of the weekend, and no-one lived there. But they did operate as important social spaces in the locales where they were built.

Community facilities and common space

In *Shopping Towns USA*, Gruen and Smith argued that shopping centre planning created

> not only stores and the buildings in which they are located but also public areas in the spaces between and around these buildings. It also brings into being community facilities, such as auditoriums and meeting rooms. This is done with the express intention of creating an environment which, if properly utilized, will establish the shopping center as the focal point for the life of a community or a number of communities.[7]

Their entreaty reflected the reformist perspective of architects involved in the early shopping centre movement in the United States,[8] although some

Australian architects felt that such approaches had not gone far enough. In 1963, Myer store architect Donald C. Ward unfavourably compared the blank external facades of American shopping centres with what he saw as more attractive developments in Europe. Ward wrote that "in English and Swedish new towns, architectural expression of community life in retail centres, offers fresh inspiration in the layout of Australian shopping centres." He argued that a closer tie between centre and community was evident in, particularly, the British new town model and regretted the lack of public–private partnerships to this end in Australia. His comments are indicative of Australia's broad interest in retail developments. While there was a general recognition within the Australian industry that an American influence predominated, notice was still taken of innovations in the United Kingdom and other markets. Ward noted that there was "much to be seen in England with regard to the relationship between a centre and its community."[9]

The SAHT was the most enthusiastic adopter of this approach in Australia. Its shopping centres at Elizabeth were notable for their inclusion of community facilities. Medical services, post offices, banks, SAHT offices, public libraries and Baby Health Centres were consciously placed in shopping centres across Elizabeth. A dance hall, billiard saloon and theatre provided centralised social infrastructure in the Town Centre.[10] The concept of the shopping centre as a community hub did not begin in Australia at Elizabeth – both Chermside and Top Ryde included a child-minding service with the latter also providing a Baby Health Clinic – but it set a benchmark, and helped channel European influences into the market. In this way, Elizabeth made an important contribution to understandings of the role shopping centres could play in Australian communities. This influenced their marketing as well as the types of community facilities that private developers included in their complexes, at times at the behest of public authorities seeking to wring more public value out of the development process.

The inclusion of community facilities by a number of Australian firms was also a strategy aimed at increasing consumer adoption.[11] The decision to invest in regional shopping centre development in the 1960s was based on a limited sample of experience. Shopping centres appeared suitable for Australian conditions but were not yet proven. Every capital city market was different, and there had been little time to assess the ongoing viability of what was a radically disruptive retail innovation. In this environment, few stones were left unturned by firms making what were very substantial investments: Myer spent £6 million building Chadstone; the Hammerson Group of Companies and Grace Bros. invested similar amounts in Warringah Mall and Roselands respectively; Lend Lease spent $17 million, developing Bankstown Square, Myer $18 million on Northland (after Australia converted to decimal currency in 1966). With so much at stake, developers in the 1960s sought to make their projects as desirable as possible to Australian consumers. Many provided the kinds of facilities and services included in the SAHT's Elizabeth centres. Baby Health Clinics were not uncommon. Professional and medical services were frequent inclusions. But developers also followed advice from figures such as Gruen and Smith about designing space to facilitate sociability. And they observed the ways in which American architects had approached this in practice.

A number of early American malls included community facilities. These varied in size and sophistication but included auditoriums as well as smaller rooms and kitchen facilities, available to community clubs and groups.[12] Many of the large regionals built in Australia during the 1960s adopted this practice in one form or another. Most had children's playgrounds with a variety of equipment such as fibreglass sculptures, spiral slides, rides and climbing blocks. Miranda Fair included a branch of the municipal library. The local council had wanted an auditorium as well but settled for a large restaurant that could be hired for organised functions.[13] This was a solution adopted at other centres like Marion, where catering operations served customers during shopping hours and were available for hire at other times.[14]

Promotions for Roselands declared that "like any city" it would "give the community all it needs – a Post Office, banks, doctors, dentists and other professionals, restaurants, health clinics for adults and children, a City Hall … and places to relax."[15] The inclusion of professional services was common in all 1960s regional shopping centres, but it was the big city retail developers that tended to offer the most comprehensive community facilities. This continued their cultural tradition of service. Like Roselands, Myer's Chadstone, Northland and Southland projects all included large, fully equipped auditoriums. Some provided dance floors and stages that could be used for ballet recitals, lectures, exhibitions, musical performances and business conferences.[16] Additional community rooms provided space for "first class receptions and social occasions," meetings and conventions. Adjacent bathrooms, dressing rooms, kitchenettes and tea and coffee making facilities added to their convenience and utility.[17] Myer claimed that the community centre at Chadstone was "one of the most-used services at the centre."[18]

Developers and retailers also invested heavily in the common areas of shopping centres, seeking to facilitate and encourage social congregation. Both these approaches built on the theory that retail space was more valuable if it was located in a network of social and cultural relations. In making this point, Gruen and Smith urged industry readers to

> remember the important and vibrant role our town squares have played in the life of our communities … sensitively observe the colorful, stimulating, and commercially busy urban scenes in the market squares of Central European cities in order to understand the contribution to community life the open spaces in our new shopping towns can make … They must be busy and colorful, exciting and stimulating, full of variety and interest. They must not only make walking enjoyable, but must also provide places for rest and relaxation … the environment should be so attractive that customers will enjoy shopping trips, will stay longer and return more often. This will result in cash registers ringing more often and recording higher sales.[19]

When designing courtyard spaces in regional malls, American architects deployed a variety of methods to suggest grandeur, harness natural light, introduce natural elements and cultivate atmosphere. Central courts were frequently landscaped with ponds, fountains, trees, flowering plants, sculptures and murals.[20] These provided a palette of ideas for Australian architects. Miranda Fair's central court extended through three levels and was roofed with a glass dome to admit natural light to greenery below.[21] Southland, opening later in the decade, similarly employed a multi-level open well around its central court that was naturally illuminated through an acrylic skylight.[22] Myer's Northland centre included three covered malls that radiated out in a cruciform design from a landscaped central plaza, creating "ideal strolling and shopping conditions."[23] The Compass Court at Marion was envisaged as the hub of the centre, extending two stories high and covering some 7,000 square feet of space. To enhance its "spacious glamour," open planning was adopted for stores facing onto the court, allowing customers to stroll through and between shops uninterrupted.[24]

Centre courts were imagined as the social anchors of shopping centres and used to define their identity. In doing so, they helped elevate the larger developments beyond a merely utilitarian collection of shops. Northland's marketers described the centre as "a kind of oasis and palace combined." Grace Bros.' marketing team declared that Roselands would "capture as never before the colour, the excitement, the lure and the bustle of a bazaar in the most beguiling 20th century setting." Such marketing superlatives should not obscure the genuine attempt by a new industry to create environments that people wanted to be in, and to mark out their own place in Australian architectural history. Roselands, like its contemporaries, was not only "designed as a place to linger in … to explore … to enjoy … to relax." It was imagined as "the hub of a new way of life."[25]

Shopping centres in this period were frequently described as "ultra-modern." Declaring that they wanted to combine efficiency with beauty, developers commissioned artists and designers to create public works of art that reflected the modernist credentials and civic contribution of their centres.[26] Gosseye and Vernon describe Chermside as an example of "Gesamtkunstwerk" – a harmonious and unified total work of art. To introduce artistic elements and develop a cohesive aesthetic across the site, Chermside's architects engaged an "Italian colour consultant and decorator," Percy Zanuttini, who had immigrated to Queensland in 1950. Zanuttini employed 24 men to integrate his custom-mixed colours throughout the centre. A highlight was "a large Mondrianesque chrome cement tableau" on an external façade, which Zanuttini claimed was "the first of its type in the world." At Top Ryde, Sydney artist Gordon Andrews was commissioned to build a 4.6-metre fibreglass abstract figure encrusted with chips of coloured glass. Myer invited ten artists to produce sculpture proposals for Chadstone. Two were subsequently installed: a concrete representation of commerce by Stanly Hammond and an abstract, painted steel work by Lenton Parr entitled "Plant Forms." Gosseye and Vernon note that "these artworks were probably the only pieces of publicly accessible contemporary sculpture in the suburbs and among the first in Melbourne."[27]

As the decade progressed, however, the commitment by developers to elevating civic good taste through the commission of modernist artworks and murals began to shift. Décor to stimulate excitement, pleasure and consumption became more prevalent.[28] At Roselands, promotional material claimed there would be

> no tensions ... acoustic control will make the sounds merge into a happy hubbub ... there will be gentle, calming water trickling from fountains and water wheels. And sunbeams will filter down from the vaulted dome ceiling ...The Centre Court will have all the exciting hustle, the breadth, the sense of a city ... but none of the congestion, the cacophony, the discomfort.[29]

In the centre court, a long copper stem supporting an open cage sprouted out of a mosaic bowl. Inside the cage, an illuminated giant rose with 15 hand-beaten copper petals revolved under a deluge of water jets. An adjacent cat-walk for fashion parades was suspended over a wide, shallow pool of water. Shrubbery and landscaping connected these elements with the most widely publicised aesthetic feature of the centre, the Raindrop Fountain. This was comprised of hundreds of fine nylon threads, which directed droplets of a special fluid directly downwards to "create the effect of a seeping rain forest." The total, 45-foot-long display formed "perhaps the most unusual indoor garden in Australia."[30]

The net effect of such exercises in interiority was to flip the traditional relationship of shop to street. Architect Martin Butterworth has argued that "a shop is an object on the street that makes its boundaries as weak as possible so shoppers can come in."[31] The shop in the shopping centre was much the same: at Marion, for example, the centre court provided common ground that connected competing retailers facing into it. This echoed the way that traders had operated around outdoor plazas and town squares for centuries. Similarly, shopping centre concourses emulated shop-lined high streets. And by condensing and intensifying the competitive environment, shopping centres encouraged retailers to invest more heavily in weakening shop front boundaries. Retail trade journals in the 1960s were filled with advice on how to deploy merchandising, lighting and display to invite and lure customers into shops. As the retail property industry professionalised, shopping centre managers formalised this advice into standards of presentation and shop fit-out that became requirements of occupancy.

Shopping centres enclosed these "boundary-less shops" within boundaries. This began as a byproduct of separating cars and foot traffic, but the development of fully enclosed, inward-facing centres that sought to meet all customer needs independently of external traders, marked a change in the relationship between commerce and urbanism. High streets had porous borders and operated in multi-functional spaces along thoroughfares. This caused problems, as has been discussed in regards to traffic, but it also produced a more direct spatial relationship between retailers and surrounding communities. Shopping high streets were not just destinations, they were part of a broader urban fabric that was shaped by a host of participants in the community. They thrived on pedestrian circulation. They were accessible by many modes of transport and did not, to their detriment, sufficiently privilege the car. They were subject to law, legislation and policy frameworks, but not to operational management regimes. By circumscribing and regulating retail space, retail property developers provided a range of benefits to consumers, including protection from the weather and comprehensive one-stop shopping, and also gained greater control over their investment. Interiority also limited the extent to which surrounding retail could leverage advantage from the infrastructure they were providing. No-one wanted to build a parking station for someone else's shops.

The housewife's square

This controlled space was also gendered. Kim Humphery argues that "while shopping has historically been defined as a female activity, the conceptualisation and management of retail environments have almost always been the province of men."[32] More research needs to be conducted into the role of women executives in Australian retailing and property development, but it is generally true that this dynamic was again at work when shopping centres were introduced to Australia.[33] Males were the predominant employees in the fields of architecture, construction, finance, market research and leasing. Entrepreneurial property development was also almost exclusively their field. Collectively, their labours developing shopping centres were viewed as a form of nation-building, fulfilling a grand modernising vision by introducing on massive scale an entirely new retail format that transformed suburbia.[34] The regional shopping centres built in the 1960s were virtually all described as the largest of their type, in their city, state or hemisphere.[35] The boldness and bravura of these enterprises were lauded by politicians and in the press. In 1957, the President of the Brisbane Chamber of Commerce declared that Allan & Stark should be "congratulated on their courage and initiative in pioneering the first drive-in shopping centre in Australia."[36] When he opened Miranda Fair, Sutherland's Shire President also commended the "rock courage [taken] to spend £3.5 million on this wonderful development."[37] Press coverage frequently described "armies" of workers, labouring day and night with cohesion and military order, usually until the eve or morning of opening day to bring the visions of developers to life.[38]

A promotional film commissioned by Arndale in the late 1960s offers further insight into the gendered dimensions of such praise. Only one woman appeared in the film – a local resident being surveyed about her shopping needs. Every other figure was male and productive. Teamwork across numerous professions and industries was emphasised, reflecting the increasing scale and sophistication of development projects in the post-war period.[39] Watching these men building "the proud and ambitious concept destined to be South Australia's most elegant city of shops," a male narrator told viewers that:

> Top executives and project planners at Arndale Developments Australia Pty Ltd met together early in 1966 to fulfil this concept ... they gave their best in skill and experience ... Survey teams worked hard to gain information ... Month followed month of planning ... Then ... Architects for this mammoth project were appointed ... Gradually the centre's concept began to take shape. Skilled draftsmen created sketches, meticulously planning every detail. These talented men used vivid, inexhaustible imaginations ... Uppermost in their minds was the ambition to build a shopping centre that would stand as a pillar of the south and provide every conceivable shopping facility.
>
> A massive construction program for Marion is launched ... 35 acres, formally thriving vineyards were cleared and prepared. Then, the heavy equipment was put to work. More than 22,000 cubic yards of soil at the site were excavated, graded and levelled. 40,000 square yards of crushed, rock hard core was formed as base for roadways. Surveying, digging, framing, concreting ... and soon the foundations for the massive concrete columns at Marion were excavated and poured ... The site became a hubbub of development. Busy workmen combined in the tremendous task. Each and every one conscious of his role in creating this ultra-modern shopping centre ... Architects, contractors, consultants, surveyors, builders, project engineers, hundreds of skilled men, all working with one common goal.[40]

While men were lauded for their role in producing what were massive and transformative retail spaces, there was an unequivocal belief that shopping centres were female spaces.[41] One Australian market researcher in the late 1960s declared that "not only are women directly responsible for a whacking proportion of all consumer purchases, but they provide the motivation behind many of the males' buying 'decisions.'"[42] This was an understanding shared in both Europe and America.[43] In Australian retail marketing archives from this time, women only appear with any regularity in analyses of shoppers. Indeed, here they dominate and are conflated to feminise any general group of consumers being discussed.[44] This set the tone for advertising and promotions that spoke to, and reinforced, existing understandings of gender roles.

All of the large shopping centres built during the 1960s were described in one form or another as a "woman's world – with the accent on mothers."[45] While centres were sometimes advertised as "family centres," the shopper was almost exclusively depicted as female. Chadstone was "planned and geared for women's needs," easily and conveniently accessible to "Mrs Suburbia."[46] In one artist's impression of a populated centre court at Northland, only two figures were discernably male (Figure 5.1). Both stood in the background,

Figure 5.1 Northland promotional brochure, ca. 1966.

accompanied by female partners amidst dozens of other female shoppers and children.[47] Bankstown Square was marketed as "the Housewife's Square."[48]

Shopping centres included services that catered specifically to women. Most notable amongst these were childcare facilities, staffed by trained carers, and available to anyone shopping at the centre for up to a few hours. It was believed, largely accurately, that women would stay for longer and enjoy themselves more if they could leave their children in a safe and pleasant environment while they shopped. This approach was not unique to Australia. In the United States, numerous shopping centres planned to included nurseries, although few actually materialised. Nurseries did not directly produce rental income and there were concerns that they could "easily lead to damage suits [rather] than gratitude."[49] Nurseries were included in a few centres such as The Discoveries in Oklahoma City and in the planned township of Levittown, where the overwhelming majority of customers were young married couples with children.[50] In most American malls, however the less expensive option of a children's play area was more common.

In Australia, childcare services were proportionally far more widespread, and were inclusions in most large regional centres built up until the mid 1960s.[51] Children's play areas and equipment were also included. At Roselands, a "TV Child Minder" was installed. Said to be the largest closed-circuit television system in Australia, it allowed parents (and everyone else) to observe their children playing in the Roselands' nursery on monitors positioned around the shopping centre. The nursery was staffed by a qualified nurse, and her cohort of "baby sitters."[52]

There was a very real pragmatism to shaping the shopping centre environment to the needs and interests of Australian women: marketers were trying to change established shopping habits and had to appeal to those who did the shopping.[53] There were also cultural frameworks at play: socially constructed ideas of femininity homogenised and caricatured the female shopping experience. Advertorials for Myer's Chadstone store described the soft vinyl tile flooring that had been installed to prevent "the imprint of women's stiletto heels." Escalator steps were given a fine grooved surface, "again to take care of those stiletto heels."[54] Whether in high heels or not, women's driving abilities were considered suspect. A "timid driver" arriving at Marion shopping centre was assured that her path was smoothed by "easy access to entry and exit points." Chadstone's parking spaces were set at 45-degree angles to prevent "embarrassing manoeuvres into small spaces."[55]

Facilitating access and shaping the centre environment for women's comfort and convenience was clearly a pressing concern for marketers. But they also knew that shopping was the bedrock on which all visits would be built. In its review of Roselands, the *Retail Merchandiser* noted that the key to its success would depend on providing the "one intangible which [female] shoppers demand: choice."

> One butcher would not be enough, or one haberdashery – Madam likes to compare competitive prices and qualities, to find some challenge to her bargain-hunting skills. Consequently, there are two or three or more of everything … As women are the principal shoppers, the planning of Roselands as a shopping-community centre was largely directed towards serving their requirements and convenience in shopping and their interests in community activities … This has been achieved in Roselands' variety of shops and household services, in its professional services, in child care, and in facilities for relaxation and entertainment. And most importantly, in the extent and convenience of car parking.[56]

An unstated premise of this advertising was that shopping was a time-consuming and labour-intensive activity. Not only were women responsible for the actual purchase of most food, clothing and household items, they were tasked with comparing, valuing and selecting these based on a range of criteria extending from household budgets to personal, familial and social expectations.[57] As one-stop shops, shopping centres were presented as an efficient technology through which women could realise this economic role. At the same time, marketing rhetoric obscured the labour involved by wrapping the new shopping experience in motifs of freedom, choice and fulfilment. Newspaper advertisements for Roselands suggested to women that:

If you believe that variety is the spice of life … if you like your fashions new … to be in on the latest … if you have a mind of your own … if you seek the latest fads, priced within your reach … if you love your man in good clothes, well cut, well maintained, if you love to dress your children up in fashion designed to show them off then you'll love Grace Bros. Roselands.[58]

Shoppers were invited to "step into tomorrow"; into "a new way of life,"[59] with the shopping centre described as a comprehensive solution to the problems of the past. The city was now in the suburbs; cleaner, more efficient, convenient and comfortable. The weather was controlled and set to year-round spring. There was no rain, no wind, no flies.[60] Cars could be driven almost to the shop door, but were nowhere in sight, smell or hearing once shopping began. In America, marketers declared that such environments turned shopping from a chore into a pleasure.[61] In doing so, they conflated all shopping trips, discretionary and non-discretionary alike, into a homologous experience that was equated with the novelty of city shopping, which had traditionally been viewed as a day out, a special event, or linked to important occasions. The idea had purchase because it masked and reframed mundane labour, while highlighting the hedonistic aspects of shopping. Australian marketers readily imported and deployed it in their own promotional efforts, offering women "the perfect day out" and the opportunity to meet with friends in convivial environments.[62]

The twin themes of pleasure and convenience were reflected in the clothes people wore to shopping centres. Casual dress replaced the stiff formality of the city, where personalised service and tradition imposed on the customer an obligation to appear respectable, lest sales staff subtly indicate their judgement of one's taste or economic status.[63] Michael Lonie, who began working for Westfield in the late 1960s and rose to senior executive positions in the 1980s, describes this as a cultural change that was aligned with, and overlaid, retail's geographic shift:

Originally, the town hall was the focal point or the central railway was the focal point of the city. That's why so many of the original retailers were always down that end of town [in Sydney]… when retail went out of the CBD into the suburbs, you really started that whole structural change … You had the Mark Foy's and you look at that building … there was an absolute style to that building but it died … I can still remember people coming into the city with their hats and their gloves and their handbags and they'd go to Coles and have afternoon tea in the Hotel Australia … They didn't have to dress to the same extent if they were going down to the suburbs or the corner store. If you were going to the regional shopping centre, I could go down casually because it was not a trip to the city. Everyone got dressed to go to the city.[64]

Some suburban shopping trips would certainly have been pleasurable, but most were still a chore. In the 1930s, the average suburban home received a stream of regular deliveries from icemen, butchers, grocers, greengrocers, milkmen, bakers and rabbitohs. The widespread adoption of the refrigerator and the car, combined with the emergence of the supermarket, changed this dynamic. Delivery services dropped as car driving became more prevalent, making shopping more labour-intensive for the shopper, especially as self-service was introduced: women collecting items from around the supermarket were doing the work previously undertaken by retail workers.[65] Such work was even more onerous for the many women yet to obtain a driver's licence or without day-time access to the family car.

Shopping for food and everyday needs was domestic labour for which "housewives" were given primary responsibility. As with housework within the home, shopping was (and is) a chore undertaken without payment, over-time rates, paid holidays or sickness entitlements. Similarly, too, there was little evidence that women saw any relief from their shopping responsibilities as they returned to the paid workforce in increasing numbers during the 1960s and 1970s.[66] Shopping was such a chore that feminist activists attempted to have it acknowledged as an economic activity in union campaigns during the early 1970s.[67] Their argument was relatively short-lived, but it formed part of a broader attempt to lift the cloak of invisibility from domestic and household labour at the time, and serves as a reminder that shopping – the procurement of the goods on which households depend – is a vital but little recognised pro-ductive role integral to the consumer economy.[68]

Employment

An irony of the "housewife" archetype was that it was maintained while women entered the paid workforce in increasing numbers (Table 5.1).[69] In 1954, just 29 per cent of women were employed in the Australian workforce. They comprised less than a quarter of working Australians. By 1978, 46 per cent of all women were employed in paid work, equating to 35 per cent of all workers.[70] The growing proportion of women staying in the workforce after marriage was one of the major features of this development.[71] This reflected international trends in what has been described as "the most important change to have affected the supply side of labour markets throughout the developed world."[72] By the end of the 1970s, more than 60 per cent of women in the Australian workforce were married.[73] Many also had young children.[74]

The growth in women's workforce participation resulted from a number of factors. The full-employment years of the post-war boom increased demand for labour. There was a broadening of employment opportunities for women in a wider range of industries (although female employment remained concentrated in relatively few).[75] Higher levels of educational attainment amongst women changed expectations about careers. Policy changes such as the lifting of bans on married women's employment in the Australian Public Service and

Table 5.1 Employed women: Selected indicators, 1954–98

Employment rates of women aged 15–64 (%)			% of employed women working part-time	Employed women as % of all employed persons			Employed women who were married (%)
Year	Full-time	Part-time	Total		Married	Not married	Total	
1954	n.a.	n.a.	29.0	n.a.	7.0	15.8	22.8	30.9
1968	28.0	13.7	41.7	32.9	17.2	14.0	31.2	55.1
1978	30.8	15.6	46.4	33.6	21.8	13.6	35.4	61.5
1988	33.3	21.1	54.4	38.7	24.4	15.9	40.2	60.6
1998	33.5	25.5	58.9	43.2	26.3	17.0	43.3	60.7

Source: ABS, *Australian Social Trends*, 4102.0, 1998, 111.

industries like banking removed obstacles to ongoing employment. The earlier completion of family formation as a result of younger marriage ages increased opportunity, as did labour-saving household technologies, and shifting social attitudes.[76]

The spread of consumerism also encouraged the pursuit of additional income. Women chose to work, incentivised by the lifestyle opportunities available.[77] A survey of married women in two large Australian retail stores in 1971 found that the overwhelming reason given for working was that it provided "essential financial support," covering the costs of running the home, educating children, purchasing consumer durables or funding holidays. However, more than half said they would continue to work even if their husband's salary increased to match their present total household income. Most also said that their husbands favoured them working – a response that indicates the value of second incomes as much as the question revealed social understandings of the power dynamics within domestic relationships.[78]

Retailing was one of the biggest contributors to the growth of women's employment. In 1962, men comprised 53 per cent of the retail workforce and women 47 per cent. The suburbanisation of retailing and the spread of supermarket chains saw this gap close by 1974, by which time there was an even gender distribution in terms of total numbers.[79] One part of this process was the mass employment of women as cashiers in supermarkets and the simultaneous displacement of male grocers and other small shopkeepers. The feminisation of retailing thus coincided with other structural changes in the sector: the rise of supermarkets and the decline of the independent grocer brought a higher proportion of wage labour; self-service introduced automation as customers were funnelled past a stationary cash register operator whose tasks were routinised and measured; and deskilling occurred as marketing and merchandising decisions became centralised in head offices.[80]

There was also a gendered division of labour across the retail sector, with men and women considered suitable for different types of selling. In 1974, women made up 68 per cent of workers in department stores, 76 per cent in variety and general stores, 60 per cent in supermarkets, 62 per cent in grocers and tobacconists and 76 per cent in clothing and footwear. Men were more likely to sell appliances, furniture, sporting goods, meat and motor vehicles. If we exclude workers selling cars and accessories for them, women comprised 60 per cent of the retail workforce.[81] This is a remarkable statistic given the broader workforce participation rates detailed in Table 5.1, and made retailing the only major industry in the country that employed more females than males.[82]

As with other industries, though, women were more likely than men to be part-time and working at the lower levels of firms. This was largely recognised as natural at the time. In the mid 1960s a senior male executive reportedly praised a woman who had run an important department for his firm by saying that "If she weren't a woman, she'd be a director." An American retailer observing such attitudes during a visit to Australia asked his professional readership to "try to think of even one woman in any retail store in this country who has a position higher than that of fashion controller." By the 1960s, a few women were making their way into marketing and buying roles, but there was a glaring female absence at executive levels. The observer noted that for an industry courting women as its predominant customers, "it remains one of the most incongruous bits of idiocy in a country which prides itself on the opportunities it offers to its citizens."[83]

Women were simply not seen as management material. Rather they offered a convenient and cheap labour force that could be disciplined to the increasingly mechanised routines of modern retailing.[84] The skills, abilities and aesthetics for which women were valued are evidenced in cash register speed and accuracy competitions that were prevalent at the time. Conducted across the country at both the firm and industry level, these competitions aimed to raise the standard and efficiency of checkout operators. Women's preparation for competition was seen to reflect "automatically on their everyday operation and performance."[85] In competition they were praised for both their skill and appearance. One male attendee at a 1969 national title reportedly "compared the speed contest between the six attractive girls as a cross between the Miss Australia contest and the Melbourne Cup" horse race.[86]

Despite these conditions, retail labour was also valued by many who obtained it. Eighty per cent of the respondents to the department store survey cited above said that "their employment conditions were generally satisfactory, and that their employers were doing enough to make working conditions convenient for married women."[87] Their service-oriented department store roles were quite different to the repetitive routine of supermarket work, but the responses do provide an indication of the value retail employment held for women and their families. Despite the onerous conditions of some retail jobs and the restrictions on advancement within firms, employment was an important economic and social contribution that shopping centres made to suburbia – a fact that developers noted when seeking construction approvals or promoting the opening of their centres.[88]

Written testimony from Sydneysiders who were teenagers in the 1960s indicates the importance of retail employment for young people as well.[89] When she was 18, Lorne found a job in the accounts section at Grace Bros. Roselands where her mother worked. "I loved working with my mother, [and] had a great time getting to know people in Grace Bros … It was like a big family (not always happy though!) but everyone knew everyone else."[90] Lorne met her future husband, Ken, when he came in to make a payment on his $10 credit account. "She offered me a lolly," Ken recollects. "I was hooked. We were engaged two months later and married four months after that."[91] Lorne and Ken held their reception "in the Rose Room which was part of Roselands … people were very kind … and helped us tremendously [in] keeping costs down etc. It was a tight little community the retail sector … in those days."[92]

With wartime babies and their post-war siblings coming of working age in the 1960s, young people like Lorne were an important source of labour for retailers.[93] Pauline was another young employee in Grace Bros.' Roselands store, joining the display department after finishing art school. She recalls that it was an unusual occupation for a girl at the time and that most of her workmates were male and gay. "I loved it and them," she recalls:

> they treated me like a favoured child teaching me everything they knew from the 'hey day' of window dressing … at Mark Foys in Sydney. They were a talented and amusing bunch and introduced me to a lot of things, 'completing' my education with ballet, films, food and fashion. I can remember going to see *Elvira Madigan* with 'Tilly' after he had taken me to the original Adam's Marble Bar [in the city].[94]

Watching the ill-fated love affair of tightrope-walker Hedvig Jensen and Swedish cavalry officer Count Sixten Sparre, they "sat and held hands and cried throughout the movie." Pauline also worked on her boss's drag outfits. One evening, she helped sew him into a ball gown covered in thousands of tiny mirrors. Gary Wotherspoon has noted that queens in the 1960s sometimes travelled to events in removal trucks to preserve the appearance of elaborate gowns and wigs.[95] Tilly was transported in a station wagon. The mirror dress prevented him from bending at the waist so he lay flat in the back of the car – much to the surprise of a toll-collector observing their passage across Sydney's harbour bridge.

Pauline and Tilly worked at Roselands at a time when display was becoming more widely appreciated in the retail industry. In the 1940s, limited funds and materials had forced staff, who were often viewed by management as odd and "arty," to manufacture their own props. In the fifties, mass-produced display items became available. By the 1960s, the presentation of merchandise was a topic of hot discussion in the retail press with managers urged to integrate store displays with other promotional material.[96] Display staff still created their own workplace cultures, however, and interactions with management were not always smooth. When Tilly received a command "to pull his finger out," he sent a mannequin's broken-off finger back to management in reply. It was also not uncommon for Pauline and her colleagues to run through Grace Bros. with a naked mannequin, shrieking with laughter as they clutched its crotch or breast.[97]

Hanging out in shopping centres

Australian youth not only worked in shopping centres, they met friends, observed fashions, shopped and entertained themselves in what quickly became a vibrant social space.[98] William Kowinski has written about this process in the United States. In *The Malling of America*, Kowinski criticised the artificial world constructed inside the mall, but recognised its importance as a social space in post-war American life, particularly for youth.[99] Young Australians, too, embraced the shopping centre. Roselands, writes Ken, was "like a magnet ... the centre of the area."[100] Robert recalls that it became "the central focus of my life and that of my friends ... Each afternoon after school and every weekend was spent meeting up within Roselands to 'hang' ... I met my first girlfriend [there] and had my first kiss."[101]

Social interactions like these were fuelled by consumer practices. The "teen market" had been discussed in the media since the late 1950s, and by the 1960s was recognised as an important demographic by marketers and retailers who were adopting age-based market segmentation.[102] Even adolescent boys were said to be "more style conscious" than ever before. Stores were advised to invest in promotions as "study after study" found that young customers looked "to their favourite store for ... fashion guidance."[103] This may have been wishful thinking by retailers hoping to dictate fashion to a market they did not truly understand, but Robert credits Roselands with introducing "fashion to my group ... [because] trends were on show that would have been unknown to those outside the complex."[104]

Teenage consumers were welcomed by retailers but also treated with suspicion. There was nothing new in such concerns: fears about anti-social youth had been expressed in public debates since the mid nineteenth century.[105] Now, caught in the anxieties of the Cold War, an older generation that had experienced the straitening circumstances of the 1930s Depression and World War Two had difficulty empathising with cultural dissidence. Ready employment and rising wages brought relief from the privations of the past, but also funded new consumerist choices for young people that clashed with older sensibilities. Teenagers embraced consumer culture and adopted American styles of music, dress and dancing. Working-class (male) "bodgies" and (female) "widgies" hung out in milk bars and on street corners exuding violence and sexual licence to a concerned middle class.[106] Selective media coverage of their activities broadened fears about an entire generation. By the late 1950s, Keith Moore argues, "many people embraced the opinion that a substantial proportion of the country's teenagers were uncontrollable."[107] There were reports in the late 1960s of gangs congregating outside shopping centres, fighting and racing cars in car parks at night.[108] Skateboarders, too, rode these vast, empty concrete landscapes on Saturday afternoons and Sundays. For retailers, though, the primary threat teenagers posed was shoplifting.[109] Articles in retail trade journals from the time contain extensive commentary on the issue. Experts provided detail on state laws, products they considered most at risk, and how to profile and identify shoplifters.[110]

If shopping centre car parks appeared dangerous, and the street was "a magnet for delinquency,"[111] interiorised retail worlds were seen by parents and even teenagers themselves as safe American imports. They were a respectable place to socialise, especially for young women.[112] Marketers reinforced this impression by providing middle-of-the-road entertainment that was fun but rarely transgressive. Miranda Fair had only just opened when pop stars Col Joy and Little Pattie visited, performed and signed autographs for young fans at Farmer's record bar.[113] Teenagers gathered for both fashion parades and rock shows at Westfield Burwood.[114] At Roselands, "the raindrop fountain was the focus." Crowds would gather all the way up to "the top floor to view the scene." Stars like Johnny Farnham and Ronnie Burns performed on the stage in the centre court far below.[115] In the late 1960s, Pauline watched Farnham sing "Sadie the Cleaning Lady," and when Tiny Tim sang "Tip Toe through the Tulips," she and her friends "stood near the stage and pelted him with plastic flowers."[116]

One teenager from Sydney's northern beaches recalls that Warringah Mall was "a very big thing to people in my age group as we had something else to do on weekends apart from going to the beach and playing sport … We all loved going to the 'Mall.'"[117] Management responded by projecting surfing movies onto the two-story wall of the David Jones department store. Local youth, schooled in beach and surf culture, watched from the car park:

> The first time I saw Endless Summer was from the roof of my boyfriend's car, which was a VW … he had pulled the two front seats out … so we would be comfortable. Imagine several hundred teenagers all sitting in the car park, which was an open-air style, either in or on top of their cars watching movies. Surfing movies of course, because we were all Northern Beaches kids who lived and breathed that stuff then.[118]

Privatised public space

Consistent amongst the developers of Australia's early regional shopping centres was a belief that making an environment attractive and exciting to people was an investment that would improve sales – whether this was presenting products of popular culture to cultivate the spending proclivities of youthful consumers; providing child-care facilities for mothers of young children who would then have more time to shop; or constructing expansive indoor courts featuring elaborate water features, landscaped gardens and modernist art to encourage and lengthen visits. There was little tangible data on how to measure the effect of these investments, which were informed by ideas and cultural tropes about gender, demographics and customer behaviour rather than any rigorous method of evaluation. But they were pursued to increase the competitiveness of the untested and disruptive shopping centre format. It was noted in 1964 that large planned shopping centres held competitive advantages in functionality, layout, parking and range of merchandise. Social and cultural facilities, however, were mainly concentrated in established district centres and high streets.[119] Shifting this balance was seen as a way to encourage consumer adoption.

Within just a few years, however, developers and retailers were reappraising their approach. Plans for Southland included "Australia's best" child-minding service, but this was abandoned before development was completed in 1968.[120] When Myer opened Tea Tree Plaza in South Australia in 1970 there was no mention of community or child-care facilities. Advertising and newspaper coverage focused exclusively on the retail offer and the comfort, convenience and appeal of the centre environment.[121] With consumers largely convinced of the advantages shopping centres offered, community facilities and even promotional concerts became seen as "incidental to the business." Reg Jebb notes that regional centres

> all started off having cake halls and boardwalks that models could walk on at all the fashion shows. But all they found was that [promotional shows] made too many traffic jams in the middle of the mall ... shoppers could not get around and businesses were adversely affected.[122]

The phasing out of community facilities coincided with the rise of specialist developers. City department stores that developed regional shopping centres still retained organisational cultures entrenched in ideas of service. Entrepreneurial developers building sites for supermarkets, as the earlier example of Jack Weinert's approach to construction indicates, were more determinably focused on efficiencies. But as the shopping centre format became more established, all retailers and developers had less incentive to invest in non-productive space. When firms did, by providing facilities like libraries, it was usually a condition of development approval. In the United States, Victor Gruen lamented this trend. In 1979, he incorrectly predicted the decline of the mall because developers had eschewed its community function.[123] Gruen had always envisaged a balance between commercial and non-commercial space. Now he saw little that was not harnessed to the ends of profit.[124]

During the course of the 1960s, the architectural form of the shopping centre was reconfigured to be more productive. Introverted centres became the dominant type, providing developers with greater control over shopping environments. Enclosure created worlds in which external influences, from the weather to competing high street retailers, were kept at bay. Ambient sound, temperature and light were curated to frame merchandise and encourage purchases. Enclosure protected investments by constraining the mobility of customers to an area from which the landlord extracted rent. This limited the extent to which outside interests could profit from the facilities provided by the shopping centre. This made shopping centre space more valuable: the better a shopping centre traded, the higher the rents a landlord could charge. If the land-lord was also a retailer, as was the case with many of the early regional centres, they also derived an obvious direct benefit by increasing shopper visits and time spent in their shops.

The early inclusion of community facilities and the scale of increasingly self-contained "shopping cities" led to claims that shopping centres might be performing a civic role in their locales.[125] Grace Bros. labelled Roselands a "one-stop city in the suburbs," called the centre manager "a sort of Ombudsman," and named its community area the "Roselands Town Hall."[126] This section of the centre contained a range of useful community spaces, but had no actual civic functions. The rhetorical sleight of hand confused some local residents, who visited Roselands under the assumption that they could conduct municipal business there. Following their complaints, Canterbury Council sought legal advice as to whether they could prevent Grace Bros. from using the term "town hall" but were advised that the Local Government Act contained no provisions prohibiting its use.[127]

The use of the term "town hall" to describe community space in shopping centres did not become widespread in Australia. But it serves as an example of a slippage that occurred between privately controlled commercial space and democratic public space. As Cohen suggests in the American context, shopping centres promoted themselves as community centres, but then defined "community" in exclusionary socioeconomic terms.[128] Similarly, Leonie Sandercock argues that American regional shopping centres were positioned as "a more perfect downtown" by excluding the weather and traffic, as well as "poor and coloured folks."[129] William H. Whyte argues that such delimited environments should not be considered true town centres, because "they do not welcome – indeed, do not tolerate – controversy, soapboxing, passing of leaflets, impromptu entertaining, happenings, or eccentric behaviour, harmless or no."[130] Such rules, determined by private companies, defined shopping centres as private spaces. So, although shopping centres in Australia quickly evolved into social meeting places and gathering points for consumers, this did not make them true public spaces. As Peter Spearritt argues: "If your access to particular public spaces depends on both your willingness and your ability to pay, then those spaces cease to be public."[131] In this regulated environment, surveillance, control and security were harnessed to provide "family friendly" environments in which shoppers felt safe and comfortable. This meant allowing access to those who complied with the codes of conduct required by landlords, and limiting access to those who didn't.

Shopping centres were in this way an early example of the private control that is exercised over modern urban spaces of mass congregation, be it football stadiums, entertainment precincts, city squares or disused industrial waterfronts that have been redeveloped for consumer tourism. Commentary on such spaces tends to historicise them as a function of neoliberalism, with public authorities from the 1980s onwards seeking to create "more public environments with less expenditure of public money."[132] Placing such sites under private control introduced new forms of regulation, while layers of consumption were added to increase returns on investment. Shopping centres provided a historical precedent for such developments, demonstrating the ways that commerce and leisure could be entwined, and how social space could be monetised within privately controlled environments.

Acknowledging the difference between public and private space should not distract attention from the role shopping centres did play in surrounding communities. As the stories from Sydneysiders quoted above indicate, the regional shopping centre became a central hub of social and economic activity in Australian suburbs. Employment shaped the lives of families. Consumption helped define who they were. Social networks passed in and through "shopping cities," which also generated new connections. Although they were not civic centres, they were important social sites for many Australians. This capacity to operate as shared spaces and social worlds was an important contributor to the adoption, success and longevity of shopping centres in Australia. It also remains one of their most important competitive advantages in the current battle with online retail.

Notes

1 White, *Inventing Australia*, 158–63.
2 O'Hanlon, "Cities, Suburbs and Communities," 177. See also Dingle, "'Gloria Soame'," 189–90.
3 *RT*, June 1965, 4–5.
4 *SMH*, 12 October 1965, 34.
5 Barrett, "Roselands," 133.
6 Bankstown City Council Library, Local Studies Collection, Bankstown Square File, Hely, Bell & Horne (Architects) Bankstown Square Shopping Centre, Fountain Court Entrance, Sydney, n.d.
7 Gruen and Smith, *Shopping Towns USA*, 257.
8 Howard, *From Main Street to Mall*, 141–2.
9 *RM*, December 1963, 26.
10 Modern Merchandising Methods, *Australian Shopping Centres* (1971 edn).
11 Beed, "Growth of Suburban Retailing," 261.
12 Redstone, *New Dimensions*, 166, 173.
13 Sutherland Shire Council Library (SSCL), Local Studies Collection, Special General Committee Meeting, Minute no. 161, 7 May 1962.
14 *AR*, June 1967, 4–5; State Library of South Australia, South Australiana Pamphlets (SLSA), Jones Lang Wootton, Marion: An Arndale Shopping Centre, 1968.
15 CMA, Box 57, The trend-setting city in the suburbs: Roselands, ca. 1965.
16 *RM*, May 1960, 10; *Property*, October 1966, 19.
17 *GSJWA*, November 1968, 8.
18 CMA, Box 1800, Northland Promotional brochure, ca. 1966.

19 Gruen and Smith, *Shopping Towns USA*, 247–8.
20 Redstone, *New Dimensions*.
21 SSCL, Farmer's Press Release, Farmer's £3½ million Miranda Project building to begin next month, 17 October 1962.
22 *GSJWA*, November 1968, 6.
23 *RM*, July 1964, 21; October 1966, 6–9.
24 *AR*, June 1967, 4–5.
25 CMA, Box 57, The trend-setting city in the suburbs: Roselands, ca. 1965.
26 Redstone, *New Dimensions*, 51; SLSA, Marion; *RM*, October 1966, 6–9.
27 Gosseye and Vernon, "Shopping Towns Australia," 222–3; *CM*, 29 May 1957, 28.
28 Gosseye and Vernon, "Shopping Towns Australia," 222–3; *RM*, October 1966, 7; *GSJWA*, November 1968, 6; *SMH*, 11 October 1966, 21.
29 CMA, Box 57, The trend-setting city in the suburbs: Roselands, ca. 1965.
30 *RM*, November 1965, 29–30.
31 *The Australian*, 8 August 1997, p. 37.
32 Humphery, *Shelf Life*, 91.
33 Humphery, *Shelf Life*, 91.
34 *The Torch*, 3 February 1965, 2.
35 Barrett, "Roselands," 124; *MD*, 6 April 1963, 1; *SGSSL*, 5 February 1964, 9.
36 *CM*, 29 May 1957, 29.
37 *SGSSL*, 18 March 1964, 5. Roselands, too, resulted from "rock courage": see *RM*, November 1965, 26.
38 *SMH*, 20 September 1966, 22.
39 Clausen, "Northgate," 145.
40 Bosisto, "Marion Shopping Centre."
41 Davison, *Car Wars*, 108; *SMH*, Roselands Feature, 12 October 1965, 2.
42 Cited in Reekie, "Market research," 18.
43 Elvins, "History of the Department Store," 142–3; Alexander, Nell, Bailey and Shaw, "Co-Creation of a Retail Innovation," 535; Alexander and Phillips, "Retail Innovation and Shopping Practices," 2209; Bowlby, "Planning for Women," 179–84.
44 CMA, Box 3294, Strategic implications of shoppers' attitudes to Target stores, November 1984; Box 1941, Target Discount Shopping Centres promotional pamphlet, ca. 1970.
45 *RM*, October 1966, 6–9.
46 *Herald*, 3 October 1960, quoted in Davison, *Car Wars*, 108.
47 CMA, Box 1800, Northland promotional brochure.
48 *BO*, 21 September 1966, 2–3.
49 Baker and Funaro, *Shopping Centers*, 261.
50 Redstone, *New Dimensions*, 154.
51 *Herald*, 17 September 1960, 14; *RM*, May 1960, 10; CMA, Box 1941, Myer Press Release, Chadstone Shopping Centre: £6,000,000 project, 19 February 1959; *RM*, May 1960, 10; *RM*, August 1966, 34; CMA, Box 1800, Northland Promotional brochure, ca. 1966.
52 Canterbury City Council Library (CCCL), Local Studies Collection, Roselands File, Explore Roselands, ca. 1965; Barrett, "Roselands," 127–8.
53 Tea Tree Plaza News, supplement to the *North-East Leader*, 16 September 1970, 2.
54 *Sun*, 4 August 1960, 26–7.
55 *The Age*, 20 February 1959, quoted in Davison, *Car Wars*, 108.
56 *RM*, November 1965, 26.

57　Alexander and Phillips, "Retail Innovation and Shopping Practices," 2205.

58　*Bankstown Canterbury Torch*, 13 October 1965, 40.

59　*The Torch*, 20 October 1965, n.p.; Sloan, "Marion," 25.

60　*RM*, December 1955, 18; *CM* 29 May 1970, 23; *SMH*, 12 November 1957, p. 19; *Bankstown Canterbury Torch*, 6 October 1965, 16–17.

61　Quoted in Malherek, "Victor Gruen's Retail Therapy," 231; Naftaly, *Northland Mall*, 8.

62　CMA, Box 1946, Chadstone News, No. 3, ca. 1960; *RM*, May 1960, 12; CCCL, Roselands File, Everything for Everybody at Grace Bros Roselands; Sloan, "Marion," 25.

63　Kingston, *Basket, Bag and Trolley*, 80.

64　Author interview with Michael Lonie, 20 December 2013.

65　Probert, *Working Life*, 82–3.

66　On housework as a female occupation, see, Probert, *Working Life*, 71–88.

67　Hargreaves, *Women at Work*, 30.

68　Probert, *Working Life*, 77.

69　For a broader discussion of issues surrounding this, see Bowlby, "Planning for Women," 180–1.

70　ABS, *Australian Social Trends*, 4102.0, 1998, 111.

71　ABS, *Australian Year Book*, 1960, 1970, 1980.

72　Lambert and Petridis, "Slow Progress," 3; *RT*, February 1966, 5.

73　ABS, *Australian Social Trends*, 4102.0, 1998, 111.

74　Probert, *Working Life*, 89.

75　Hargreaves, *Women at Work*, 25.

76　*RT*, October 1964, 31.

77　Hudson, "1951–72," 541.

78　*AR*, May 1971, 10–12.

79　Hargreaves, *Women at Work*, 23–5; Game and Pringle, *Gender at Work*, 63.

80　Game and Pringle, *Gender at Work*, 63–7.

81　ABS, *Retail Census*, 1962, 1974.

82　*AR*, February–March 1971, 20.

83　*RT*, March 1964, 5–6.

84　Game and Pringle, *Gender at Work*, 59–79.

85　*RW*, 12 November 1969, 3.

86　*RW*, 12 November 1969, 7.

87　*AR*, May 1971, 10–12.

88　*The Torch*, 7 December 1961, 15–16; *SGSSL*, 5 February 1964, 9; CMA, Box 142, Letter from E. L. Byrne to V. Upson, 11 September 1961; Minutes of meeting in Mr A. H. Tolley's office 10am, Tuesday 9th August, Reference: Sydney Branch Development.

89　Survey conducted by the author, 2006–8. Records are indicated by respondent's name, Written Testimony (WT) and month submitted.

90　Author correspondence with Lorne, 3 October 2006.

91　Author correspondence with Ken, 4 December 2006.

92　Author correspondence with Lorne, 3 October 2006.

93　*RT*, December 1963, 29–30; Arrow, *Friday on Our Minds*, 49, 59.

94　Author correspondence with Pauline, 20 April 2006.

95　Wotherspoon, *City of the Plain*, 135.

96　*AR*, February 1968, 4–7.

97 Author correspondence with Pauline, 20 April 2006.
98 Bailey, "Inside Suburban 'Persian Bazaars'"; Beth, WT, January 2007; Dianne, WT, January 2007.
99 Kowinski, *Malling of America*.
100 Author correspondence with Ken, 4 December 2006.
101 Robert, WT, January 2007.
102 Arrow, *Friday on Our Minds*, 62–5.
103 *RT*, December 1963, 29–30.
104 Robert, WT, January 2007.
105 Bailey, "Ill-natured cartels"; Moore, "Bodgies, Widgies and Moral Panic."
106 Arrow, *Friday on Our Minds*, 46–53.
107 Moore, "Bodgies, Widgies and Moral Panic."
108 Bailey, "Retailing and the Home."
109 *AR*, May 1968, 17–19.
110 *AR*, July 1967, 5–9; *AR*, July 1967, 27; *AR*, April 1972, 5.
111 Trentmann, *Empire of Things*, 217.
112 Deborah, WT, January 2007; Beth, WT, January 2007; author correspondence with Lorne, 3 October 2006.
113 *SGSSL*, 16 March 1964, 15.
114 Maire-Louise, WT, January 2007.
115 Robert, WT, January 2007.
116 Author correspondence with Pauline, 20 April 2006.
117 Ros, WT, January 2007.
118 Ros, WT, January 2007.
119 Beed, "Growth of Suburban Retailing," 261.
120 CMA, Box 1800, Southland promotional brochure, ca. 1968.
121 Tea Tree Plaza News, supplement to *North-East Leader*, 16 September 1970; *Advertiser*, 17 September 1970.
122 Author interview with Reg Jebb, 23 February 2015.
123 Hardwick, *Mall Maker*, 219.
124 Gruen, "Sad Story."
125 *Property*, October 1966, 33.
126 *SMH*, 12 October 1965, 34.
127 CCCL, Town Clerk's Report, 65/ 5766, 7 December 1965.
128 Cohen, "From Town Center to Shopping Center," 1059. See also White and Sutton, "Social Planning for Mall Redevelopment," 69; Allan, "Marion," 124.
129 Sandercock, "From Main Street to Fortress," 28. See also Friedberg, "Les Flâneurs du Mall," 7; Cohen, *Consumers' Republic*, 265; Brown-May, *Melbourne Street Life*, 215.
130 Whyte, *City*, 208. See also Webb, *City Square*, 206.
131 Spearritt, "Suburban Cathedrals," 96.
132 Brill, "Transformation," 23–5.

6 Sub-regional shopping centres and the discount evolution

The emergence of supermarkets, shopping centres and city department store branches in suburban locations marked the first phase of retail's response to the disruptive influence of the automobile. By the end of the 1960s, after a decade of strong economic growth, shopping centres were serving as commercial and social hubs in suburbs across Australia. Coles and Woolworths had cemented their positions, alongside Myer, at the top of the Australian retail hierarchy. The latter's move into shopping centre development had proved strategically sound, consolidating its position as the country's largest department store firm. Despite these successes, challenges remained and new threats loomed. The most significant retail competition arrived in the form of discount department stores (DDSs), a format that used the logics of the supermarket to sell department store merchandise. Notably, for Australia's largest retailers, DDSs attacked the market shares of both variety and department stores.

DDSs refined and professionalised a concept started by cut-price discount merchants in the United States in the early 1950s.[1] Martin Chase, a gift-ribbon manufacturer operating out of an old weaving mill in Cumberland, Rhode Island, was one of the early innovators. Facing strong competition from a larger, more efficient nearby firm, he decided to liquidate his stock and explore other business opportunities. He set up a temporary system in which customers selected quantities of ribbon, placed them in a bag and paid as they left. As had been the case with supermarkets, shoppers appeared willing to do without service in return for lower prices. Chase extended his product range and, in the process, developed a low-margin, high-turnover retail format. Growth followed and began to draw attention from retailers across the country. This included national chains and entrepreneurs such as Sam Walton who would later found Walmart.[2] Chase was one of a number of entrepreneurial innovators developing similar retail operations. Their methods were picked up and spread during the 1950s. Often unconventional in their approach to systems, administration, book-keeping and marketing, they opened outlets in cheap locations like abandoned industrial buildings. Some, like E. J. Korvette, expanded into large chains.[3] By the end of the decade, discount retailing in the United States garnered sales in excess of $1 billion per annum.[4]

The success of discounters threatened established retail chains such as S. S. Kresge, North America's second largest variety store chain. Its 700 variety stores were largely located in downtown areas that the middle class was leaving behind for the suburbs. At the same time, supermarkets were cutting into sales.[5] Bevan Bradbury later recalled that S. S. Kresge's

> profits had been going steadily downwards from about 1955 onwards. They were typical of a large number of American variety chains that were simply going out of business. Harry Cunningham [the President of S. S. Kresge] … was virtually given a free hand to go round and see what the future lay for the S. S. Kresge chain because it was in dire trouble … it was the days of the "white glove" men where men used to don white gloves and go around and pat places up on the top shelf and see whether there was any dust. And they were great on getting rid of dust but they weren't very good at that stage at getting customers into their stores. They were concentrating on the wrong things.[6]

Cunningham was one of the many retail executives to visit Chase's store in Rhode Island. After touring the country examining other operations, he concluded that S. S. Kresge should embrace discounting, but implement it more professionally than the newcomers currently eroding his firm's market share. Another early mover was the Dayton Corporation, which recognised the threat discounters posed to its traditional department store operation and, similarly, concluded that it should embrace rather than compete against the selling format.[7] S. S. Kresge and Dayton's respectively developed Kmart and Target. They had the resources to build large, purpose-built stores and to quickly establish national chains. In doing so they were able to offer broader and deeper product ranges than the early discounters which they now characterised as low-rent competitors.[8] In 1966, Cunningham described the latter's stores as "converted factory building[s] with a miscellaneous assortment of cheap, close-out or inferior merchandise displayed on rough wooden counters or pipe racks on a dirty floor and staffed by unkempt, ill-mannered personnel."[9]

The American Kmart and Target stores were clean and tidy, utilised mass-produced display stands, and employed professional staff training programmes. They operated on a single level, contained approximately 80,000 square feet (7,500 square metres) of retail selling space, and were configured to handle large volumes of customer traffic with minimal service. Customers collected their goods from around the store and paid for them at cash register checkouts arrayed in banks near the front entrance.[10] These operating efficiencies allowed DDSs to offer goods at lower prices and generate higher turnover than conventional department stores.[11] DDSs were generally located outside of inner urban areas and provided free car parking, making them highly convenient for their lower and middle-class, car-driving customers. The first Kmart and Target stores both opened in 1962. Kmart expanded rapidly to a chain of 233 stores by 1968.[12] Drawing on the company's cultural history in the department store space, Dayton's positioned Target above Kmart as a "quality discounter." Target expanded more slowly, but was still a highly profitable venture.[13] Both firms would play an important role in the transfer of the DDS format to Australia.[14]

Discount department stores in Australia

The reshaping of the United States' retail landscape raised a number of issues for Australia's biggest retailers. Coles and Woolworths had established the largest national supermarket chains, but faced tightening margins on food as they competed against a range of smaller chains including Franklins, Flemings, Tom the Cheap, Safeway, Jack the Slasher and Half Case Warehouse. This made it even more important to deal with the ongoing question of variety stores, which remained a large component of their operations (Table 6.1). Supermarkets had evolved to include a targeted scope of general merchandise, cutting sales from variety stores. It was clear from America, also, that variety stores would not remain competitive against the DDS format, which stocked a far wider range and depth of merchandise, and were less labour-intensive to run.[15] Established general merchandise retailers, including traditional department stores like Myer, Boans, Grace Bros. and John Martin's, were also aware of the impact DDSs could have on their market share. On the flip side, DDSs offered a growth opportunity in a concentrating industry.

Concerned that one of the larger United States retailers would develop a DDS chain for the Australian market, both Myer and Coles began planning national chains of their own.[16] Woolworths elected to postpone development. The firm has recently been criticised for presiding over one of the worst financial disasters in Australian retail history in its failed experiment with the Masters Home Improvement hardware chain during the 2010s. This failure echoed its inability to successfully introduce the DDS format in the 1970s and 1980s. As with Masters, Woolworths ceded first-mover advantages to Coles, allowing its rival preferential site selection across the country and, when finally introducing its own chain, bungled implementation. Woolworths' Big W DDS chain lost millions of dollars for 15 years before finally turning a profit in the early 1990s. It did so by acquiring, for virtually no transactional cost, operating expertise from Walmart through personal connections established by individual Woolworths executives.[17]

Coles and Myer were far more successful, and followed a familiar Australian retail pattern to develop their DDS chains. They observed international developments, particularly in the United States. They engaged in personal communication with their peers in foreign markets. And they set up meetings and visits designed to elicit knowledge and information about retail operations. As former Coles' executive Thomas North later noted: "You invariably find that what's good for the American retail industry is good for Australia ... This country has, you know, copied America in many ways in retailing."[18] Coles was the first of the Australian firms to develop concrete plans for a DDS chain, possibly because of their long-running association with S. S. Kresge from whom they had garnered valuable advice about variety store operations in the past. Harry Cunningham harboured a desire for international expansion. When he became aware of Coles' plan to move into discounting, he suggested a joint enterprise.[19] Following a series of reciprocal visits, Kmart (Australia) Limited was established in January 1968 as a subsidiary company of S. S. Kresge, which held 51 per cent of shares.[20] For Coles, the partnership brought capital, administrative systems, operational expertise and international buying networks.[21] Geoff Tate, who was the General Manager of Coles Variety Division in the early 1970s, later recalled that without S. S. Kresge "we would have been floundering for years … it gave us such a start over all our opposition."[22]

Acutely aware of the dangers posed by Coles' interest in general merchandise discounting, Myer determined that it, too, would enter the field. It began with the acquisition of a small soft goods retailer, Lindsay & McKenzie, based in the city of Geelong, south-west of Melbourne. Since the late 1950s, Lindsay & McKenzie's major shareholder and managing director, Geoffrey Betts, had been attending Bernardo Trujillo's seminars in the United States. Betts sent his senior managers to Trujillo's seminars as a key component of their training, and held numerous personal discussions with the American guru. Drawing on technology purchased from National Cash Register, as well as the philosophies of low-margin retailing expounded by Trujillo, Lindsay & McKenzie opened shops in the high streets of regional towns, as well as in shopping centres where there was a ready market for streamlined low-priced clothing store. By the late 1960s, the Geelong firm had grown to a chain of 14 stores by implementing discount retailing principles, but it lacked the capital to expand further.[23]

Lindsay & McKenzie offered Myer a base from which to build a discount chain. In a friendly takeover, Myer acquired all the ordinary shares in Lindsay & McKenzie Pty Ltd, retained the existing Lindsay's management team, and set about developing a DDS chain.[24] In 1969, Betts, Baillieu Myer and a small team undertook a study tour of Europe and the United States to develop additional buying networks and acquire more detailed information about the operation of large-scale discount stores. While in the United States, they attended one of the MMM seminars that had shaped the Lindsay & McKenzie strategy, inspected a wide range of American discounters, and visited the Dayton brothers in Minneapolis. A personal friendship between Baillieu Myer and the Daytons facilitated knowledge transfer about the American Target chain's operations, and an agreement that enabled Myer to use the Target brand and logo.[25]

Australian sub-regional shopping centres

The first Australian Kmart opened in Burwood, Victoria, on the site the Myer brothers had purchased when they were scouting locations for Chadstone. Coles had purchased the land "for a song," but was frustrated in gaining development approval for their proposed stand-alone store.[26] Lance Robinson later noted that:

Council wouldn't approve because it wasn't a shopping centre, and they'd never heard of Kmart, never heard of it ... So I dealt with our legal boy. I said "I want that site" ... I said "now we'll draw up our plans." I said "put a wall around it ... and put a big aisle up the centre and it is a shopping centre. You get that approved." He got it approved ... we just pulled the walls down, so we got it in. We finally got it after a long battle.

No. 2 site was in Sydney. Blacktown. There were about 38 houses on the property we had to wipe off ... and No. 3 was in Adelaide. When we went to see the site in Adelaide, there was nothing but sheep around. No houses at all. Hal Lane [from S. S. Kresge] couldn't believe it ... He looked at it and said, "There's nothing but bloody sheep here. How are we going to do business here?" Jack Weinert said, "I promise you. I tell you. Within 12 months you'll see a lot of houses here. You can't see any now, but they will come." Hal said to me "We're crazy to build a Kmart here" ... [but] boy you wouldn't believe it. In 12 months the houses that were around that place. We did very well out of Store No. 3.[27]

While Kmart (Australia) initially tried to build stand-alone stores as S. S. Kresge had done in the United States, Myer envisaged its DDS chain as an anchor for a new retail form. It branded these as Target Discount Shopping Centres. To build them it sought "sites of a minimum of ten acres on major highways and intersections in the fast-growing suburbs being developed by young families."[28] Target Discount Shopping Centres were comprised of a Target DDS, a restaurant, a few snack food outlets and a Target supermarket. The restaurant catered to customers, but was also conceived as a moderately priced eating destination for nearby residents outside of shopping hours.[29] The Target supermarket was an ambitious and potentially risky strategy for a department store firm that had little experience in food retailing. But with supermarkets established as anchors across all levels of shopping centres in Australia, including in Myer's own developments, the firm pursued further growth through horizontal integration. A supermarket chain would generate greater value from Myer's vertically integrated property development arm, which at the time was facilitating the expansion of supermarkets owned by other retailers. The model was established in three early developments in South Australia at Edwardstown, Newton and Fullham Gardens between March and November 1970. Myer planned to build 25 such centres in five years – an ambition described as "the largest single development project in the company's history."[30] The goal was never achieved. In 1981, only 14 of Target's 63 stores were located in Target Discount Shopping Centres.[31]

Target Discount Shopping Centres, like the Kmart stores Lance Robinson struggled to get approved, did not align easily with Australian planning regimes (Figure 6.1). Sites that were suitable from a marketing point of view were unlikely to be zoned for retailing. Arthur Coles later noted that this meant acquiring or gaining control "over property that you think you can influence the authorities to rezone ... and it's not easy to do."[32] This raised challenges

Figure 6.1 Target Discount Shopping Centres brochure, ca. 1970.

getting development approval for large retail stores or shopping centres, but once they were built it offered protection by limiting new surrounding retail construction. American malls had no such protection, leading to oversupply and the more recent phenomenon of "dead malls."[33] Richard Clarke, former managing director of Lend Lease Retail, argues that:

> the main unique feature of Australian shopping centres is that they are a protected species. The zoning laws in Australia really did not allow for random, laissez-faire development that was available more or less in America … If you wanted a shopping centre in Australia, and it was not

zoned correctly, it was very, very difficult, if not impossible, to develop a competing facility to the one that was already there.[34]

By limiting the supply of potential sites, planning also intensified competition for these locations. This had a significant impact on the form and function of the shopping environments constructed in Australia during the 1970s and 1980s. Stand-alone stores could, in places, generate higher sales per square metre than equivalent stores in shopping centres,[35] but for any given site, developers could extract greater value from a shopping centre than a retailer could from a stand-alone store. The rentals developers could garner from specialty stores allowed them to outbid retailers for sites, driving up the cost of land.[36] This encouraged both retailers and developers to reimagine the earlier community centres that sat in the middle of the tripartite typology of centre forms. The general merchandise anchor in community centres had been small-scale, 'junior' department stores, which contained none of the efficiencies of DDSs and were not big enough to adapt through merchandise remixing.[37] With planning regimes constraining development opportunities, the DDS was reappraised as an anchor that could generate strong customer traffic. Through this process a unique Australian retail form was created: the sub-regional shopping centre – although it was not named as such until the 1990s.

Big retailers thus adapted to a development model that relied on specialty retailers to subsidise costs. They employed agents to find land that they could develop themselves and also provided lists of desirable locations to prospective developers.[38] In doing so, they continued their established practices of facilitating finance and outsourcing construction to "can-doers" with the contacts and capacity to negotiate development approvals, as well as the skills to build rapidly at low cost.[39] Jack Weinert again provides an instructive example of this dynamic though his work for Coles in South Australia. Robinson recalled that "he got the K mart sites when we couldn't get them anywhere else. He was a goer … He made more money for G. J. Coles than any other individual." This was in part due to his unique capacity to establish and maintain connections, particularly with government authorities. "You don't ever have to worry about Jack to go and get an appointment, he just walks straight into an office," Robinson noted. At the SAHT, "Jack could go in there and get almost anything."[40] This provided Kmart (Australia) with insight into future population densities and the related value of prospective trade areas, which informed locational decision-making for developments that Weinert would then build.

Warren Anderson was another important figure in the development of Kmart stores and shopping centres. Anderson was a farmer from Western Australia who turned his hand to retail development. Between 1970 and 1978 he developed more than 30 projects in the state either directly for Coles or with Coles supermarkets as anchors. This progressed Coles from having virtually no presence in Western Australia to being the dominant supermarket operator in the state.[41] Many of Anderson's builds were stand-alone stores – Woolworths, in contrast, favoured shopping centres in Perth, taking space in

Boans' regional centres as well as numerous smaller neighbourhood and community developments. Looking to expand his field of operations, Anderson moved to the eastern states. He was most active in New South Wales, where he "was able to get approvals that others could not."[42] This was significant for Coles, which from its home base in Victoria had struggled to obtain planning approval for developments in NSW. In 1986, one former Coles executive argued that

> we were terribly fortunate to have him ... a great percentage of the sites we have built in the last 10 years in New South Wales have been [due] to Warren's efforts in getting the original site together and dealing with councils and so forth.[43]

For Anderson, Coles' commitment to take tenancies in his centres allowed him to obtain finance for construction.[44]

By the early 1980s, most of the centres Anderson was building for Coles included a proportion of supporting specialty tenants and complementary national chains, although Kmart and Coles still dominated. As with traditional department stores in early Australian regional shopping centres, Kmart stores accounted for up to half the retail floor space of the centres they anchored. Supermarkets were allocated around 18 per cent of centre floor space, while specialty and other non-Coles traders comprised less than 30 per cent. Highlighting their importance for the financial viability of centres, however, the specialty stores contributed approximately the same amount of rent as the two main anchors, despite occupying far less floor space.[45] DDSs also joined established regional shopping centres as additional anchors. By the end of the 1970s, there were regional shopping centres in all states that included both a traditional department store and a DDS.[46]

Growth and expansion of DDSs

By adapting their development strategies, both Kmart and Target were able to establish and consolidate their positions as national chains relatively quickly. Target expanded rapidly between 1970 and 1975, by which time it had opened 52 stores, and Target's share of Myer's total retail space had climbed to 22.5 per cent.[47] This was faster than the Kmart rollout, because of the foundation provided by the Lindsay & McKenzie store network, the access Myer had to sites through its existing shopping centre portfolio, and the firm's willingness to adapt the Target model to a variety of store footprints ranging from 3,000 to almost 9,000 square metres in size.[48] Many of these early stores were smaller than Australian Kmarts, and had a merchandise mix more highly concentrated on soft goods. While this flexibility allowed the firm to rapidly expand its store network, the lack of standardisation arguably made Target a less focused retail format than Kmart, which from the beginning had a clear merchandising identity.[49] Between 1970 and 1979, Kmart increased its selling area from 7.48 per cent to 29.68 per cent of Coles' total selling area, and was inundated with offers from developers to open in shopping centre complexes.[50] By the end of the decade, Kmart had almost the same number of stores as Target (Table 6.1) but occupied far more retail floor space across the country. Kmart was an immensely profitable operation, going from strength to strength as the decade wore on.[51] Its success, combined with concerns about the administrative costs of running a dual-ownership operation, encouraged Coles to buy out S. S. Kresge's share of the chain in 1978 – exchanging it for 20 per cent of Coles' total operation.[52] The editor of industry journal *Inside Retailing*, Phillip Luker, described it as one of the most important and valuable transactions in the company's history.[53]

Marketing and staffing DDSs

One of the early challenges for Australia's biggest retail firms was to convince Australians to adopt the new form of shopping that DDSs represented. By the late 1960s, self-service had been largely embraced in the grocery sector, where supermarkets dominated sales.[54] The still ubiquitous variety stores also placed an increasing emphasis on self-selection by shoppers.[55] However, marketers were aware that shoppers still relied heavily on staff advice when purchasing many of the products sold in DDSs, including apparel, footwear, electrical goods, homewares and hardware. They employed extensive advertising campaigns to sell the new format, and to convince customers that cheap prices did not equate to poor-quality merchandise (Figure 6.2).[56] Single-floor layouts, computerised stock control, self-service and scale buying power were all explained in newspaper advertorials as operational efficiencies that reduced the price of goods for the benefit of the consumer.[57]

As with supermarkets, these savings were derived, at least in part, by a transfer of labour from retail firms to shoppers. And again, it was recognised that women would supply the bulk of this labour and that marketing should thus be directed towards them. When Target was launching its Discount Shopping Centre at Newton, South Australia, for example, its marketers advised that prominent women should be recruited to feature in opening promotions. They sought "a local 'heroine' rather than a mayor, councillor or other governmental VIP ... a suitable lady who would have the wholehearted support and emotional interest of all the local residents."[58]

While DDSs were pitched to female consumers, they also helped reshape women's paid employment in retailing by extending the logics of labour efficiency that had been ushered in with supermarkets. This occurred amidst the growth in female workface participation examined in Chapter 5, and coincided with the development of equal pay legislation in Australia. This meant that big retailers introduced more labour-efficient, capital-intensive systems at the same time as they faced the prospect of paying higher wages to female staff. Inside shopping centres, tenancy mixes were including increasing numbers of specialty shops and fashion outlets, as well as supermarkets and DDSs. Women thus continued to comprise a significant share of employees working in shopping

Table 6.1 Selected Coles, Myer and Woolworths chains, 1973–95

Year	Coles			Myer				Woolworths				
	Food markets	Variety stores	Supermarkets	Kmart	Dept. stores	Target supermarkets	Target	Food stores	Variety stores	Super-markets	Family Centres	BIG W
1973	125	245	179	11	45	3	27	348	102	300	24	0
1980	39	159	320	56	51	18	57	209	118	280	0	21
1985	19	121	368	103	109	0	71	183	88	360	0	41
Coles Myer												
1990	11	203†	491	138	79	0	79	xx	xx	xx	0	57
1995	0	149	497	163	70	0	99	67	3(71)	526	0	63

Sources: G. J. Coles & Coy Limited, Myer Emporium Limited, Coles Myer Limited and Woolworths Limited Annual Reports (1973–1995); *IR*, 4 June 1973, 10; *IR*, 30 June 1980, 11; *IR*, 28 January 1991, 7; *IR*, 7 August 1995, 5.

Notes:

Years selected based on available data.

xx = not reported

† In the late 1980s, Coles Myer converted variety stores into Fosseys stores – a downmarket family apparel chain that Myer had acquired with its takeover of Grace Bros in 1983. The figure here includes a large number of Fosseys stores. Many Fosseys stores were later rebranded as Target Country stores, offering budget apparel in regional areas.

‡ By the mid 1990s, there were only three Woolworths variety stores in operation. Seventy–one had been converted to a new discount chain under the Crazy Prices brand, and the remainder closed.

Figure 6.2 Kmart marketing brochure, 1969.

centres. When Myer was promoting its early Target Discount Shopping Centres, it boasted that its development programme would generate "new job opportunities … around Australia, a high proportion of which will be filled by part-time women."[59] These women were usually cashiers, administrators and floor staff, although by the 1980s a rare few had progressed through to store management positions.[60]

Some women also found career paths within the shopping centre industry itself, graduating from newly introduced training programmes and moving into centre management positions. Understandings of their skills were distinctly gendered: women were said to be more in tune with shoppers, attentive to the needs of tenants, and meticulous with "housekeeping." Despite this, they earned between $5,000 and $10,000 less for managing a regional centre than the average male, whose salary in 1985 sat at around $40,000. Women also reported having a limited role in leasing, which was increasingly being handled by head offices, and had to contend with sexism from male managers and retail proprietors.[61]

As with other industries, the predominance of women employed at the lower end of firms left them open to exploitation. In a promotional newspaper insert for the opening of the Karatha City Super Kmart shopping centre in regional Western Australia in the mid 1980s, an advertisement for the Briar Rose specialty fashion store featured a youthful retail assistant, "delightful Debbie." Debbie was pictured in one of the store's "luxurious little items," reclining in a cane lounge draped with a cotton floral throw. Accompanying text provided her full name, and described the "slinky negligee and underthings" that she and other women would be selling in the store. Her appearance contrasted sharply with a photograph of the manager of Karatha City a few pages earlier. The moustached "man at the top" was middle-aged and fully clothed, albeit with an impressive display of dark chest hair pushing past the broad collar of his half-buttoned shirt. His image was juxtaposed with commentary on the scale of the centre, the size of estimated turnover and the importance of the development for the surrounding Pilbara community. The buying public were offered certainty that the new development was in safe, mature male hands, which managed the retail environment where Debbie and hundreds of other women worked for minimum wages and with the possibility they might be asked or encouraged to lend their faces and bodies to promotional activities.[62]

These contributions that women made to retailing – including their work within shops – had always been monetarily undervalued. In the 1960s they worked under wage awards that paid them less than men, and which were conditioned by earlier legislative decisions that privileged men as household "breadwinners."[63] In 1969, the year the first Kmart opened in Australia, the Commonwealth Arbitration Commission awarded women equal pay to men, provided they were doing work of the same or like nature.[64] Further advances were made through decisions in 1972, when the principle of equal pay for work of equal value was established, and 1974, when the Commission set an equal minimum wage for men and women. In the retail industry, where wages formed such a large component of costs in traditional business models, the move towards equal pay was treated with considerable alarm. Retailers had been warning against the deleterious impacts and "economic oddity" of equal pay "vote-catcher" legislation since the late 1950s.[65] In the early 1970s, equal pay legislation was opposed on the basis that it would render firms unprofitable.

Equal pay highlighted the fact that retail employers had traditionally been able to extract a higher profit margin from female labour than they could from men.[66] Legislation forced firms to return this differential margin to the women who generated it, but also incentivised modifications to staffing and operational systems to minimise the impact of this transfer. One result was an increase in casualisation. Between 1972 and 1982, part-time and casual employment in retailing grew by more than 75 per cent, even as full-time employment dropped slightly as a percentage of overall retail employment. Retailers also hired a greater proportion of juniors than they had previously.[67] A retail industry report in 1976 claimed that the previous year had seen an "alarming" rise in costs because of equal pay legislation, but pointed out that:

> Among the well-managed retailers, wage-bills have been held down by retrenching staff, by making greater use of part-timers, and by improving the productivity of existing employees through the introduction of such techniques as area-wrap centres and check-out points.[68]

In some cases, equal pay for equal work was simply avoided by obfuscation. One union report found that women who were acting as managers of branches in chains did not always receive equal pay with their male peers because they had not been "confirmed" in their roles. Benefits were only provided to confirmed appointees, but women continued to be denied this status despite ongoing employment as managers and with equivalent responsibilities to their male peers who enjoyed higher salaries.[69]

In terms of operations, equal pay encouraged retailers to push self-service innovations further, or to reconceptualise their approach to staffing.[70] DDSs were opportune in this regard: the labour efficiencies the format generated aligning neatly with rising wage costs. During the 1970s, the growth of retail floor space far outstripped increases in retail employment.[71] Faced with mounting competition from the discounters as well as rising wage bills, some of the traditional department stores sought efficiencies by cutting service staff. This reduced costs, enabling them to compete more strongly on price, but denied them their natural competitive advantage of in-store, personalised selling. Australian retail executives clearly understood the importance of price for consumers, and had watched traditional stores lose market share to discounters in the United States, but not all agreed with the strategy of cutting customer service. One Myer executive, for example, was scathing in an internally circulated analysis:

> We have literally forced our customers into expecting to have to wait to be served or look after themselves; [we have accepted] a lack of knowledge of products on the part of staff; [and] that if our store doesn't have the goods the customer will have to go elsewhere, and so on. The customers who didn't like our treatment or expected more from us just didn't come back and we … didn't really care, or if we did we had reached the conclusion that we couldn't do much about it anyway.[72]

By the mid-1980s there was a recognition that this had been a mistake and department stores like Myer and Boans made strategic decisions to reinvest in the quality and service image with which their brands were traditionally associated.[73] There was no reverse, however, in the conditions that had driven the decisions to cut staff. The price competition brought by discounters proved a more powerful lure to shoppers than the customer service they missed but were unwilling to pay for. Reflecting this, the traditional stores also never reversed in any substantive way their drift away from floor service staff – a feature of their operations that remains a chief complaint of customers today.

The impact and influence of the DDS format in Australia

The introduction of DDSs to Australia coincided with the collapse of the postwar boom. Along with other industrialised countries, Australia entered a period of economic hardship as global competition eroded its manufacturing base, and it transitioned to a service sector economy. High unemployment and a lack of real income growth produced difficult trading conditions for retailers. While this brought challenges for firms seeking development finance, it also created an environment highly conducive to cut-price selling.[74] Tony Dimasi argues that this extended into the early 1980s when "K mart was the darling in general merchandise and [cut-price supermarket chain] Franklins was the darling in food. The consumer was quite easy to predict because everyone wanted more or less the same thing; that was that discount-focussed retailing."[75]

In this environment, the impact of DDSs on traditional department stores was marked. While the latter maintained advantages in product categories like cosmetics, fashion accessories, fabrics and quality fashion, the discounters made deep inroads into sales of toys, children's clothing, small electrical appliances, linen, kitchenware and even some fashion items such as skirts and blouses.[76] Specialty stores and chains that traded on targeted branding, staff product knowledge and customer service also contributed to the decline in market share of conventional department stores. The financial model of DDS development, which required small retailers and chains to help finance the shopping centres they anchored, facilitated the spread of all these retailers (as did the growth of regional centres, which also increased their dependence on specialty stores during the 1980s). Variety stores, though, could not compete. Although still profitable in the 1970s and even, in places, in the 1980s, they were too small and labour-intensive to run, and were gradually phased out (Table 6.1).[77]

Between 1973/4 and 1980/1 the market share of Australia's six largest traditional department store chains dropped from 11 per cent to 8 per cent of all retail sales in the country. This amounted to a loss in effective retail sales of around $1.1 billion. Over the same period the main DDS chains increased their market share from 2 per cent to around 4 per cent of all retail sales. Figure 6.3 provides figures on each format's respective share of department-store-type merchandise. Traditional department stores dropped from 27 per cent in 1974 to 9 per cent in 2000, after being overtaken by DDSs during the 1990s.[78] The success of DDSs, as well as the rapid spread of supermarkets that also grew considerably in size, helped Australia's largest retailers consolidate their market dominance. The clear winner was Coles, which now rivalled Woolworths as the leading supermarket operator (Table 6.1) and trounced their main competitor with the early and successful introduction of Kmart. In 1970/1, Coles held 3.1 per cent of total retail sales in Australia. By 1980/1 the firm held almost 10 per cent.[79]

DDSs also instigated a further evolution in the locational dynamics of Australian retailing. In the mid 1980s, after 15 years of DDS development, Myer conducted a review of its traditional department stores. Many of its poor performers were located in traditional high streets and faced increased competition from new or redeveloped shopping centres anchored by DDSs. Some, such as at Strathpine and Carindale in Queensland, were located in established shopping centres but were competing against DDSs that had taken up tenancies in these centres. The underperformance of particular department stores, combined with the broad decline in market share, had the effect of accelerating ownership concentration amongst the traditional department store firms.[80]

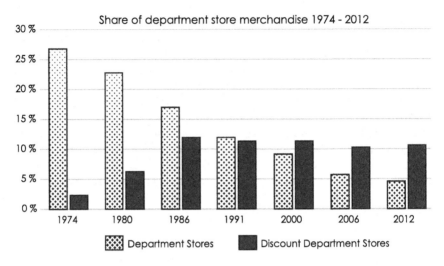

Figure 6.3 Market share of department store merchandise, 1974–2012.

At the end of the 1970s, research coming out of the American Kmart Corporation claimed that "no deterrents to continued preference for discount self-service establishments can be found in the emerging demographic trends."[81] In Australia, DDSs did not increase their overall market share of sales from the mid 1980s onwards, but maintaining their share in the face of new entrants as traditional department stores continued to fade indicated their appeal to Australian consumers. Their inability to further increase market share, however, suggests that the expansion of their store networks during this time served as a defensive strategy, and that emerging competitors were able to assemble appealing value matrixes through various combinations of price, product range and convenience. DDSs were also entrenched in the networks of shopping centres that by the 1980s had taken command of Australian retailing. In the early 1990s, Woolworths launched an aggressive campaign to expand through sub-regional shopping centre development under the brand of Woolworths Marketplaces, fuelling further competition and growth.

By 1995, just over 25 years since the first DDS opened in Australia, there were more than 170 sub-regional shopping centres across the country. This was a unique Australian retail form. The DDS format had been imported to Australia but reshaped to local conditions. The difficulty of obtaining sites forced a compromise in approaches to development, encouraging shopping centre construction and the uptake of tenancies in established centres. In 1995, sub-regional shopping centres accounted for more than 3.2 million square metres of retail space, covering more ground than the 65 regional shopping centres at the top of the retail hierarchy. Constraints over the availability of sites meant that once each of these centres was established it was protected from competing developments. Each was thus invested with a natural advantage that incentivised redevelopment and expansion. From the mid 1980s onwards, this would become the most important avenue of growth for the Australian retail property industry.

Notes

1 Sammartino, "Retail," 179.
2 Spector, *Category Killers*, 19–20; Rowley, *On Target*, 117.
3 Howard, *From Main Street to Mall*, 168–71.
4 *Discount Store News*, 17 February, 40.
5 Spector, *Category Killers*, 19–20.
6 CMA, Box 2927, Stella Barber interview with Bevan Bradbury, 18 December 1985, transcript, 10.
7 Rowley, *On Target*. On the threat to department stores more broadly, see Howard, *From Main Street to Mall*, 171.
8 Bentley Historical Library, University of Michigan, S. S. Kresge Company Records, 1912–78 (BHL), Microfilm Roll 6, Harry B. Cunningham, An address before The National Conference of the Financial Analysts Federation, New York City, 23 May 1966.
9 BHL, Cunningham, An address before The National Conference of the Financial Analysts Federation, New York City, 23 May 1966.
10 Magretta, "Why Business Models Matter," 7; CMA, Box 3035, Guides for Growth – Target, ca. 1980.
11 Chandler, *Scale and Scope*, 29–30; Christensen and Tedlow, "Patterns of Disruption in Retailing," 43–4; CMA, Box 3035, Target DDSs: An Introduction, ca. 1981.
12 BHL, Microfilm Roll 6, S. S. Kresge Annual Report, 1968.
13 Blackwell and Talarzyk, "Life-style Retailing," 9.
14 Bailey, "Marketing to the Big Middle."
15 CMA, Box 634, Store financial results, 1982/3.
16 Author interview with Bruce McIntosh, 2 March 2016.
17 Bailey, "Absorptive Capacity."
18 CMA, Box 4763, Stella Barber interview with Sir Thomas North, 11 October 1985.
19 CMA, Box 2927, Stella Barber interview with Bevan Bradbury, 18 December 1985, 22.
20 CMA, Box 464, Articles of Association of Kmart (Australia) Limited, 1 December 1967; CMA, Box 464, Form provided to the American Consulate General, Melbourne, 24 April 1968; CMA, Box 3515, Shareholders' agreement between S. S. Kresge Company, G. J. Coles & Coy Limited, Kmart (Australia) Limited, 31 January 1968; CMA, Box 465, Letter from Harry Cunningham to Sir Edgar Coles, 29 December 1971; CMA, Box 1738, Sir Edgar Coles, Proposal: A partnership in the third dimension, 1966; BHL, Microfilm Roll 6, S. S. Kresge, 57th Annual Report, May 1969, 4–5.
21 Author interview with Bruce McIntosh, 2 March 2016; CMA, Box 464, Template letter from J. L. Bishop, Secretary, Kmart Australia Limited, 1 March 1973; CMA, Box 1505, Stella Barber interview with Lance Robinson, 29 November 1985, transcript, 15.
22 CMA, Box 4765, Stella Barber interview with Geoff Tate, 28 June 1986.
23 Betts, *Birth of Target Australia*, 28–43.

24　Betts, *Birth of Target Australia*, 40–3; Bailey, "Absorptive Capacity."

25　Author interview with Peter Wilkinson, 11 December 2015.

26　CMA, Box 1505, Stella Barber interview with Lance Robinson, 29 November 1985, transcript, 15.

27　CMA, Box 1505, Stella Barber interview with Lance Robinson, 29 November 1985, transcript, 20.

28　CMA, Box 3035, Target Discount Shopping Centres, Press Release, 24 November 1969.

29　CMA, Box 388, Target Discount Shopping Centres marketing strategy memo, 7 May 1970.

30　CMA, Box 3035, Target Discount Shopping Centres, Press Release, 24 November 1969.

31　CMA, Box 1941, Target, Australia Pty Ltd, 15 January 1981.

32　CMA, Box 4097, Stella Barber interview with Arthur Coles, 24 February 1988.

33　www.deadmalls.com, accessed 1 December 2019.

34　Author interview with Richard Clarke, 24 March 2015.

35　BHL, Microfilm Roll 6, S. S. Kresge, 57th Annual Report, May 1969, 8–9.

36　Author interview with Bruce McIntosh, 2 March 2016.

37　Howard, *From Main Street to Mall*, 171.

38　CMA, Box 4097, Stella Barber interview with Arthur Coles, 24 February 1988.

39　Author interview with Reg Jebb, 23 February 2015.

40　CMA, Box 1505, Stella Barber interview with Lance Robinson, 29 November 1985, transcript 2, 6.

41　CMA, Box 4767, Stella Barber interview with Jim Thomas, 22 January 1988; *AFR*, 2 January 1979.

42　Author interview with Reg Jebb, 23 February 2015.

43　CMA, Box 4765, Stella Barber interview with Geoff Tate, 28 June 1986.

44　*AFR*, 2 January 1979.

45　CMA, Box 580, Shopping Centre Portfolio no. 1 market analysis by R.T. Jebb & Associates Pty Ltd, August 1982, 21.

46　BOMA, *Directory of Australian Shopping Centres*.

47　*IR*, 16 February 1976, 9.

48　CMA, Box 512, R. T. Jebb and Associates, Target Strategy Report, October 1984.

49　Bailey, "Marketing to the Big Middle," 422–7.

50　CMA, Box 493, Kmart Corporation Proposal, 1978.

51　CMA, Box 493, Overhead projections for a talk by L. R. Robinson, 1969; CMA, Box 456, Sunnybank Kmart – A Revolutionary Principle, Press Release issued by G. J. Coles & Coy Limited, ca. 1973.

52　CMA, Box 764, Letter from Tom L. North, Managing Director, G. J. Coles & Coy Limited to Robert E. Dewer, Chairman and CEO, Kmart Corporation, March 1978; *IR*, 31 July 1978, 11.

53　*IR*, 5 March 1979, 11. This sentiment was echoed in the Chairman's address to shareholders later that year. See CMA, Box 1352, G. J. Coles & Co Chairman's Address, 15 November 1979.

54　Rosewarne, "Political Economy of Retailing," 23.

55　Kingston, *Basket, Bag and Trolley*, 86.

56　Bailey, "Marketing to the Big Middle," 422–5.

57　*Guardian*, 17 June 1970, 1; CMA, Box 2509–11, Target Discount Shopping Centres promotional strategy document, ca. 1970.

58 CMA, Box 388, Target Discount Shopping Centres marketing strategy memo, 7 May 1970.

59 CMA, Box 3035, Target Discount Shopping Centres brochure, ca. 1970.

60 *North Shore Times*, 27 January 1988, 27.

61 *IR*, 26 August 1985, 6. See also *IR*, 26 March 1984, 4. For an in-depth discussion of leasing, see Chapter 10.

62 *North West Telegraph*, 1 August 1986, 1–15.

63 Probert, *Working Life*, 97–8.

64 ABS, 1301.0, *Year Book Australia*, 1970, 264.

65 *JRTANSW*, August 1958, 23; November 1958, 23.

66 Prerost, 'Technological Change,' 134.

67 Fisher, "Assessing Economic Impact," 45–50.

68 *IR*, 19 January 1976, 8–9.

69 Hargreaves, *Women at Work*, 115.

70 Fisher, "Assessing Economic Impact," 45.

71 *VSCAN*, June 1984, 3.

72 CMA, Box 3323, Myer internal correspondence, c.1983.

73 CMA, Box 3323, Myer Queensland Stores, ca. 1983; Hough, *From Clogs to Clogs*, 247–8.

74 Humphery, *Shelf Life*, 144; CMA, Box 580, Shopping Centre Portfolio no. 1 market analysis by R. T. Jebb & Associates Pty Ltd, August 1982, 12–13.

75 Author interview with Tony Dimasi, 3 November 2014.

76 CMA, Box 340, Critical issues: Specialty store retailing, February 1981, 10.

77 CMA, Box 4765, Stella Barber interview with Geoff Tate, 28 June 1986.

78 Unpublished figures supplied to the author by Urbis, www.urbis.com.au. Includes all Myer/Grace Bros. (excluding Megamart and Good Buys), David Jones (excluding Warehouses), Aherns, Harris Scarfe and Daimaru Stores. For the parallel process in the United states, see Howard, *From Main Street to Mall*, 192.

79 CMA, Box 580, 'Shopping Centre Portfolio no. 1 market analysis' by R. T. Jebb & Associates Pty Ltd, August 1982, 14.

80 *IR*, 5 December 1983, 16.

81 *RW*, 5 September 1979.

7 Investment, growth and specialty retail

With a smaller retail footprint and lower price points, DDSs could survive and even thrive in less affluent areas and within smaller trade areas than traditional, large-scale department stores and regional shopping centres. They were thus able to expand into the working-class outskirts of the major cities and well beyond into hinterland and regional areas. Indeed, many of the sub-regional centres that emerged from this process were constructed outside of the capital cities.[1] They brought scale competition to areas that had traditionally been served by local retailers, including small department stores. Many of these were put out of business by the price competition, range and convenience provided by Kmart, Target and Big W, serving to further concentrate the retail industry.

In Queensland, the Kern Corporation was highly active, building several neighbourhood and community centres. The firm had been started by Ron Kern with a contract to build mining infrastructure in the mid 1950s. He soon diversified into residential construction, while also supplying ready-mixed concrete and quarrying stone. By 1977 he had moved into shopping centre development, building the Kin Kora Centre in Gladstone, 550 kilometres north of Brisbane, and Mt View Shopping Plaza, a further 800 kilometres north near Townsville. In just over ten years, the firm built some 28 small and medium-sized centres across the state. Kern Corporation was Woolworths' developer of choice for building shopping centres anchored with Big W DDSs in regional Queensland towns like Earlville, Caneland, Buddina Beach and Bundaberg.[2] It was also among a diverse range of developers that built centres in Western Australia, where DDSs also drove retail development in regional towns and cities such as Bunbury, Karratha, Geraldton and South Hedland.

Kern had been born in Perth, served Australia in World War Two and returned to carve out a living in his preferred state of Queensland. Many of his contemporaries, like the developer entrepreneurs of the 1960s, were immigrants or children of immigrants – particularly in New South Wales and Victoria. Like Kern, several began as construction specialists before diversifying into higher-value fields of development. The Grollo Group was started by Italian immigrant Luigi Grollo in 1928 as a concrete paving business in Melbourne. His son Bruno joined him at the age of 15 and, along with his brother Rino, expanded the business into sub-contracting concrete formwork for high-rise buildings before moving into property development, including shopping centres. In these enterprises they frequently collaborated with Ted Lustig and Max Moar. According to Ruth Ostrow, "it was said that Lustig and Moar conceived of projects and negotiated the financing while Bruno Grollo used his men and industrial muscle to build shopping complexes in record time."[3] Grollo avoided industrial disputes by providing good working conditions for a highly loyal workforce, declaring in later interviews that his background in the hard grind of the concrete industry made him sympathetic to the lot of labouring men.[4]

The Grollos also cultivated a relationship with Builders Labourers Federation (BLF) president, Norm Gallagher: along with developers Maurice Alter and George Herscu, they were later charged with paying secret commissions to Gallagher to gain favourable industrial outcomes. The developers each received $5,000 one-year good behaviour bonds. Gallagher's systematic corruption saw him sentenced to four years and three months jail in 1985 and the BLF deregistered in Victoria, NSW and the ACT in 1986.[5] The Fitzgerald Inquiry into corruption in Queensland later charged Herscu with bribing the Queensland Minister for Local Government and Main Roads, Russ Hinze, to resolve a dispute with Brisbane City Council about traffic access to his Sunnypark community shopping centre in southern Brisbane.[6] In 1990, Herscu lodged what might have been Australia's largest personal bankruptcy debt of almost half a billion dollars following a debt-fuelled shopping centre investment spree in the United States.[7]

Most of Herscu's peers managed their affairs legally and more circumspectly. Ted Lustig, who was born in Vienna, grew up in Poland and moved to Israel to study civil engineering, immigrated to Australia in 1956. He worked for a local architecture firm before setting up his own construction business. In 1971, he was joined in the business by his Israeli-born son-in-law Max Moar. During the 1970s, Lustig and Moar built community shopping centres in Richmond, Boronia, Box Hill and Wendouree in Victoria, with the firm flourishing in the 1980s, building and often retaining ownership of office towers, hotels and shopping centres. This included Sydney's Chatswood Chase, which they co-owned with Marc Besen and Maurice Alter.[8]

Alter had immigrated from Poland in the 1950s, worked his way into property development and established Pacific Shopping Centres in 1979. The group built, purchased and extended numerous centres, including the Kmart-anchored Lansell Plaza in Bendigo in 1979, the Target-anchored Wodonga Plaza in 1984 and Tooroonga Village Shopping Centre in East Hawthorn. Rumanian-born Besen had been the co-owner of the Sussan fashion chain with his brother-in-law John Gandel. Gandel's grandmother, Fay, a Jewish immigrant from Poland, had established the business with her husband Sam in 1939. Following the pattern of the biggest retailers, Gandel and Besen used shopping centres as a vehicle for rapid expansion, building Sussan into a chain of more than 200 stores. In the process and after paying millions of dollars in rent, they recognised the long-term value of retail property ownership. They built experience in retail property by acquiring smaller centres.[9] Partners in these centres included

Lustig, Moar and Abe Goldberg, another Jewish immigrant from Poland who had made his fortune in clothing and textiles manufacture.[10]

Gandel and Besen's own sales data demonstrated the trading strength of regional shopping centres, encouraging further property investment.[11] Besen's daughter, Carol Schwartz, recalls that:

> they were both big travellers, and John in particular spent a lot of time in Los Angeles and really was sold on the idea of shopping centres. He could see the way they were working. Also there were so many similarities between, particularly Melbourne city and Los Angeles, because they are car cultures – at that time. I think Melbourne has become a lot more focused on public transport, but at that time everyone was driving in cars. So if you provided free parking, and a fantastic retail offer, you basically were fulfilling customer needs.[12]

In 1981, Besen and Abe Goldberg bought the Highpoint Shopping Centre, 10 kilometres north-west of Melbourne's CBD. In 1983, Gandel bought Chadstone and Northland for $37 million each from Myer. Two years later he sold his share of Sussan to Besen for an estimated $100 million to concentrate more fully on retail property, describing fashion as a business "for younger people." Besen retained ownership of two small shopping centres owned by Sussan, continued to run the fashion chain, bought Goldberg's share of Highpoint in 1987 and expanded it into the country's largest shopping centre by the early 1990s. By this time his children had taken up major roles in the company: Carol Schwartz ran the company's property interests, and became the first female president of the Victorian Building Owners and Managers Association (BOMA) and the Australian Shopping Centre Council; another daughter, Naomi Milgrom, became chief executive of the Sussan chain.

Gandel had been able to acquire Chadstone and Northland because Myer was financially stretched. Its traditional department stores faced declining market share, with one executive describing them as "the dinosaurs of retailing." The firm responded through a costly diversification strategy.[13] Target was the most prominent example of this, but Myer also acquired several specialty chains, including Red Rooster (takeaway chicken), San Remo (liquor), Dynamite (fashion) and Country Road (fashion), all of which were placed on growth trajectories through national expansion. Myer had also sunk money into a tele-shopping venture called Videonet. The cost of these moves, as well as the rollout of Target Discount Shopping Centres, had left the company with significant debts subject to rising interest rates in a difficult retail environment. By 1983, Myer had sold off, abandoned or reduced its investment in most of its specialty store ventures as well as in Target supermarkets.[14] It also sold the stock, fixtures and fittings and transferred the leases of its NSW department stores to Grace Bros.[15]

Myer's multi-pronged investment strategy, and especially its heavy investment in Target, had diverted funds away from its regional shopping centres, most of which saw little redevelopment during the 1970s.[16] In this way it was out of step with its competitors in the industry. The imperative of DDS construction ensured ongoing shopping centre development across the country, but with limited sites available in Australia's major cities and high costs associated with new construction, a substantive shift of focus towards the redevelopment, refurbishment and expansion of existing centres was also occurring.[17] This process supports Patrick Troy's argument that over time, established interests seek to maximize their competitive advantage in urban environments by enhancing the value of their initial investment.[18] While such strategies had been underway since the 1960s, redevelopment had not been a defining feature of an industry that was still spreading geographically. By the mid 1980s, redevelopments were becoming a central plank of capital growth and market expansion strategies.

Planning continued to play an important role in this process. Although there were variations across the states, Australian planning generally sought to concentrate urban development in designated zones to improve the efficiency of private and public transport and reduce traffic congestion.[19] It was thus far more practical to further develop established retail complexes in these zones rather than seek out new sites.[20] Writing for an international readership in the early 1980s, John Dawson noted the advantages of redevelopment: existing sites were likely to be well located, have an established identity, and face fewer regulations on zoning or environmental impacts. Redeveloping an existing centre cost less than building a new one, and allowed developers to reconfigure and expand tenancy mixes with the aim of increasing overall retail sales and the value of their asset.[21]

Within the Australian industry there was also a pressing urge to keep pace with population growth as well as shifts in customer expectations. The former involved expansion, the latter, refurbishment to align with contemporary tastes.[22] John Schroder, former CEO of commercial property at Stockland, argues that "there is a finite timeframe [before shopping centres] become obsolete. You have to address it and redevelop them."[23] During the redevelopment of Bankstown Square in 1989, Peter Smith, the Managing Director of GPT, declared that if

> you stick to the old, when people demand the new, your asset will diminish in value. It needs to change with the times. With a large Super Prime regional … you need to exploit its dominance as opposed to resting on its laurels.[24]

Former Myer executive, Graham Terry, recalls that in the early 1980s Myer "had huge plans for Chadstone, huge plans for Eastland, huge plans for Southland, Tea Tree, Chermside. You ought to have seen the plans, they were magnificent."[25] But the company couldn't afford them and decided to sell segments of its portfolio, which contained considerable latent value. Chadstone, for example, was still dominated by the Myer department store, had comparatively few specialty stores for a regional centre at the time, lacked sufficient anchors to activate the whole centre, contained open-air sections from the original design, and experienced traffic and parking issues. Much of this was fixable with an expansion that would create capital value and build on the strengths of the centre: it was the most profitable of Myer's Victorian shopping centres, had a strong brand, faced no nearby threat from a competing regional centre, and had a permit to expand retail space by 33 per cent on what was a comparatively large site.[26]

Myer approached Westfield and AMP offering centres for sale.[27] Terry recalls

> being at meetings where they tried to sell assets, to get out of the debt situation at Myer, and save the company ... They went to Westfield to buy and they said no. They went to AMP and they said no ... then John Gandel came out of the Sussan's organisation ... he bought Northland and Chadstone, and he could not even get finance from the banks ... Myer had to partly finance him to do the deal, and he had to pay Myer back. But a lot of people say that John got an absolute steal: Chadstone and Northland at ridiculous prices.[28]

Gandel was a private buyer who recognised the value in the Myer portfolio. Westfield and AMP, despite turning down Chadstone and Northland, soon also became purchasers of Myer centres at a time when corporate raiders were already targeting entire retail companies, seeking to capture both their cash flow and their property assets. In June 1980, the Adelaide Steamship Company (Adsteam) took a controlling interest in David Jones. Bond Corporation, run by flamboyant entrepreneur and later bankrupt Alan Bond, bought Waltons department store chain in March 1981. Both Adsteam and Bond also sought control of Grace Bros., with the latter accumulating 45 per cent of stock. Myer also acquired 45 per cent of Grace Bros., in part funded by its sale of Chadstone.[29] Westfield owned 5.3 per cent of Grace Bros., which it sold to Myer to ensure the chain stayed in the hands of a retailer.[30] Myer, though, soon faced takeover pressures of its own from raiders such as Larry Adler's FAI Insurances group, as well as from Coles.[31]

In July 1985, Coles placed a bid for control of Myer, raising interesting questions for the major shopping centre landlords whose interests were intertwined with those of their largest tenants. The big anchors underpinned rental levels, drove customer traffic, helped determine the value of centre brands and were fundamental to overall retail performance. In 1985, Myer, Grace Bros. and Target (all owned by Myer) occupied 15 anchor tenancies in Westfield's 17 shopping centres. The Coles takeover would create a retail super group with which landlords would need to negotiate, but it would also help stabilise a sector under siege from non-retailers. Believing that a corporate raider was unlikely to share its interests, Westfield echoed its approach with the Grace Bros. takeover, accumulating 12 percent of Myer stock.[32] Frank Lowy, now a member of the Myer board, was in a pivotal position to influence proceedings and supported the Coles bid.[33] He later recalled that: "The paramount question for Westfield was the financial stability and strength of the retail business. While a choice of retailers might have been better, at that time there was no choice."[34] Coles Myer Limited began trading in January 1986. The "dominant force in the country's retail industry,"[35] it employed approximately 130,000 people in 1,368 stores, and held one-fifth of the Australian retail market.[36] In 1987, Coles Myer leased 51 per cent of Westfield's total gross leasable retail space.[37]

The merger of Coles and Myer created a super company but did not shift the general trajectory towards property divestment by big retailers.[38] This indicated structural forces beyond the firm-level dilemmas faced by Myer. The collapse of the post-war boom had brought a downturn in consumer spending, while discounters ushered in a price war.[39] This eroded margins, encouraging larger firms to pursue greater shares of the existing market, including through acquisitions and development activity. But falling profits and rising interest rates necessitated rationalisation. Rather than cut back on retail expansion programmes, the big retailers sold their shopping centre interests and leased back the stores they held within them. Corporate raiders also stripped portfolios to extract value from property: shortly after Adsteam took control of David Jones, it sold its Garden City centres at Upper Mount Gravatt in Queensland, Booragoon in Western Australia and Kotara in New South Wales to AMP which, along with Westfield and Lend Lease, had become one of the dominant firms in the industry.[40]

Jack Rich, who was Managing Director and Chairman of AMP Capital in the early 2000s, as well as the first president of the Shopping Centre Council of Australia, says that AMP

> decided pretty early in the piece that we wanted to build … our own shopping centre company team, with retailers and shopping centre specialists … I guess you could summarise it by saying that we had a lot of our investable funds in there, and we wanted to make sure the assets worked as well as possible, generate the best returns. And we concluded that the best way of doing that was having our own team, our own trusted team, of specialists. And that was the genesis of a lot of the shopping centres.[41]

AMP continued to acquire centres in the eighties and nineties, including from the Hammerson Group of Companies when it exited Australia following the early 1990s property crash. In "one of Australia's largest ever property transactions," AMP bought Hammerson's entire Australian portfolio in 1994 for $544 million.[42] Warringah Mall, then the second-largest regional shopping centre in the country, dominating "an unassailable market on Sydney's middle-class northern beaches," was described as "the jewel of the holding."[43]

The divestment of property by the big retailers was also about specialisation. Reg Jeb notes that the development firms

> were property people, not retailers. And a shopping centre is a property development and it has got to be a property development that caters to

retailers and their market. So across a whole range of fronts – design, costs, their own building companies, their access to capital, their ability to deal with local councils – all of those things they were better at than the department stores, which in any event, were in decline.[44]

His views on the differences between the capabilities of department store firms and those of developers are supported by analysis produced by Myer itself. In a 1983 report, the Myer Property Division suggested that:

> Large organisations seem to experience difficulties in successfully implementing development opportunities ... other major companies and the institutions also appear to be uncompetitive with the up and coming entrepreneurs who avoid over analysis, act decisively, can take short cuts to achieve ends and are willing to suffer short term decline in profits to achieve long term gains.[45]

The same report, written within a few months of the sale of Chadstone, recommended reducing the firm's portfolio further – from $566 million worth of assets to around $275 million. The report was clear that the most valuable assets on Myer's books were its city stores and regional shopping centres: the former because of the size and street frontage of sites that held unique retailing value and "(long term) development" potential; the latter because of their capacity for capital growth through expansions, rental income from additional stores, their appeal to consumers, and their protection from competition under planning regimes. Myer could not afford to hold all its assets, but also wanted to retain either full or part ownership of some regional centres. One mechanism for doing so was a joint venture co-ownership vehicle with Westfield, the WestMyer Trust, into which Myer initially sold the Southland and Tea Tree Plaza shopping centres.[46] This proved a temporary position: in 1994 Coles Myer sold its 50 per cent stake in the WestMyer Trust to AMP, which became the joint owner of Southland and Tea Tree Plaza with Westfield.[47] This fitted AMP's growth strategy, giving them an ownership stake in "scarce assets, with proven track records."[48]

The WestMyer Trust was an example of changes in the retail property industry during the 1970s and 1980s, which saw trusts and institutional investors take an ever-larger role in shopping centre ownership. During the 1960s, Australia's capital market had broadened, providing a financial framework that helped fuel a property boom in the late 1960s and early 1970s. Finance companies became far more ambitious in the scope of their lending and permanent building societies expanded substantially. By 1975, 9 of the largest 25 finance companies had at least 50 per cent of their loan portfolios invested in property. Major institutions also expanded their property interests in response to demand for funding by Australian developers who faced competition from well-financed British firms during a boom in office development in the late 1960s. For example, in 1962 the AMP society had just 6 per cent of its assets in real estate. By 1974 this figure was closer to 20 percent.[49]

Changes in legislative frameworks also played a role: the Commonwealth Superannuation Act 1976 introduced amendments that allowed superannuation funds to invest in property.[50] The Act also established the Commonwealth's Superannuation Fund Investment Trust, superseding the Superannuation Board that had administered the Commonwealth Superannuation Fund since 1922. In its first year of operation, the new Commonwealth Trust purchased six shopping centres in Adelaide, Melbourne and Brisbane at a cost of $39 million, on the basis that they had "established rental incomes and sound potential for growth." These included a number of centres owned by Arndale, which moved out of Australia when the economic climate soured in the 1970s.[51] From its early forays, the Commonwealth Trust built its property holdings up to $201.2 million in 1980, which accounted for 13.2 percent of its total portfolio.[52] By 1985 this had grown to $1,051 million, or 41.5 percent of the portfolio.[53]

The complexity of shopping centre management, however, required specialised managers so, in what was to become standard industry practice, the Trust signed head lease arrangements with experienced industry operators.[54] This became another area of specialisation in the industry, with a number of management agencies such as Jones Lang Wootton, Savills, Richard Ellis Retail Management, Byvan Management, Knight Frank Hooker and Colliers Jardine providing expertise that facilitated institutional ownership. Many of these firms had been servicing the industry for years. Real estate firms like Raine & Horne and Richardson & Wrench also provided management services for smaller neighbourhood shopping centres. At the regional level, the big established players like Westfield and Lend Lease offered their vast management experience to institutional owners – particularly those they had sold shopping centres to. Institutions thus required no operating expertise to own complex and dynamic retail assets with strong capital growth potential. Nor did they need to deal with thorny issues such as disgruntled tenants.[55] This separation of powers suited the investment institutions. In 1985, the Commissioner of the Commonwealth Superannuation Fund Investment Trust declared that the division of responsibilities between owner and manager was "directed towards achieving maximum returns from individual properties."[56]

In 1972, of the major shopping centres that it had built, Westfield owned Hornsby, Indooroopilly, Miranda, Toombul and 50 per cent of Liverpool; and had built, sold and leased back Burwood, Eastwood, Figtree and Doncaster. The sell-and-lease-back system earned Westfield a profit on the design, construction and sale of the site as well as ongoing management fees, while "the cash flowing into superannuation schemes from rising, wage-indexed salaries" offered ongoing opportunities for expansion.[57] Westfield preferred ownership of sites, but the lease-back option allowed the company to ride its liquidity and adjust to the costs of external finance.[58]

Lend Lease and Westfield also set up their own property trusts while continuing to develop and manage properties. Established in 1971, Lend Lease's General Property Trust (GPT) was Australia's first listed property trust.[59] Richard Clarke recalls that:

> GPT became the end recipient of a lot of developments that Lend Lease did. As did MLC, because MLC and Lend Lease had cross-shareholdings. MLC was the custodian for life insurance funds, and needed to invest them in all sorts of things including property, and became the end-owner of a number of shopping centres … Lend Lease was never a vehicle that wanted to own property long term. It might have owned them as a warehousing-type situation. GPT remained the owner, as did MLC.[60]

In 1978, Westfield began a complex and highly profitable restructure. It had its property assets revalued, causing its share price to almost triple by the year's end when it announced that it would be forming a property trust.[61] In July 1979, Westfield Ltd was delisted, replaced by Westfield Holdings Limited and the Westfield Property Trust. Westfield's company history suggests that its sale of shopping centres into the trust "constituted what was at the time probably the largest-ever property transaction in Australian history."[62] While most of the shopping centres were sold into its own trust, some properties were purchased by the Commonwealth Superannuation Fund Investment Trust with Westfield retaining management rights.[63] Westfield also purchased the head lease on two Adelaide shopping centres owned by the Commonwealth Trust, taking responsibility for their management and development.[64] Retrospective tax legislation prevented the continuation of Westfield's new model, but this spurred the company to achieve similar ends through another complex restructure. A new trust was floated in 1982.[65]

The growth of specialty retail

By the early 1990s, property trusts and superannuation funds owned the majority of regional shopping centres in Australia.[66] At the same time, the scale of investment being undertaken necessitated a high degree of certainty.[67] Retail firms with established, tested systems were less likely to fail than inexperienced operators and would also elevate the presentation of centres. In the late 1980s, Lend Lease Retail leasing executive, Tony Taylor, described tenant selection as his biggest challenge:

> We want top operators who can cater to a volume market, who can present well, display their range, market their produce … we're beyond just filling shops – concept, range, quality, fit-out, uniforms, packaging, style – they're all the features we need to focus on.[68]

A decade earlier such retailers had been difficult to find in any great number. Erica Allan, the manager of the Floreat Forum shopping centre in Perth, described the industry as too thinly spread, reliant upon "inexperienced, second-rate retailers" paying high rents to sustain it.[69] Reg Jebb notes that:

> if you go back to the sixties, to developers or retailers, they would say that you could not have more than 50 shops in a shopping centre, because there were not 50 good retailers to put together ... even if you [could get] all the good ones.[70]

Richard Clarke, recalls that:

> The classic example was a bloke who, at the age of 50, retires or was made redundant from his job. His wife is an okay cook, so he says, "Okay darling, we will open a coffee shop." They go off to open a coffee shop, but it is a mum-and-dad operation that does not have the professional marketing ... even the architecture of the thing is normally bit out of the garage, work bench type stuff. And as a result, they were not turning over what they could have been turning over, and therefore, they could not pay the rent they should have been paying ... So by redeveloping and remixing it with good tenants who were more professional, you get a higher rent, you get a lower cap-rate on the thing, and you multiply the two, and the leverage is enormous. And that is what was happening in Penrith, Charlestown, Casuarina, Maroochydore, all around the place where we had shopping centres. So we were pretty much achieving that – increasing the value from 100 to 200 for the cost of 50.[71]

Professional operators, employing systems and pursuing scale, had been increasing in number since the 1960s. All the early regional shopping centres had housed national specialty chains. In the 1970s more emerged in categories such as footwear, fashion, toys, sporting goods and electrical appliances. In a 1980 survey in Chermside, Queensland and Blacktown, New South Wales, shoppers were asked to name the type of store they would usually visit to purchase certain listed items. The key story emerging was the extent to which DDSs had infiltrated the traditional department store market in little more than a decade (Table 7.1). But the survey also showed that in 1980, specialty operators had established footholds in both Chermside and Blacktown. From here, the sector experienced considerable growth as Australia's maturing market, high home ownership and marriage rates, as well as growing white-collar employment brought changes in shopping behaviour.

Shopping centres were deeply implicated in this rise of specialty retailers and, by collating them within a single site, their capacity to lure customers away from the big department stores. The survey report noted that:

Table 7.1 Division of shopping between store types (%)

	Chermside			Blacktown		
	Department store	Discount dept. Store	Specialty store	Department store	Discount dept. Store	Specialty store
Cosmetics	54.6	11.5	5.1	51	14.7	3.2
Men's casual shoes	30.5	21	10.8	27.9	12.2	46.5
Children's shoes	18.3	23.7	16.6	26.9	18.6	30.8
Fashion accessories	57.3	16.3	8.5	55.1	10.6	24.7
Skirts and blouses	26.1	35.9	18	38.5	22.8	24
Children's clothing	11.5	56.9	1.4	29.8	44.9	4.5
Men's sportswear	36.6	25.1	5.8	47.1	21.2	19.9
Furniture	22.4	2.4	45.1	53.2	5.1	33
Toys	6.4	44.1	21	18.3	52.6	13.8
Small electricals	18.6	43.1	14.6	46.5	35.3	14.4
Linen	33.6	42.4	2.4	59	29.2	1.9
Men's knitwear	33.6	25.1	5.4	58.3	16.7	9.6
Fabrics	36.6	16.3	15.6	32.4	23.4	18.6
Kitchenware	30.8	48.8	2	49.4	42	2
Sporting goods	21.4	22.7	17.3	20.2	26.9	36.5

Source: CMA, Box 340, Critical issues: Specialty store retailing, February 1981, 10.

Note: The figures do not tally to 100 per cent, perhaps because of an unreported "don't know" response.

> Historically, department stores have enjoyed a number of advantages when compared with specialists. This has greatly changed since the development of the suburban shopping centre. Virtually all of their traditional advantages have significantly deteriorated over time as a result of shopping centre proliferation.[72]

Like department stores, the mall operated as a one-stop shop, allowing customers to obtain access to a complete range of goods by visiting numerous stores. In this way, the smaller stores benefited from agglomeration: grouped together and with supporting anchor stores, they gained access to greater customer foot traffic. City department stores had offered facilities such as restaurants, toilets, creches and baby change rooms. They also ran promotional events like fashion shows. The shopping centre now did the same. And it offered a form of out-sourcing for site selection, with developers providing a steady stream of poten-tial locations to expanding chains.

Specialty chains competed strongly against department stores. They developed scale buying power. Some adopted vertical integration to generate efficiencies and gain control over supply lines and manufacturing processes. In fashion, specialty retailers used market segmentation to target defined customer profiles, offering complete ranges of distinctive sets of merchandise sold by staff who (ideally) held a good knowledge of the products being sold.[73] Gandel and Besen had followed this path with Sussan. Other entrepreneurs like David Bardas (Sportsgirl), Joseph Brender and Sam Moss (Katies), John Homann and Graeme Maher (Suzanne Grae) and Craig Kimberley (Just Jeans) did likewise, establishing some of Australia's most distinctive mass-market fashion brands. Former Myer leasing executive Graham Terry recalls that these retailers formed an important second tier in the leasing process after the major anchors had been secured: "we would laugh … back in those days, we would say you would put Just Jeans in one corner, Katies on another, Sussans in another and once you got those, you would backfill from there."[74]

The first Katies store opened in Rundle Mall, Adelaide in 1954. It expanded into a seven-store chain across three states before listing as a public company in 1962. By the mid 1970s it had moved into manufacturing, and achieved substantial growth in the second half of the decade with sales climbing from $30 million in 1976 to more than $70 million in 1979 when it ran a network of more than 100 stores. Katies leased most of these and by the end of the decade could "be found in all the major shopping centres throughout Australia as well as in the major cities of each state."[75]

Many chains also operated stand-alone stores in shopping strips and took advantage of the lower rents available in country towns. However, expanding nationally invariably meant engaging with shopping centres. Greg Chubb, the Retail CEO of Charter Hall, whose career included executive roles in the property divisions of Coles, Mirvac and Lend Lease, argues that:

> the vast majority of mainstream retail businesses, whether it be here in Australia or overseas, have only been able to grow and grow successfully with scale because of the evolution of the shopping centre market. I do not think you would find too many retail businesses that have only grown in high street environments. You will find that the majority of retail businesses that have grown, and grown successfully, have done so in shopping centres.[76]

The trajectory of Suzanne Grae is illustrative of this process. Like a number of other retail entrepreneurs who succeeded in the 1980s and 1990s, Graeme Maher had come out of big retail. He had worked his way into management at Woolworths but harboured a strong desire to operate his own business. He joined John Homann who had four women's fashion stores in Wagga Wagga, a regional city in the Riverina region of NSW. The pair expanded to 65 stores in country areas before ever opening a capital city store. Maher notes that:

> we grew through shopping centres … we opened in Riverdale shopping Centre, and when I say it was a success I mean it was massive. Cars went

right over the Macquarie river to West Dubbo and down Wellington Road – it was huge. These were the marketplaces that Woolworths became famous for in country towns ... there weren't many marketplaces that they opened which we didn't put a store in. Then Kern's in Queensland ... they were very strong in regional areas through Rockhampton, Mackay. All through there, we had stores. These sub-regional shopping centres were very important to us.[77]

By 1989, Suzanne Grae had grown to a chain of 145 stores. That year it was purchased by Marc Besen's Sussan Corporation, which had 185 Sussan stores of its own.[78] Craig Kimberley's Just Jeans had also grown into a 140 store chain.[79] Kimberley had visited the United States in the late 1960s and recognised the growing appeal of specialty jeans stores. He brought the concept to Australia, opening his first store in 1970 in Chapel Street, Prahran in Melbourne's southern suburbs. He notes that the department stores "did not have the [anti-establishment positioning] concept like we did." He describes the first stores as

all American Pie, Uncle Sam ... they were all pro-American. And that was where Australia was at that time, with American flags, or American music and it just took off like a rocket ... and the family they poured thousands of dollars into the business, I think within three months we had three shops ... [The firm then opened in shopping centres, including Chadstone.] And that really added a huge increase in sales and really made it more commercial. We could then afford to advertise.

The specialty stores that became major chains in Australia tended to provide a practical retail offer to the middle-market shopper. Shopping centres, too, thus largely remained middle-market retail environments. Michael Lloyd notes that:

There weren't any Gucci there. I mean Katie's and Sussan's was top of the range. When I was leasing shopping centres, Katie's was tops. And, Sussan's was number two. That's who you went for when you started leasing fashion; you just went straight to Katie's. If you got them, the others would follow. Things like Lowes Menswear, which wasn't Lowes Menswear then – it was Manhattan, and other things, they were quite utilitarian. These were shops selling stuff for kids' clothing, working overalls, working clothes for men. A lot of Katie's fashion just had smock dresses. So our centres provided the retail needs of the community. Whereas the American [regional] centres provided the retail wants.[80]

Other fashion retailers with a substantive shopping centre presence included Cherry Lane, Country Road, Esprit, Laura Ashley, Noni B, Portmans, Sportscraft, Sportsgirl, Sportique and Witchery. General Pants and Jeans West pursued the market leadership of Just Jeans. Kay's Bags and Strandbags sold accessories; Angus & Coote as well as Prouds, jewellery; Fays, Mathers, Williams the Shoeman and

Payless Shoes, footwear; Dick Smith, electronics; Brashs, music; Copperart, decorative brass and copper goods; Best and Less, discount fashion; Cut Price Deli, small goods. The presence of such chains also helped leasing managers rent space to upcoming retailers who modelled their business concepts on successful chains, or saw advantages in being located in close proximity to them.[81]

While some of these chains were fully company-owned, others operated as franchises. At the end of the 1960s, franchising had been one of America's fastest-growing business sectors, but in Australia, small business people still distrusted the model – in part because they associated it with failed pyramid selling schemes.[82] The rise of chains, though, had brought new levels of sophistication to retailing operations, inventory control and marketing, making retailing an increasingly difficult field to enter successfully.[83] In this context, franchising offered small entrepreneurs the promise of support through the administrative and operational systems of large and sophisticated businesses. Franchisees paid for research and development, brand recognition, marketing strategy, product display and production.[84]

By the 1980s, with large-scale shopping centre construction an intrinsic component of Australia's retail landscape, sites were readily available for franchise operations. Retail franchises occupying shopping centre tenancies included the Bra Shop (lingerie), Darrell Lea (chocolates), Angus & Robertson (books), Knitwit (knitting classes and fabrics), Najee Menswear, Chic Jewelry and Watches, Snap Instant Printing, Tandy Electronics and Radio Shack.[85] The Cut Price Deli chain was started by Enzo Sgambellone and Frank Rechichi, who bought their first delicatessen in 1974, expanded to 16 Cut Price Deli stores by the early 1980s, and launched a franchise programme in 1983. By 1988 they franchised more than 141 stores across Australia that garnered an annual turnover of approximately $80 million. This rapid growth was achieved by locating stores in shopping centres next to supermarkets to capture customer foot traffic. Sgambellone noted at the time that: "It took us a while to get recognition from the shopping centre developers, but now we are approached all the time and are offered prime sites in the new shopping centre developments."[86]

Redeveloping and expanding shopping centres

Redevelopments that added space for specialty retailers, franchises, supermarkets and DDSs increased the value of assets and allowed landlords to compete more strongly with surrounding retail – whether this was located in other shopping centres or on high streets. It thus became a key strategy of Australia's most successful retail property firms.[87] Simon Rumbold, a Director at Urbis, notes that:

> in terms of investment performances [the retail property sector] … has been a dominant player for a long, long time in Australia and out-performed other property sectors. I think a lot of that has been about leveraging the value of the real estate they have. When you've got real estate in the right

location with the right planning designation it's an extremely valuable asset. What they do ultimately is just increase the density of development on the site.[88]

Successful developers made their sites work harder. In its official company history, Westfield notes that once it acquires "a new shopping centre, it does not leave it to tick over quietly. Rather it begins immediately to improve it on every possible level for retailers, for shoppers, for stakeholders and for investors."[89] The firm demonstrated this capacity repeatedly. In 1979, for example, Westfield purchased Marion in South Australia from the original developers, Arndale, in partnership with Commonwealth Funds Management. The centre spent much of the 1980s under redevelopment with new sections opened in 1982 and 1989. When Marion opened in 1968 it housed 33,445 square metres of retail space. By the late 1990s it had been expanded to 109,000 square metres in size. The original two traditional department stores, unusual at the time, had been joined by all three major discount department stores and the number of specialty shops had increased from 80 to 250.[90]

A similar approach characterised Westfield's launch in the United States.[91] After much scouting, the firm purchased a single shopping centre in Trumbull, an affluent town in Fairfield County, Connecticut, and immediately began planning for "several phases of renovations, expansions and aesthetic upgrades." Over fifteen years a centre that had not been clearly positioned for its trade area was transformed from "a disjointed mishmash of 60 small merchants anchored by a local department store and a failing discount store ... into a heavyweight shopping centre destination with four powerhouse anchors and 200 popular specialty retailers." The redevelopments increased the value of the centre from its purchase price of US$21 million in 1977 to US$190 million in 1992.[92] Further purchase and redevelopment projects followed in both America and Australia. In 1990, Westfield's Australian portfolio comprised 21 shopping centres housing around 3,600 retailers. By the end of the decade it held 30 Australian shopping centres with approximately 6,350 tenants. Sixteen of these centres had undergone redevelopment over that time span, at a total cost of more than $2.7 billion.[93] Former Chief Operating Officer of Westfield in America, John Schroder, argues that:

> a lot of the innovation over there came from here: roof top parking, they didn't know what roof top parking was in the States. Putting discount department stores like Walmart and Target in your shopping centre. When we started talking about that they looked at us like we had two heads. We were used to it: supermarkets in shopping centres, we were use to it. America, within retail, there were sub-sectors within the sector. Super regionals: fortress malls, mainly fashion orientated, department store orientated and homewares orientated. Then lifestyle malls; Power Centres; Community Centres; Food Centres. There's a lot more diversity

within the asset class. Yet, over here we've had 30–40 years of having all of that in the one centre. When I talk to our shareholders in America who haven't been to Australia and I describe to them the composition of one of our shopping centres, they look at me … And I go, "Yeah, that's why we have 10 million people who go through the Mall a year rather than 4 million."[94]

This approach of redeveloping and improving centres, vastly increasing the number of retailers they housed, was a feature of the industry more broadly. In 1983, Lend Lease bought Monaro Mall in Canberra back from AMP and the MLC insurance groups to which it had originally sold the centre. Since that time Lend Lease Investments had continued to manage the centre, and in 1981, advised AMP and MLC to upgrade what was seen as an aging asset anchored by a David Jones branch that the retailer itself described as an "embarrassment." AMP and MLC had hesitated to act,[95] encouraging Lend Lease to acquire the centre in order to capture the unrealised value that fresh construction could unlock. This process took longer than initially envisaged, but by the mid 1990s Monaro Mall had tripled in size. It contained 144 specialty shops and, in an evolving trend, multiple department store and DDS anchors.[96] Around the time it opened, Coles Myer and the Colonial Mutual Group were completing a redevelopment of the Galleria Morley in Perth. The project brought "30 eastern States retailers to the Perth market for the first time."[97] This offers another instructive example of the way that shopping centres facilitated chain expansion on a national scale: the population and density of the eastern states produced bigger chains that could move across to the distant Western Australian market without having to develop intimate knowledge of local retail geographies.

By 1995, 1,049 shopping centres had been built in Australia's mainland states. They contained 10,469,676 square metres of retail floor space and more than 40,000 specialty shops. Australia's 65 regional shopping centres leased, on average, more than 150 specialty retail stores. New categories of regional centres were introduced: major regional centres and super regional centres respectively averaged 184 and 277 specialty retail tenants. The largest centre in the country, Westfield Shoppingtown Parramatta, contained 370 specialty retailers, spread over five floors and 113,814 square metres of retail floor space. Sites like these represented a staggering increase in scale in just a few decades. Chadstone, which was seen as monumental in 1960, contained less than 70 specialty stores when it opened. Chermside had launched with 25 specialty stores, the same number housed, on average, in neighbourhood shopping centres in Australia's eastern states in the mid 1990s.[98] What was even more remarkable, was that site expansions through redevelopment were only really beginning. Planning regimes continued to limit the number of new centres that could be built, investing established sites with a latent value that could be realised as new opportunities emerged in the market.

Notes

1 BOMA, NSW Division, *Shopping Centre Directory NSW & ACT*; BOMA, Victorian Division, *Directory of Shopping Centres, Victoria*; BOMA, South Australian Division, *Directory of Shopping Centres, South Australia*; BOMA, Western Australian Division, *Directory of Shopping Centres, Western Australia.*

2 BOMA, Queensland Division, *Directory of Shopping Centres, Queensland*; Sullivan, "Kern, Ronald Gerald."

3 Ostrow, *New Boy Network*, 44.

4 *Australian*, 22 March 2014, 18.

5 *SH*, 25 June 1989, 16.

6 *Australian*, 21 December 2013; Fitzgerald, "Report of a Commission of Inquiry," 111; *Age*, 20 December 2013, 22.

7 *AFR*, 12 July 1990, 1.

8 BOMA National Council of Shopping Centres, *Directory of Australian Shopping Centres*; *BRW*, 17 May 1991, 51.

9 *VSCAN*, April 1983, 1.

10 *BRW*, 24 November 1989, 95.

11 Author interview with Reg Jebb.

12 Author interview with Carol Schwartz, 18 February 2015.

13 *VSCAN*, October 1982, 10.

14 *VSCAN*, April 1983, 1.

15 *VSCAN*, February 1983, 2.

16 CMA, Box 4097, H. L. L. Leach, Myer Properties Limited: Report to Corporate Board, Friday 4th November 1983.

17 White, "Changing Nature," 2; *IR*, 21 July 1986, 16.

18 Troy, "Introduction," 12.

19 Australian Government Productivity Commission, "Market for Retail Tenancy Leases," 62.

20 Atkinson, "Business Improvement," 4.

21 Dawson, *Shopping Centre Development*, 84–5. See also *IR*, 4 August 1975, 9.

22 *MD*, 27 March 1985, 21; Peter Walichnowski (Director Lend Lease Retail) quoted in *SCN*, August 1989, 18–19.

23 Author interview with John Schroder, 4 March 2015.

24 *SCN*, August 1989, 18.

25 Author interview with Graham Terry.

26 CMA, Box 2763, Phased Development of Chermside Shopping Centre, 1984; *VSCAN*, April 1983, 1.

27 CMA, Box 4097, H. L. L. Leach, Myer Properties Limited: Report to Corporate Board, Friday 4th November 1983, 4.

28 Author interview with Graham Terry.

29 CMA, Box 766, News Release, 27 June 1983; Rosewarne, "Political Economy of Retailing," 30–1; *IR*, 11 April 1983, 2; *BRW*, 16–22 April 1983, 78; *BRW*, 14–20 July 1984, 95; *Age*, 16 June 1984, 21; Margo, *Frank Lowy*, 192–9; Humphery, *Shelf Life*, 152–3; *Sun*, 17 February 1983, 53; *AFR*, 15 November 1984, 11.

30 Westfield Holdings Ltd, *Westfield Story*, 82.

31 *SMH*, 9 July 1985, 21.

32 Margo, *Frank Lowy*, 192–9.

33 *SMH*, 10 July 1985, 29.

34 Margo, *Frank Lowy*, 197.

35 *SMH*, 8 August 1985, 2; Cardew, "Retailing and Office Development," 34.

36 Margo, *Frank Lowy*, 196; *SMH*, 10 July 1985, 1.

37 *IR*, 6 April 1987, 11.

38 Cardew, "Retailing and Office Development," 34; *SMH*, 10 July 1985, 1.

39 Rosewarne, "Political Economy of Retailing," 24–8; Humphery, *Shelf Life*, 147–8.

40 *AFR*, 10 March 1988, 61; 23 May 1991, 32.

41 Author interview with Jack Rich, 24 March 2015.

42 *SMH*, 18 October 1994, 49.

43 Anon., "Hammerson PLC," 165–6; *AFR*, 18 October 1994, 1; 26 September 1994, 46.

44 Author interview with Reg Jebb.

45 CMA, Box 4097, H. L. L. Leach, Myer Properties Limited: Report to Corporate Board, Friday 4th November 1983, 14.

46 CMA, Box 4097, H. L. L. Leach, Myer Properties Limited: Report to Corporate Board, Friday 4th November 1983, 5–6.

47 *Reuters News*, 28 November 1994.

48 Author interview with Jack Rich.

49 Daly, "Finance."

50 *IR*, 24 January 1977, 11.

51 Annual Report of the Superannuation Fund Investment Trust, 1976/7, 1, 3, 11; *CT*, 26 February 1977, 3.

52 Annual Report of the Superannuation Fund Investment Trust, 1979/80, 6.

53 Annual Report of the Superannuation Fund Investment Trust, 1985, 27, 33.

54 Annual Report of the Superannuation Fund Investment Trust, 1984/5, 33.

55 *BOMA (NSW) News*, June 1986, 17.

56 Annual Report of the Superannuation Fund Investment Trust, 1985, 33. See also Queensland Committee of Inquiry, "Report," 15.

57 Rivkin and Company, *Westfield Limited*, 6–7; Westfield Holdings Ltd, *Westfield Story*, 57.

58 Rivkin and Company, *Westfield Limited*, 8.

59 Australian Stock Exchange, "Property Trusts," 13.

60 Author interview with Richard Clarke.

61 Westfield Holdings Ltd, *Westfield Story*, 57–8.

62 Westfield Holdings Ltd, *Westfield Story*, 58.

63 *IR*, 9 July 1979, 16.

64 *IR*, 16 October 1978, 12.

65 Westfield Holdings Ltd, *Westfield Story*, 58.

66 JLW Research and Consultancy, "Examining Investment," 6–7.

67 Sax, "If You Build It"; Guy, *Retail Development Process*, 49; Cohen, *Consumers' Republic*, 263; Spearritt, "Suburban Cathedrals," 104–5; *BOMA (NSW) News*, June 1986, 17.

68 *SCN*, August 1989, 20.

69 *IR*, 15 September 1980, 7.

70 Author interview with Reg Jebb.

71 Author interview with Richard Clarke.

72 CMA, Box 340, Critical issues: Specialty store retailing, February 1981, 21.

73 Cardew and Simons, "Retailing in Sydney," 153.

74 Author interview with Graham Terry.

75 Katies Annual Report, 1979, 3–6.

76   Author interview with Gregg Chubb, 18 March 2015.
77   Author interview with Graeme Maher, 17 September 2014.
78   *BRW*, 12 April 1989, 17.
79   *BRW*, 12 May 1989, 110.
80   Author interview with Michael Lloyd.
81   Haselhurst, "Leasing Newtown Mall."
82   *AR*, October 1969, 9; *IR*, 15 September 1975, 6.
83   *IR*, 12 August 1974, 7.
84   *AR*, October 1969, 9; Voyce, "Privatisation of Public Property," 255–6.
85   *VSCAN*, April 1981, 8–9; June 1981, 13.
86   *BRW*, 31 March 1989, 52.
87   Author interview with Peter Holland.
88   Author interview with Simon Rumbold.
89   Westfield Holdings Ltd, *Westfield Story*, 68.
90   Allan, "Marion," 117.
91   Sammartino and Van Ruth, "Westfield Group," 311.
92   Westfield Holdings Ltd, *Westfield Story*, 66.
93   Westfield Holdings Ltd, *Westfield Story*, 110.
94   Author interview with John Schroder.
95   *CT*, 11 February 1984, 3.
96   BOMA National Council of Shopping Centres, *Directory of Australian Shopping Centres*; BOMA, NSW Division, *Shopping Centre Directory NSW and ACT*; *CT*, 6 June 1989, 17; 11 February 1984, 3.
97   *AFR*, 10 February 1994, 30.
98   Compiled from BOMA, NSW Division, *Shopping Centre Directory NSW & ACT*; BOMA, Victorian Division, *Directory of Shopping Centres, Victoria*; BOMA, South Australian Division, *Directory of Shopping Centres, South Australia*; BOMA, Western Australian Division, *Directory of Shopping Centres, Western Australia*; and BOMA, Queensland Division, *Directory of Shopping Centres, Queensland*.

8 Shopping for entertainment

The dramatic expansions of large-scale shopping centres from the mid 1980s onwards not only added space, they also helped reposition centres within a changing landscape of consumption.[1] This was conditioned by two structural shifts: the deregulation of retail trading hours and a longer-term shift in consumption expenditure from goods to services. Suburban growth had transformed the geographic framework of retailing. Longer trading hours now shifted its temporal boundaries. One result was an expansion in the productive hours of retail property assets. Able to work their sites harder, shopping centre landlords diversified tenancy mixes to attract a wider share of the consumer dollar. This was a direct and strategic response to a drift in consumer expenditure towards services and leisure experiences. Redevelopments of the bigger centres targeted this shift by incorporating multiplex cinemas, games arcades and food courts, repositioning shopping centres as leisure destinations.[2] Understanding that they were in the "environment creating business,"[3] landlords elevated design, restoring a commitment to amenity that had been lost under the rational utility of discount-orientated development during the 1970s.

Trading hours

In the nineteenth century, shop trading hours internationally were largely unregulated. From the 1850s onwards, even as consumers were enjoying greater purchasing power and increased access to consumer goods, the hours in which they were allowed to shop began to be shortened. Regulations varied widely but were generally instituted in response to lobbying from churches and trade unions. The patterns established lasted into the post-war period when retailers began pushing for deregulatory reform, beginning in the United States in the early 1960s.[4] When big retailers in Australia began seriously agitating for longer shopping hours in the early 1980s, they pointed to the greater freedom to trade in the United States and Europe. Many viewed their sites as underutilised, "lying idle" for 16 hours a day, most of the week, and barely used on the weekend. Although longer hours would mean having to pay penalty rates, these could always be challenged in the future. Meanwhile, mechanisms for controlling labour costs had been established with self-service operations, casualisation strategies and the hiring of junior staff. This made the value of trade outside of standard business hours compelling. One estimate as early as 1958 suggested that Saturday morning shopping accounted for between 10 and 20 per cent of sales in what was around 7 per cent of available trading hours.[5] By 1980, Thursday or Friday night and Saturday morning were by far the busiest shopping times in Australia.[6]

For consumers, the growth of women's workforce participation made it ever harder for families to access shops. Saturday morning degenerated into a mad rush of procurement. Shopping became "a frantic and earnest activity, losing any of the social, leisurely or expansive connotations it had once had."[7] Couples purchasing big ticket items had to cram shopping time into brief windows. Retail car parks were clogged during late night weekday and Saturday morning shopping.[8] Women, who remained the predominant shoppers, juggled shopping with workforce roles, fitting it in around part-time jobs or buying a few rushed items during lunch hours. Bev Kingston argues that "extended shopping hours would probably have come earlier had the idea of shopping not been so deeply ingrained as women's work."[9] In 1980, the *Australian Women's Weekly* illustrated the challenges women faced:

> Saturday morning goes at a gallop in most Australian households. No time for lying in. It's up and down to the shops for meat, fruit and bread, and if you're a working woman, probably groceries, too. One child has to be taken to football, another to music lessons, or ballet or tennis. Then round to the hardware shop for paint; mustn't forget to pick up the picture from the framers; on to the chemist for more cough syrup, and the dry-cleaners, and oops, Jenny has a party next week, have we time to nip along and see what's around in the way of children's dresses? But wait! Stop, everybody. It's 12 o'clock. The shops are shutting, time to go home.[10]

Australia's biggest retailers believed that the challenges people faced fitting shopping around other commitments was negatively impacting sales.[11] Trading had been sluggish in the second half of the 1970s. In a difficult economic climate, retail sales grew by just a little over 1 per cent a year.[12] Temporal expansion offered an avenue of growth. Longer trading hours would provide access to the weekend consumer dollar, which new entrants to the industry were targeting, uninhibited by the restrictions shackling traditional retail.[13] During the 1980s there was considerable growth in street markets, "factory outlets" and "seconds shops," all operating on weekends. These distribution formats had low overheads that translated into cheap prices.[14] For traditional retailers, including those locked into the high-cost structures of shopping centres, this was seen as a form of expenditure leakage – sales going untapped because they could not open their doors to compete.

From the early 1980s, coalitions drawn from the largest retailers devised public relations campaigns to lobby for extended hours. They contacted manufacturing industry groups, individual manufacturers and specialty retailers, with varying degrees of success, to add weight to the cause.[15] They appointed executives to manage government relations and formed numerous associations and lobby groups across the country.[16] They attempted to change the terminology from "extended shopping hours" to "convenience shopping time."[17] And they tried to show that the issues were broader than their own interests. Chief General Manager of Coles, Graeme Seabrook, believed that emerging and reconfigured distribution formats operating on weekends posed a threat to all traditional retailers:

> We need to make everyone … understand that the people who benefit from restrictions on our trading hours are people outside the industry. Small retailers particularly need to be convinced to stop opposing us in this area, because if traditional retailers don't give our customers what they want then someone else will. It is already happening, and the next phase will include tele-shopping from home computers.[18]

Prescient as they were, such arguments had little material impact on the views of small retailers who had little appetite for deregulation. Mark Paterson, former CEO of the Retail Traders' Association of NSW, notes that:

> There were lots of contexts amongst retailers at the time. Large retailers wanted to trade. Half the specialty retailers wanted to trade. Many of the small retailers didn't, either because they already traded seven [days] and didn't want competition or didn't trade seven and didn't want to work seven. So, there were lots of competing economic and lifestyle decisions that were influencing it.[19]

Many small retailers could already open longer than their bigger competition.[20] Extending trading hours would simply erode one of the few comparative advantages they then held over larger chains. It would also entail longer hours for proprietors and higher staff wage costs. In 1985, the Western Australia Shopping Centre Retailers Association used survey data to claim that small retailers in New South Wales had seen little improvement in business since Friday night and Saturday afternoon trading had been introduced there. Moreover, it argued that because shopping centre leases usually required all shops in a complex to open during "normal shopping hours," small retail tenants would be forced to open during the hours being pushed by the larger chains with little financial benefit.[21] Unions representing the interests of shop-floor employees in large firms opposed any extension of weekend trading on the basis that it would negatively impact workers, accelerate casualisation, fail to improve trade, increase prices and undermine leisure time central to the Australian way of life.[22] Church groups claimed, as they had in other countries, that Sunday trading would lead to a decline in spiritual and moral values and would prevent those who wished to worship from doing so.[23]

In response, big retailers called for freedom of choice in a "pluralist society."[24] The industry rebuffed the union assertion that longer trading hours would see a decline in full-time employment, suggesting that in fact more jobs would be created.[25] When unions argued that staff would be coerced into working on the weekend, the extended hours movement pointed to groups of workers such as students that this might suit.[26] Not all large firms took this stance: Boans in Western Australia argued against deregulation, convinced that overall trade would not increase, but the cost of doing business would.[27] The larger eastern state chains were more bullish, although all brought different interests to the debate. Some sought all-day Saturday trading. Others, like the supermarkets, wanted full weekend shopping, including Sundays. The debate was extended and at times acrimonious. In a 2006 review of trading hours in South Australia, the chief investigator Alan Moss noted that:

> at the end of the interview process I was left wondering how it could be that a group of pleasant, intelligent, genuine and well meaning persons could be so completely opposed. The answer is probably a complex mixture of ideology, self-interest and a genuine belief that their views are in the best interest of the community.[28]

Consumers and consumer groups tended not to make strong representations to government inquiries, leaving their interests to be claimed and articulated by other stakeholders.[29] The evidence deployed often took the form of surveys, although as Margetts has noted, "the community opinions on retail trading hours tend to depend on how survey questions are asked."[30] As a result, survey data were produced that supported both sides of the debate.[31] An opinion poll conducted by McNair Anderson in 1980 reported a majority favourable to Saturday afternoon trading, with the strongest support coming from those under the age of 40.[32] A Queensland government report delivered in October 1981, in contrast, argued that "the vast majority of small businesses, employees and consumers do not need or desire extended trading hours in Queensland." Of 6,470 people surveyed, 65.3 per cent responded "No" to the question "Do you see a general need for extended trading hours." Of 1,711 employees of small retail businesses, 81.1 per cent answered "No" to the same question.[33] Employees of large firms do not appear to have been surveyed. Two years later, a NSW inquiry did examine the experiences of chain employees in a pre-Christmas trial of extended Saturday shopping and found no ill-effects. It noted that at a time of high unemployment most seemed willing to volunteer for weekend shifts.[34] A poll by *The Age* newspaper in Melbourne in 1991 found 70 per cent approval for Sunday trading.[35] The industry continued to urge authorities to "let the people decide when they want to shop."[36]

One significant problem was that hundreds of retailers simply flouted trading hour regimes. Prosecutions had failed to prevent the practice, not least because a blind eye was also regularly turned. Gerry Harvey, for example, reportedly opened Harvey Norman Discounts on weekends from its initial launch in 1982.

A year later he claimed that this accounted for 25 per cent of his trade and that no warnings had been issued by government inspectors. The General Manager of Ikea-Scandinavian Living, Keith Williams, declared in 1983 that his firm had never seen a government inspector and made 25 to 40 per cent of its sales on Saturdays and Sundays. Other large retailers chose to remain just within legal boundaries by partitioning their stores to restrict customer access to items legally saleable on weekends.[37] Mark Paterson recounts a case in Victoria where traders were allowed to sell books on Sundays but not billiard tables. One creative retailer started selling books for $3,000 on Sundays and giving away free billiard tables with them. Paterson claims that:

> You had the bizarre situation down in the ACT [Australian Capital Territory] where the award provided a penalty rate for trading legally and a different penalty rate for trading illegally. They had a penalty rate if you were entitled to trade on a Sunday, and if you weren't then it was a different penalty rate, which meant that a legal instrument authorised illegal activity and paid a different penalty rate to employees who did it.[38]

Such inconsistencies in the application and prosecution of the law suggested that change, if only for clarity, was required. Over time, the campaign by big retail achieved "gradual but durable success in watering down" restrictions on trading hours. Legislation was under the jurisdiction of the various states, resulting in a patchy mosaic of laws. South Australia and Western Australia retained the most stringent regulations, while other states like Victoria and Tasmania became largely deregulated.[39] Clarity may not have been achieved but shopping hours were extended through Saturday and then later, and unevenly, Sunday. Studies conducted in the early 1990s suggested that extended trading hours not only benefited the larger retailers but planned shopping centres as well. Longer hours reduced dormant periods, expanded shopping centres' operational capacity, made them more productive, and brought in more customers. Consumers were more likely to travel further to shopping centres and to decrease the regularity of visits to high street shopping precincts.[40] Weekend shopping also broadened shopping demographics. The housewife had always been the central figure of retail marketing campaigns, and women remained the most important customers, but with shopping now available during time traditionally set aside for leisure, new opportunities beckoned. Able to cater to weekend family shopping trips, shopping centre landlords looked for ways to encourage longer visits, by men as well as women and children, and to broaden the types of consumer experience they offered.[41]

Leisure spending

Extended trading hours allowed retail to compete more effectively with other industries for a share of the consumer dollar.[42] From the 1960s onwards, services and experiences became a major area of growth in industries like tourism and hospitality.[43] As early as 1970, analysts in Australia were arguing that despite the benefits that economic growth had delivered to the retail industry, adaptation would be required to maintain proportional shares of expenditure. According to one, "in an expanding economy with rising incomes, more and more will be spent on services rather than goods … spending money on services such as entertainment and travel appeals to an affluent society."[44] This was less a problem for utilitarian providers like supermarkets than it was for discretionary retailers. In 1978, the chairman of Grace Bros. department store, B. A. Grace, declared that "the average consumer has tended to concentrate his spending on food and basics with a noticeable transfer of the spending dollar going towards travel and leisure."[45]

Recreational spending continued to grow as a proportion of total consumer expenditure. Between 1984 and 2010, purchases of food and non-alcoholic beverages dropped from 19.7 to 16.5 per cent; clothing and footwear, from 6.5 to 3.6 per cent; and household furnishings and equipment, from 7.7 to 4.7 per cent.[46] Researchers writing for the Reserve Bank *Bulletin* estimate that between 1986 and 2013 "household spending on goods decreased from around half to one-third of total spending, while the share spent on services increased from around half to two-thirds."[47] In 1996, an article in *Business Review Weekly* claimed that "mainstream retailing is sick, the manufacturing sector is under pressure from rising costs and low inflation, and media companies are battling flat advertising revenue, but the entertainment and leisure industry is booming." This included rapid growth in sales of entertainment hardware and software such as computers, electronic gaming devices, hi-fi equipment, televisions, newspapers, magazines and comics, compact discs and records, books, and photographic equipment.[48] Regional shopping centres responded by including record store chains like HMV and Sanity, and chains selling home entertainment equipment like Dick Smith Power House.[49]

Shopping centre landlords also invested more directly in entertainment facilities. Some added bowling alleys and ice-skating rinks, but the most consistent and widespread expression of this development was the introduction of multiplex cinemas to regional shopping centres. This marked a progression from the social amenities included in the early "shopping cities." These had provided non-commercial space and infrastructure designed to encourage visitation. Marketers now sought to monetise the shopping/leisure dynamic more directly. By adding multiplex cinemas to tenancy mixes, retail property developers strategically broadened their sites' appeal and pushed into new categories of consumer spending.[50] Cinemas and another new addition, takeaway food courts, attracted more people to shopping centres and kept them there longer.[51] Cinema operators also benefited. Shopping centres provided viable and productive sites in suburban areas, revitalising an industry that was heavily concentrated in urban cores and struggling against the home video revolution.

Cinema attendance had been in decline since the 1950s. In 1953, three years before the introduction of black and white television to Australia, there were 15.7 cinema admissions per head of population in the country. Per capita annual attendance dropped to 3.8 in 1969 before recovering a little to 5.0 in 1974. With the arrival of colour television in 1975, annual admissions in Australia dropped to 2.1 per head of population.[52] In 1976 videocassette recorders (VCRs) were introduced to Australia, providing further competition.[53] Echoing cinema in its heyday, video offered cheap, accessible, escapist entertainment, with areas of high unemployment recording correspondingly high levels of video usage. Collins argues that the comfort and convenience of video movie watching was a natural fit for suburbia: an environment centred on the home and socially constructed around the increasingly time-poor nuclear family.[54] Managing director of the Greater Union exhibition chain, David Williams, argued that exhibitors were in "a major fight against a drive to turn the lounge room into the ultimate entertainment centre."[55]

In the United States, this situation had encouraged logistical and techno-logical innovation to produce a new exhibition format, the multiplex cinema. These incorporated air-conditioning, comfortable seats, wide screens and high-quality sound systems into complexes that contained at least five or six screens to offer frequent screenings of, usually, mainstream movies.[56] A very gradual uptake from the first multi-screen complex in 1964 turned into a wave of development through the 1980s when almost 7,000 new screens were added to sites across the country.[57] From the late 1970s multiplexes were introduced to malls. Between 1980 and 2000 the number of screens in the United States jumped from 17,590 to 37,396.[58] The model was emulated in other markets and out-of-town multiplexes became the dominant form of cinema construc-tion in industrialised countries.[59] By most accounts, they reinvigorated the exhibition industry, turning around a long downward trend in attendances.[60]

For Australian exhibitors, multiplex cinema development offered an oppor-tunity to rectify an imbalanced geographic distribution of cinema screens in metropolitan areas.[61] After thirty years of suburban sprawl, when middle and outer ring suburbs were still attracting the highest rates of population growth, and the inner city and suburbs had declining or stagnating populations,[62] city-based cinema complexes still dominated the exhibition sector (Table 8.1).[63] This centralised distribution network magnified the convenience of video. Echoing earlier department store decentralisation, city exhibitors saw shopping centres as a vehicle for cinema to be brought "back to the people. In the suburbs … with good screens, good sound and parking."[64]

Multiplex development transformed screen distribution in Australia.[65] Table 8.1 indicates a considerable increase in total screen numbers between 1980 and 2015, even as the number of theatres housing them declined. The early 1980s saw the most theatre closures, with a large drop in seating cap-acity recorded over the decade. Capacity climbed in the 1990s, accompanying a big increase in the number of screens: while theatre numbers never recovered, the total number of screens more than doubled over the period. The overall increase in screens and decline of theatres indicate closures of small single and twin screen operations. The other big change was the growth in suburban screen numbers, driven by multiplex and then later megaplex development.

Table 8.1 Australian cinema screens by location, 1980–2015

Year	Total screens	Seating capacity	Theatres	City screens	Suburban screens	Country screens
1980	829	378,000	713	Figures not available		
1985	701	324,000	573	128	167	406
1990	791	295,000	510	119	322	350
1995	1082	332,000	557	113	500	469
2000	1778	453,000	554	129	949	700
2005	1943	466,000	519	108	1056	779
2010	1992	455,388	474	73	1112	807
2015	2080	443,000	493	68	1137	845

Source: Screen Australia, www.screenaustralia.gov.au/fact-finders/cinema/industry-trends, accessed 12 November 2019.

In 1980 there were 128 screens located in major cities. This dropped to 68 in 2015, even as suburban screens rose from 167 to 1,137. The distribution of screens was reflected in box office takings. Between 1988 and 2010, Australian suburban box office shares increased from 31 per cent ($68.5 million) to 63 per cent ($710 million) of total receipts. The city, by contrast, declined from 39 per cent ($87 million) to 6 per cent ($72.6 million) over the same period.[66]

By the late 1980s, multiplexes were being used to reposition many of the country's regional shopping centres. Retail property insiders predicted further and significant growth in what was described as a "logical extension to retailing."[67] For exhibitors, shopping centres were close to their market and provided strong existing infrastructure. Their substantial parking stations and existing footprints made development approvals easier to obtain and allowed for relatively low up-front construction costs.[68] By 1995, regional shopping centres housed around half of all suburban cinema screens in Australia. Arrangements varied in detail, but the general pattern was for retail developers to build an outer shell as part of a site redevelopment, with a major exhibitor paying for the auditorium itself and all the equipment and facilities within it.[69] The net benefit for retail property firms was substantial: one enthusiastic industry report in 1997 claimed that multiplexes brought an improvement to shopping centre turnover of between 2 and 5 per cent.[70]

The success of the partnership encouraged the development of more and larger cinema complexes in regional and, in places, sub-regional shopping centres across the country. In 1997, Village Roadshow opened what they claimed was the largest cinema in the world – a 30-screen "megaplex" at Marion Shopping Centre in South Australia. The firm reported more than 60,000 admissions in the first week of operation, declaring that "these massive destinations of entertainment are the way of the future."[71] One industry consultant suggested that "retail is becoming more like entertainment and entertainment is becoming more like retail."[72] A year later, Managing Director of Westfield, Steven Lowy, was reported offering a similar analysis. Westfield had been an early and pro-active adopter of multiplex cinema tenancies in Australia, drawing directly on its experience in the American market. Lowy argued that in the future, retailing would merge with entertainment, extending the concept of the one-stop shop to enable the community to meet, shop, eat and be entertained in one convenient location.[73] Such developments were not always welcomed: residents around Roselands opposed its redevelopment to include a cinema complex in 2001 on the grounds that the enlarged car park would impact on surrounding properties, that the cinema would attract "noisy teenagers" late at night, and that the area was already well served by cinemas in nearby district centres.[74] They were successful in staving off development, leaving Roselands as one of the few regional shopping centres in the country without a multiplex cinema presence.

Reflecting the same logics that drove specialty tenant selection, shopping centre operators had a clear preference for major exhibitors. In 1995, four chains accounted for almost all shopping centre cinemas in Australia: Hoyts ran 13 cinemas containing a total of 92 screens; Village, 8 cinemas housing 50 screens; Greater Union 7 cinemas with 55 screens; and Birch Carroll & Coyle, 5 cinemas with 46 screens. Smaller operators, such as Australian Multiplex Cinemas, which operated 37 screens in south-east Queensland, complained that the "long standing relationships" between the major retail property developers and dominant cinema chains created barriers to entry and restricted their own capacity to grow.[75] Even the United States' entertainment group, Reading Cinemas, was frustrated in its attempts to enter the market. Its initial strategy of constructing free-standing complexes and surrounding them with bookshops, restaurants and other family-style amusements was frustrated by Australian planning regimes, which required cinemas to open in shopping centres or within designated town centres.[76] Reading also faced considerable opposition from the major Australian exhibitors that contested virtually every development application it submitted.[77] By the late 1990s, Reading had managed to obtain locations in shopping centres, and today is a well-established presence in the Australian market.

The decision by already dominant cinema chains to embrace expansion through shopping centres proved strategically sound. Echoing the experience of DDS chains, exhibitors found that the first-mover advantage of securing prime locations was amplified in a marketplace where planning regimes restricted the availability of sites. Ross Jones, who headed an Australian Competition and Consumer Commission inquiry into the cinema industry in 1997, argued that the objective of the dominant firms appeared to be "to secure as many sites as possible over the next few years to prevent the expansion of Reading and the independents." The major firms' expansion plans, he said, vastly outstripped the rate of growth in demand, indicating that they were "willing to endure low or negative rates of return in the short run to maintain dominance." Such strategies allowed these firms to maintain their hold over the market. In 2018, the dominant firms of the early 1990s, Hoyts, Greater Union, Birch Carroll & Coyle and Village respectively operated 16, 13, 12 and 10 per cent of cinema screens in Australia.[78]

Games arcades, teenagers and family values

Around the cinema complex, landlords introduced complementary architecture. One example of this, which flourished briefly in the mid 1990s, was the the games arcade. Arcades offered a direct audiovisual adjunct to the multiplex. Both operated as local distribution points for global cultural production and appeared to offer similar benefits as monetised entertainment formats that would draw customers to shopping centres.[79] There were questions, though, about how seamlessly games arcades meshed with the shopping centre environment. Owner of Leisure & Allied Industries, Malcolm Steinberg, was equivocal about the fit. He had started a chain called Timezone in 1976 after building pool tables in the 1950s and operating individual games arcades in Perth during the 1960s. With Timezone, he rationalised the gaming arcade concept, opening clean, brightly lit stores that offered a point of difference with less salubrious pinball parlours.[80] By the early 1990s, Timezone was the largest games arcade business in Australia. Leisure & Allied's national marketing manager, Chris Blackman, argued in 1992 that "Timezone is to the coin-operated games business what McDonald's is to the hamburger: clean, safe, dependable and no surprises."[81]

Despite his chain's aesthetic alignment with the shopping centre environment, Steinberg was wary of the costs involved. He was particularly sceptical of the financial viability of large-scale, ride-based amusement concepts. Working space hard and efficiently had become central to shopping centre operations for both landlords and tenants. Large leisure precincts did not align with this formula. Steinberg argued that while they could play a valuable anchoring role by attracting foot traffic, landlords would need to discount rents for them to be viable.[82] Even for his own format, which ran on a smaller physical footprint, the high street remained preferential because of its lower occupancy costs, although Timezone did join some shopping centres, such as Northland in Victoria and Innaloo in Queensland.

However, other figures within the retail property industry, as well as some retail game operators, believed that entertainment and leisure would define the future shopping centre. There was initial hesitation by the former. Ian Newtown, Westfield's general manager (leasing), told *Business Review Weekly* in 1991: "I'm of that era when pinball machines were the domain of hoods." But he and others were converted by the apparent appeal of games arcades to family shoppers in the early 1990s. Steve Nicoll, Highpoint shopping centre's general manager (leasing), agreed with Steinberg that monetising larger entertainment attractions would be challenging but argued that they would become a necessary drawcard for families. A centre without such facilities, he suggested, would be akin to a "newsagent without cigarettes and Tattslotto."[83] Michael Solomon, a director of Associated Leisure Pty Ltd, predicted that entertainment precincts would become a standard feature of all new and expanding shopping centres in Australia. He lobbied Westfield for five years, "banging on the door" before the firm agreed to pilot his Playtime leisure centre in Queensland's Toombul mall in 1991. Marketed as a children's entertainment centre, Playtime emulated American formats. It offered rooms for children's birthday parties and consciously attenuated its games "machine mix" to individual locations. This was described as a micro version of the shopping centre tenancy mix, with the games machines in each outlet curated for their respective markets. The largest Playtime took up 3,000 square metres of floor space, housing an 18-hole mini golf course, a carousel, a pirate ship play area, and a small train that wove its way along tracks threaded between them. After Toombul, Playtime opened outlets in Westfield's Tea Tree Plaza, Liverpool and Indooroopilly as well as in a number of other centres owned by other firms and institutions.[84]

Playtime marked the emergence of a strategy to create "one-stop major leisure destinations" within shopping centres. In 1994, after monitoring the performance of Playtime in Australia, and observing broader trends in America, Westfield announced a joint venture with Village Roadshow and the Nine television network, Village Nine Leisure (VNL). Its remit was to develop indoor theme parks in shopping centres under the Intencity banner.[85] Intencity outlets were pitched towards families, offering amusement rides and children's areas as well as coin-operated games machines.[86] They were very large, ranging from 3,200 to 5,200 square metres in size – almost half the size of some of the largest discount department stores at the time. Intencity was launched in 1995 at Westfield's Hurstville complex, with plans to open a further 20 outlets within a few years.[87] Parallel strategies were pursued by other firms. In 1997, Highpoint shopping centre introduced Cinemotion, which provided immersive simulated "rides" where patrons watched short films from seats that moved in response to the action on screen.[88] The Highpoint expansion produced the city's first 16-screen megaplex in a self-contained entertainment precinct that in addition to Cinemotion also included Fun Zone game machines, a Pancake Parlor food outlet, a Playtime games arcade and a miniature golf course.[89]

Marketers positioned such entertainment precincts as family-oriented spaces, but were challenged by old prejudices. The polished and rationalised aesthetic of the new games arcades could not erase community and retailer concerns about "hoods" loitering, shoplifting and disrupting the pleasant shopping experiences of women and families. Rob White and Adam Sutton argue that the management of shopping centres "and what happens within them often are premised upon the exclusion of certain young people and other disadvantaged groups."[90] In this context, games arcades were a paradoxical tenant because they appealed to an undesirable clientele. When an arcade was being proposed for one Sydney shopping centre in 1994, the Parents and Citizens' Association (P&C) of a nearby high school argued that it would "attract gangs of youths and lead to an increase in petty crime."[91] The P&C's attitude provoked heated debate that extended to the halls of the state parliament, largely because games arcades remained indelibly linked to a "hoodlum element." The conflation of gaming and crime made some young people feel unwelcome in shopping centres that by the 1990s had become their "traditional locale". Sixteen-year-old Ferhad Mukri told one reporter:

> Once I was standing outside Playtime. There were three or four of us.
> Security came and bossed us around because there was a group of us. But
> I prefer walking with more people, because it's safer from danger. You get
> targeted if you're on your own more than if you're in a group. It's safety in
> numbers. But then you get called a gang.[92]

"Merv" didn't have this problem. In 1993, he told a reporter interviewing
him in Chadstone that he had been visiting the centre 6 days a week for
33 years since it opened. Now retired, he arrived each day at 9am and left at
4pm, meeting a group of friends he never saw outside the centre.

> It's nice and warm in winter time. In summer time, it's nice and cool. It's
> a very clean centre. Spotless … What's the use of sitting inside at home
> looking at the walls? I live in a unit. We all live in units. I'd go stupid.

His friend Nancye joked: "When he's not here, everyone thinks he's dropped
dead or something."[93] Retirees like Merv and Nancye had grown up with
shopping centres in the same generational cohort as Pauline, Lorne and Ken
who worked at Roselands in the 1960s. By the 1990s, this demographic group
accounted for a substantial proportion of shopping centre visitors. Some even
took up "mall walking," a fashion that had emerged in America during the
1980s. This involved older customers utilising shopping centre car parking and
weather protection to take group exercise walks, concluding with a drink, food
or shopping.[94]

Like the teenagers meeting outside Playtime, these customers accounted for
a disproportionately low level of expenditure in shopping centres. Both groups
shared a social and relatively non-commercial interest in the shopping centre
space, but only young people were constructed as a problem.[95] Merv's friend,
Jim, voiced approval for a ban on skateboarding and roller-skating because they
attracted "riff-raff." In another interview, a couple who had also been visiting
Chadstone for years compared it favourably with the city, for which they
professed "a profound disdain." Ms Cieslak, a university telephonist, described
Chadstone as "clean." "From the family point of view," she said, "there are no
ruffians. We won't go near Melbourne at night. Mainly it's just the young people
hanging around the streets. I am quite frightened in the city. I have given up on
Melbourne."

Her husband concurred, saying "If they could make the city area one big
Chadstone, that would be great … It's just a different atmosphere. It's like
chalk and cheese to me."[96] Such attitudes, real and imagined, and the actions
of security guards removing young people like Ferhad and his friends, helped
establish a symbolic and material sense of security for middle-market shoppers.
Not too rich. Not too poor. Not too aberrant. These customers, across the
very broad middle of Australian society, brought money into centres. Teenagers
occupied the fringes of this market, had little disposable income, and were
accommodated only to the extent that they were not disruptive.

As drawcards for such "riff-raff," games arcades produced moral anxiety, but also, and probably more significantly for their longevity, inadequate revenue. Steinberg's concern that the more ambitious entertainment offerings would be difficult to monetise was proven correct relatively quickly. Intencity

> was hugely capital intensive and that meant the price [of rides and games] was pretty high. It was the sort of thing that the kids came and played a few times but they weren't going to come in every week. Once they'd played the game, even though it cost you a fortune to put in and you had to charge them $15–20 to have a go, [after] two or three times they'd want the next thing. You couldn't rip it out and put in another one because it was way too expensive.[97]

The Intencity mega complex at Hurstville was closed down after just two years of operation. In 1998 Westfield wrote down its $20 million investment in the VNL consortium to zero, concluding that Intencity's products were too expensive and that "the idea of mega-stores had failed." Plans remained for smaller stores, but these were wiped out by prevailing competitive headwinds that would also buffet Timezone.[98] One obituary for Intencity noted that "the timing of the venture was terrible," arriving on the cusp of an enormous growth in home computer purchases, the spread and commodification of internet usage and the development of sophisticated home gaming platforms like PlayStation, Nintendo and Xbox.[99] Timezone, although less exposed with lower capital costs in smaller stores, saw its Australian network shrink from 40 stores in 1997 to just 16 in 2002.[100]

Cinemas had been able to combat product innovations in home entertainment by offering to a wide range of consumers a comfortable, high-quality audiovisual experience that enhanced the appeal of blockbuster movies designed to take advantage of the technological innovations of the format. Gaming, in contrast, appealed to a narrow demographic with limited disposable income. The experience offered in store was not tangibly different from that available at home, and the latter was far cheaper. Larger, more experiential offerings like rides and virtual reality attractions could not operate at price points that worked for both consumers and landlords. Games arcade models that survived, and that still operate today, differentiated their offer from home-based gaming, leveraging the experiential possibilities of physical stores efficiently from small retail footprints. The broader lesson from the gaming experiment, however, was that retail rental levels were not transferable to every potential use of shopping centre space.

Food courts

The success of the Playtime centre when it was piloted at Toombul was attributed to the vibrant and bustling environment that it joined. This included a busy food court containing McDonald's and Sizzler restaurant outlets.[101] Although less exciting than the grand visions of indoor theme parks, food courts like that at Toombul were a widespread innovation that transformed the Australian shopping centre from the late 1980s onwards. Functional, utilitarian environments, they housed high-volume food retailers. These were far more attuned to the logics of the shopping centre environment than games arcades, which had a limited turnover ceiling because they sold a product in which customers purchased time on an activity. It was far harder to scale or generate efficiencies selling these experiences than it was for food, which also catered to the entire customer base, from teenagers, to families, to retirees. By the 1990s, takeaway food was arguably the most dynamic area of growth in the retail industry.

The inclusion of eateries to enhance shopping trips was not a new development in Australia or abroad. Australian department stores provided customers with restaurants and cafeterias from at least the 1930s. Coffee shops were included in the early shopping centres. Australia's 1960s "shopping cities" all provided eating options to enhance leisurely consumption and to fuel utilitarian shopping trips. Some, such as those at Roselands, Bankstown Square and Marion, were recognisable antecedents of later food courts, comprising shared seating for a number of takeaway food outlets serving Australianised versions of international cuisine.[102] These outlets did not have distinctive individual branding, instead being collectively grouped under banners conceived by landlords, such as Marion's nautically themed Quarter Deck, which Arndale hoped would "become the principle rendezvous of the [Adelaide] southern suburbs."[103] But at a time when most meals in Australia were produced in homes,[104] takeaway food was a relatively minor component of most early shopping centres.

By the 1980s, food culture in Australia had changed. Eating meals outside of the home – a habit "scarcely imaginable to earlier generations that rarely ate out for pleasure" – had become a staple activity for most social classes.[105] Women's growing participation in paid employment was one contributing factor. Studies in the early 1990s, both internationally and in Australia, indicated that increases in paid work did not change the gendered distribution of domestic household labour, with women still overwhelmingly responsible for food preparation, cleaning and shopping. These studies also found that as time in paid work increased, time spent preparing food decreased.[106] Takeaway food offered one avenue for domestic food preparation to be outsourced. By 1982, a quarter of the money spent on food in Australia went on meals prepared outside of the house. By 1986 the figure was closer to 30 percent.[107] By the mid 1990s, Australians were spending an average of $700 eating out each year, with takeaway food taking a growing share of this trade.[108]

The Australian retail property industry looked to meet this market. As was its practice, it closely observed American trends but was also cognisant of developments in other countries. The food court had been introduced to American malls in the early 1970s, and exported to other markets such as the United Kingdom by the mid 1980s. Its transferability as an innovation was tied to its utility as a new type of anchor. The food court targeted a growing area of consumer demand and acted as a kind of supportive scaffolding for shopping. Food court eateries were convenient and efficient, broadened the scope of the one-stop shopping trip, and encouraged customers to spend more time and money in centres.[109] An American research report in 1987 found that food courts kept shoppers in centres for, on average, an additional 35 minutes, and that over 60 percent of customers visiting a centre made a food purchase.[110] A 1994 survey, also in America, found that 60 percent of respondents consumed a snack whilst visiting malls, and 30 percent a full meal.[111]

By 1995, the majority of regional shopping centres in Australia included food courts. Some seated as few as 100 customers; others more than 1,000. The number of outlets also varied widely, with some landlords opting for gradual adoption by including only a few, and others like Lend Lease providing space for more than 30 at Penrith Plaza when it redeveloped the centre in the early 1990s. Most food courts contained between 10 and 20 outlets, with seating for 400 to 700 people.[112] Those regional centres that did not contain food courts were simply at the back end of redevelopment phases. As each was upgraded, a food court and, usually, a cinema, were automatic inclusions.

The food courts in Australian shopping centres contained both independent and, increasingly, chain operators. The latter included international fast food brands, which had been operating stand-alone stores in Australia since the late 1960s. Kentucky Fried Chicken (KFC) was the first to arrive in Australia opening in Guildford, NSW in 1968. It was followed by McDonald's, Hungry Jack's (Burger King) and Pizza Hut. These firms had started as individual road-side stalls in America, developing over decades into multinational corporations operating international franchises.[113] With products foreign to Australian tastes, sales for the big fast food chains were initially slow, but by the late 1970s, KFC, McDonald's and Pizza Hut were firmly established. Social researcher Hugh Mackay notes that if McDonald's began in Australia as a means to "eat and run," it became a social space where families and people could "stop and talk to each other."[114] He argues that for perhaps the first time, working-class people could eat out, not worrying about how they were dressed, and be served in comfort.

Fast food's relationship with shopping centres began on their fringes in the 1970s: built on ground floors, adjacent to car parks, providing access to patrons seven days a week and outside of regular shopping hours. By the late 1980s, most large shopping centres had at least a couple of the major fast food chains perched on their perimeter.[115] The issue of access was critical to these chains, whose business models were based on high and constant turnover. This drove their demand for exterior locations rather than spaces within centres. The architectural logic of enclosed shopping centres, though, privileged internal locations by funnelling customers from car parks directly to inside retailers. This environment challenged the established practices of the fast food chains. Former managing director and chief executive of

McDonald's Australia, and later president of McDonald's China, Guy Russo, notes that:

> McDonald's, are all the same operationally, if you forget the dining room, the playground, the drive-through and the car park, which are all the things that are not in a food court ... I know there are dining rooms in food courts but they weren't ours ... The reason I mention those four things is that it was those four things which made us most nervous ... The traditional McDonald's, the successful McDonald's if you like, really had half its customers go through the front counter and the other half of its customers go through the drive-through. When you're offered this option about no car park, no Sunday trade, no night trade, no drive through and no playground, you say, well what kinds of sales are we going to do inside a shopping centre? It was easy to do the maths and say, well the drive through is worth 30% of your business. After-five o'clock is worth 20% of your business. You'd get down to nothing. It wasn't so much an operation change that needed to be done so much as a worry about the economics. Would there be enough revenue to be able to make them a viable model for the company or for the franchisee? ...
>
> We were hesitant, but when we realised how well they did and how successful they were, we wanted to be in them a lot more. Still, we wanted to be in the float of the food court. The float meaning the beginning, where you came in. Then, I remember about 10 years later when Westfield's were renovating all their centres we couldn't do a float anymore, they drew a brand new food court and had us at the back ... We said, "we don't like it at the back." They said, "well good, if you don't like it at the back then don't bother coming in." If I took you around ten shopping centres, you'd see how firstly we were right at the front and then they were so successful that Westfield's used to complain that no one could get into the back, because our lines were so long ... They put McDonald's and KFC and all those guys at the back. They said, you guys can draw them in.[116]

Russo would later bring the McDonald's approach of rational utility to the Australian Kmart operation, turning around the fortunes of a chain that by the time of his appointment in 2008 had become bloated and inefficient. His recollections about the introduction of McDonald's to food courts indicate the challenges of adapting to a new distribution environment, but also the transferability of fast food systems. Methods of customer access to stand-alone McDonald's stores were replaced by shopping centre infrastructure, with no significant alterations required to the internal logics of their operations. Branding also remained a key strength. But even firms of the scale of McDonald's had to cede power to the largest retail property landlords when it came to site selection. The shopping centre format was so effective that by the late 1990s, the latter could dictate at least some terms, increasing the value of retail space by using the drawing power of the big fast food chains to send customer foot traffic past lesser-known food retailers.

By 2002, chains such as McDonald's and KFC accounted for 28 per cent of outlets in shopping centre food courts. They acted as anchors for food precincts, which in turn socially activated retail environments, quickly becoming important contributors to the overall health and productivity of shopping centres.[117] Food courts were also a significant revenue generator in their own right. Intensely productive spaces, their rents were often higher than those of other tenants. *Shopping Centre News* (*SCN*) estimated in 1993 that food courts could "account for up to 10% of the specialty rental component" of shopping centres. This, and their appeal to customers, encouraged an expansion of their role. *SCN* reported that in the United States almost a quarter of all food courts had been renovated within the previous two years. Given the projected growth in Australia, it mused that "it's not far-fetched to consider Eateries as big a draw card for shoppers as is the department store of today."[118]

This led *SCN* to consider how the aesthetics of food courts could be elevated, citing international precedents as inspiration for developing more sophisticated offers. The journal reported on operations such as the scattered mini food precincts of Berlin's KaDeWe; Meadowhall in the UK, which heralded themed food courts that were seen as an escapist accompaniment to virtual reality games centres; and Water Tower Place in Chicago where customers were "invited to meander along flagstone paths to … clusters of food stands … under boughs of foliage."[119] It noted that KaDeWe

> has, at part of the counter, a few stools, each with a place setting at the counter. For example, at the fish counter are mountains of superbly displayed fresh fish, eels, shellfish, clams and so on, with the shoppers busy buying. Right there are a handful of people sitting and eating just two or three king prawns with a slice of bread and a glass of white wine. It's not only good business, but it's attractive too. It's a bit of theatre, action, interest, and it's the same on all the other counters from the butchery to the deli to the cheese.[120]

This musing reflected a broader shift in the industry, which was evolving to produce more pleasing retail environments.[121] Through the seventies and eighties, the rise of developer entrepreneurs and the proliferation of DDS-based developments had coincided with a rationalisation of designs and a focus on efficient uses of space. This marked a departure from the grand aesthetic visions of earlier department store developers, whose organisational cultures were informed by historically constituted ideas of service and presentation. Department stores that had their roots in the nineteenth and early twentieth centuries had grown during a time when retail floor space was not a unit of rent, but an opportunity to imbue merchandise with a sense of theatre. Their cultural history helped produce the "shopping cities" of the 1960s, replete with fountains, atriums and public art. Strategies focused on the productive and efficient usage of space, in contrast, resulted in bland, repetitive architectural forms. By the 1980s, the design and appearance of shopping centres were undergoing critical scrutiny. Brisbane town-planning consultant, Vic Feros, for example, claimed in 1980 that modern shopping centres had no soul, and that the spirit of a socially interactive marketplace needed to be reinvoked:

> Shopping areas should be convenient, engaging and inviting, instead of a mish-mash of third-grade architecture in oceans of asphalt ... Victor Gruen ... envisaged them to be centres of community focus ... The failure of his dream is tragic. Shopping centres date back to 500 B.C. and all we've got to show for 2,500 years of planning is inferior development.[122]

If this was elite critique, market research suggested that shoppers at the time also wanted improved amenity in retail environments.[123] In the second half of the 1980s, architects and designers of regional shopping centres responded with more sophisticated décor, indoor gardens, and skylights to bring natural light back to cavernous interiors. Redevelopments and refurbishments introduced more quality materials. Fluorescent lights were faded out.[124] Centre exteriors were softened to complement interior designs and to meet changing planning requirements.[125] Garden boxes were deployed in a futile attempt to disguise the austerity of decked car parks.[126]

Tenancy mixes also shifted in response to the market. One of the principal innovators in this regard was John Gandel who, by the early 1990s, was probably the largest private owner of retail property in the country.[127] Coming from a retail background in his Sussan women's clothing chain, he used a series of upgrades to reimagine Chadstone as a fashion destination. By improving fixtures, fittings and layout, and introducing design-oriented retailers that had only ever previously located in the city, he brought a fashion culture to suburban retail development. Reg Jebb argues that this "set a benchmark that said, you can have a lot more retailers, you can go upmarket, you can get higher rents, you can attract a more well-heeled clientele."[128] This had an influence across the industry and reinforced the positioning of regional shopping centres as leisure environments.[129]

The general result of these changes was to make highly utilitarian and functional shopping environments more pleasant and inviting to consumers who were now familiar with the format, but who either wanted more from it or could be attracted when more was offered. This marked a material shift from "the gun barrel mall, with the K mart at one end and the Coles at the other, the Franklins in between and 30–40 shops spread out along the way."[130] When Coles Myer launched a redevelopment of Eastland in 1994, its architects claimed that it would provide Melbourne shoppers with "an elegant and refined space, a retail centre that captures the essence of modern classicism." Targeting an affluent and still rapidly growing trade area, marketers suggested that the fountain and landscaping in the new food court "set the scene for a European garden."[131]

Architectural imagination and market repositioning like that at Eastlands established the model for the mature Australian shopping centre between the mid 1980s and mid 1990s. Entertainification was central to this process, and proved a strategically sound innovation, aligning with broad trends in consumer expenditure and the extension of shopping hours that big retailers had lobbied for so determinedly. Not all experiments were successful, with the failures revealing of the forces that underpinned retail property profitability. Intencity, for example, occupied too much space, forcing up the price of its offer that targeted a niche demographic without strong spending power. The retailers that did best were positioned to the middle market and ran high-volume operations.

The process of adding monetisable entertainment services, however, illustrated the capacity of the shopping centre industry to adapt to the market. The shopping centre format was flexible enough to horizontally expand, absorbing new types of tenants to diversify revenue streams. This demonstrated that although it had begun as a retail format, and retailing remained its core business, the shopping centre was not simply a collection of shops. It was a sophisticated piece of urban infrastructure with logistical competitive advantages that produced highly valuable space. This space was the product. It was initially rented to retailers, but offered opportunities for other firms that required physical access to consumers. The question for these firms was whether they could extract sufficient value from shopping centre sites to pay the rental costs – an issue that became increasingly pressing as shopping centre occupancy became ever more expensive.

Notes

1 On landscapes of consumption, see Zukin, *Landscapes of Power.*
2 For an analysis of this process, see Bailey, "Shopping for Entertainment."
3 *VSCAN*, August 1981, 10–11.
4 Trentmann, *Empire of Things*, 477–9; Armstrong and Ong, "Deregulation of trading hours"; Baker, "What Hours," 103.
5 *JRTANSW*, November 1958, 3.
6 *AWW*, 24 September 1980, 34–7.
7 Kingston, *Basket, Bag and Trolley*, 114.
8 CMA, Box 458, K-mart Burwood – Traffic Survey, 1972.
9 Kingston, *Basket, Bag and Trolley*, 114.
10 *AWW*, 24 September 1980, 34–7.
11 CMA, Box 509, Letter from Richard Thomas, Director Corporate Affairs, Coles Myer to Rev. G. Kerrie Graham, The Uniting Church of Australia, 29/07/1991.
12 *AB*, 16 July 1981, 73.
13 *BRW*, 21 February 1992, 27.
14 CMA, Box 1723, MINTEL, Casual clothing: Economic management report, Volume 23, April 1991; *BRW*, 21 February 1992, 26; CMA, Box 1166, Major convenience stores operating extended trading hours, ca. 1980–2.
15 CMA, Memo from B. P. Sloan, Results of discussion with Mr R. Aitchison and ACAM, 28 August 1981.

16 CMA, Box 1723, Coles, Shop trading hours activity report, 8 November 1991.
17 *AB*, 16 July 1981, 74.
18 CMA, Box 4111, Memo from G. Seabrook, Non-store retailing, 2 December 1983.
19 Author interview with Mark Paterson, 9 June 2017.
20 *AB*, 16 July 1981, 74.
21 *West Coast Retailer*, May 1985, 2.
22 *RT*, March 1965, 9; *BRW*, 8–14 October 1983, 42.
23 Price, "Extending Trading Hours," 134–5.
24 CMA, Box 509, Letter from Richard Thomas, Director Corporate Affairs, Coles Myer to Rev. G. Kerrie Graham, The Uniting Church of Australia, 29/07/1991.
25 *AB*, 16 July 1981, 74.
26 Price, "Extending Trading Hours," 135.
27 Hough, "From Clogs to Clogs," 253–4.
28 Moss, "Report of the 2006/07 Review," 23.
29 ACIL Australia, "Trading Hours," 3.
30 Margetts, "National Competition Policy," 77. On the ways that industry lobby groups approached survey design, see Baker, "What Hours," 100.
31 *AWW*, 24 September 1980, 34–7.
32 CMA, Box 1509, Why Victoria needs Saturday afternoon shopping NOW, ca. 1980.
33 Small Business Development Corporation, "Investigation into the Issue of Extended Retail Trading Hours," iii, 75, 85.
34 CMA, Box 2035, James J. Macken, Report to the Minister for Industrial Relations, NSW, October 1983, 9.
35 *Age*, 22 May 1991, 13.
36 CMA, Box 509, Letter from Richard Thomas, Director Corporate Affairs, Coles Myer to Rev. G. Kerrie Graham, The Uniting Church of Australia, 29/07/1991; *The Standard* (Warrnambool), 8 October 1986, 1.
37 *BRW*, 8–14 October 1983, 36–42. See also CMA, Box 2035, James J. Macken, Report to the Minister for Industrial Relations, NSW, October 1983.
38 Author interview with Mark Paterson.
39 Heino, "Trading Hours Deregulation," 97–9.
40 Baker, "What Hours", 99–100.
41 *AFR*, 3 November 1994, 33.
42 CMA, Box 757, Let's Go Saturday Committee: Retail Shopping Hours, June 1981.
43 White, *On Holidays,* 167–73; Davidson and Spearritt, *Holiday Business,* 283–358; Altman, *Rehearsals for Change,* 19.
44 *AR*, June 1970, 5.
45 *Australian*, 18–19 November 1978, 11.
46 Australian Bureau of Statistics, *Household Expenditure Survey 2009–2010: Summary of Results*, 6530.0 (Canberra, 2011), 30.
47 Beech, Dollman, Finlay and La Cava, "Distribution of Household Spending", 15.
48 *BRW*, 28 October 1996, 47.
49 *BRW*, 28 October 1996, 47.
50 *BOMA Bulletin*, June 1992, 3; Cardew, "Retailing and Office Development," 39.
51 On the American development of entertainment facilities, see Zukin, "Urban Lifestyles," 830.
52 Screen Australia, www.screenaustralia.gov.au/fact-finders/cinema/industry-trends, accessed 12 November 2019.
53 Doyle, "Return of the Super Cinema," 3.

54 Collins, *Hollywood Down Under*, 265–8.
55 Milliken, "Lost Picture Show."
56 Collins, Hand and Ryder, "Lure of the Multiplex," 485.
57 Paul, "K-Mart Audience," 491.
58 Maltby, *Hollywood Cinema*, 187, 203.
59 Athique and Hill, "Multiplex Cinemas," 108–9.
60 Cunningham, *Hungarian Cinema*, 153; Hubbard, "Fear and Loathing at the Multiplex," 56–7.
61 Milliken, "Lost Picture Show," 35.
62 Baker, Coffee and Hugo, "Australia: State of the Environment."
63 *SH*, 20 January 1991, 30; *SMH*, 11 January 1990, 19; Milliken, "Lost Picture Show," 35.
64 Chairman of the Motion Picture Distributors' Association of Australia, Mike Selwyn, quoted in *SMH*, 16 November 1994, 7.
65 Bailey, "Shopping for Entertainment."
66 Screen Australia, www.screenaustralia.gov.au/fact-finders/cinema/industry-trends, accessed 12 November 2019.
67 David Lowy quoted in *AFR*, 30 March 1989, 58.
68 *IR*, 26 April 1999, 9.
69 *Age*, 12 Septembe 1997, 37.
70 *AFR*, 15 April 1997, 41. Another estimate in 1996 suggested 2–3 per cent increases. See *SCN*, June/July 1996, 28.
71 Australian Stock Exchange Company Announcements, ASX-Village Roadshow Limited (VRL.AX), Chairman's AGM Address to Shareholders, 25 November 1997.
72 Graham Kwan, design director of entertainment consultants Attractions International, quoted in *WA*, 2 April 1997, 62.
73 *Foodweek*, 10 May 1999.
74 *DT*, 21 June 2001, 8.
75 *SMH*, 4 February 2002, 31.
76 *Age*, 5 December 1997, 43.
77 *SMH*, 4 February 2002, 31.
78 Screen Australia, www.screenaustralia.gov.au/fact-finders/cinema/industry-trends, accessed 12 November 2019.
79 Panelas, "Adolescents and Video Games," 54–8.
80 *BRW*, 17 May 1991, 46.
81 *BRW*, 20 March 1992, 76.
82 *BRW*, 10 May 1991, 72.
83 *BRW*, 10 May 1991, 72.
84 *SCN*, October/November 1993, 20.
85 *AFR*, 3 November 1994, 33.
86 *AFR*, 29 April 1996, 39.
87 *HS*, 18 Aug 1998, p. 29.
88 *Age*, 3 January 1997, 14; *WA*, 2 April 1997, 62.
89 *HS*, 26 December 1997, 82.
90 White and Sutton, "Social Planning," 65.
91 *NDT*, 15 June 1994, 2.
92 *SMH*, 26 February 2000, 1.
93 *Age*, 9 October 1993, 1.
94 *IR*, 17 March 1986, 9.
95 White and Sutton, "Social Planning," 68.

96   *Age*, 9 October 1993, 1.
97   Author interview with Tony Dimasi.
98   *Advertiser*, 18 August 1998, 9.
99   *SGSSL*, 14 August 2019; *WA*, 18 December 2004, 79.
100   *WA*, 18 December 2004, 79.
101   *SCN*, October/November 1993, 20.
102   *SMH*, Bankstown Square Feature, 21 September 1966, 8; CCC, Roselands File, Grace Bros. promotional brochure, Corners at Roselands Shopping Centre, ca. 1965; *Torch*, 13 October 1965, 20.
103   *AR*, June 1967, 4–5.
104   *SCN*, October/November 1993, 20.
105   Walker and Roberts, *From Scarcity to Surfeit*, 148.
106   Patterson and Porter, "Are We Contributing?"
107   Walker and Roberts, *From Scarcity to Surfeit*, 148.
108   *SCN*, June/July 1996, 28.
109   Humphery, *Shelf Life*, 153.
110   White, "Changing Nature," 81.
111   Bloch, Ridgway and Dawson, "Shopping Mall as Consumer Habitat," 30.
112   Collated from BOMA, NSW Division, *Shopping Centre Directory NSW & ACT*; BOMA, Victorian Division, *Directory of Shopping Centres, Victoria*; BOMA, South Australian Division, *Directory of Shopping Centres, South Australia*; BOMA, Western Australian Division, *Directory of Shopping Centres, Western Australia*; and BOMA, Queensland Division, *Directory of Shopping Centres, Queensland*.
113   Murray, "Faster Taste."
114   Mackay, *Reinventing Australia*, 284. See also Walker and Roberts, *From Scarcity to Surfeit*, 147; Gare, "Fast Food Phenomenon."
115   White, "Changing Nature," 80–1.
116   Author interview with Guy Russo, 7 April 2015.
117   *SCN*, October/November 2002, 10, 16.
118   *SCN*, October/November 1993, 52.
119   *SCN*, June/July 1996, 28, 32; October/November 1993, 52.
120   *SCN*, June/ uly 1996, 28–30.
121   Cardew, "Retailing and Office Development," 38.
122   Quoted in *IR*, 15 September 1980, 16.
123   Bryan and Stuebing, "Natural Light," 299.
124   White, 'Changing Nature', 68–9.
125   *The Concrete Constructions Group*, March 1981, 1; Simpson and O'Connell, "Chatswood Town Centre," 9.
126   White, "Changing Nature," 71–2.
127   *BRW*, 17 May 1991, 51.
128   Author interview with Reg Jebb.
129   Author interview with Tony Dimasi.
130   Author interview with Tony Dimasi.
131   *SCN*, April/May 1994, 36.

9   Power and property

The rapid spread and growth of shopping centres raised questions, as early as the mid 1970s, about whether too much retail space was being built in Australia.[1] One anonymous specialty chain executive claimed that all of Australia's capital cities and most of its country towns had an excess of retail development. He warned that "street after street [would be turned] into retail wastelands unless local councils and developers [were] stopped from building more and more shops for the fewer and fewer retailers who [could] profitably operate them."[2] In 1973, Perth's Metropolitan Region Planning Authority launched an inquiry into the city's retail development because it "felt the number and size of shopping centres was becoming out of balance with the rest of the development of the metropolitan region."[3] In 1974, a Westfield executive described both Sydney and Melbourne as "fairly well ringed with major regional shopping centres" with little room for expansion.[4] Indeed, one of the motivations for the firm's move into the American market, which began in 1977, was a view that opportunities in Australia were becoming more limited.[5]

Impacts on high streets

Concern was also expressed about the decline of traditional high street retailing. This became a hot topic in the 1980s, but debate over the impact of shopping centres had been underway since the 1960s. Following the construction of Chadstone, it was quickly recognised that the high street's advantage of proximity to customers was rendered obsolete by the car. A survey of 100 female shoppers in 1960 indicated that available parking at the end of the journey was more important than whether they "had to drive one mile or two miles or three miles" to get to the shops.[6] A study in 1969 of the Mitcham and Unley shopping centres in South Australia found that they adversely affected approximately 65 per cent of retail businesses located within three-quarters of a mile – although the researchers noted the possibility of other external forces as well as exaggerated claims by shopkeepers. A second study in the same year found that regional shopping centres in Melbourne impacted negatively on city and suburban shopping strips that fell within their trade catchment areas. In 1979, research on three shopping centres in Queensland found that they had impacted on approximately half of nearby shopkeepers whose services were duplicated by the centres, but that the remainder of traders had not been adversely affected. Again, the researchers noted that quantifying the impact of new developments was complicated by other external forces, including macroeconomic trends.[7]

The collapse of the post-war boom in the mid 1970s impacted the fortunes of most retailers dependent on discretionary spending, but the continued proliferation and growth of shopping centres made it difficult to dismiss perceptions that high street retailing in particular was under siege. In 1984, one development consultant described high street shopping precincts as "rotting," unable to compete in a saturated market. He argued that the resulting abundance of retail space had "reduced the average level of trade," leaving strip shopping precincts to "here today, gone tomorrow" first-time retailers, takeaway bars and non-retail businesses.[8] A year later, geographer and industry commentator, R. J. Stimson, argued that shopping centres had brought an identifiable decline in the market share of small retail businesses.[9] Tony Dimasi argues that shopping centres were a feature of this process but not the only or even principal cause:

> the shopping centre was a manifestation of other changes … Unless the high streets did something themselves then they were going to keep on going backwards in the same way that department stores lost their relevance and their significance to a degree … It couldn't be the case that those people living in those outer suburban areas, in their relatively modest 3-bedroom homes, would go back to Puckle Street, Moonee Ponds [in Melbourne] to do their shopping, let alone Double Bay or Oxford Street [in Sydney]. Those areas themselves weren't growing, the inner-suburban areas. No one really wanted to live in the inner suburbs, we were having depopulation, particularly in Melbourne. All the bulge was happening in the outer-suburbs. The facilities were going to have to be built for those people in the outer suburbs. Those facilities were not high streets because we had this new package called the shopping centre.[10]

By the mid 1980s, the retail property industry largely accepted that its growth had coincided with "economic casualties." R. O. Powys, the national director of the Building Owners and Managers Association (BOMA), expressed a view representative of industry figures both in Australia and internationally when he argued this was true of "any process of change in which more efficient methods overtake outdated procedures." He suggested that the modernisation of shopping had "diverted trade from all prior existing forms of retailing," particularly city centres and the older high street shopping precincts. The corner store, he said, had "virtually disappeared." He declared that shopping centres had been largely welcomed by shoppers, retailers and investors.[11] This was, in many cases, true, but it did not prevent residents, consumers, small retailers, planners and local councils voicing concerns about their impact. A meeting of independent traders in 1969 in Ashburton, Victoria, noted that "retail trade along each side of arterial roads in every city and every town in Australia was threatened by a diminishing flow of actual shopping traffic." It noted that the car contributed "to most of the difficulties," and that this was a problem shared in "all affluent societies with a large 'car' population."[12]

Recognition of this conundrum led Australian planners to once again look for solutions overseas, where pedestrian malls were being established by closing streets to car traffic. This was seen as a way to revitalize inner-city cores, reduce traffic congestion and improve amenity – all with the aim of encouraging increased pedestrian activity.[13] These ideas had emerged in Western Europe, and were popularised after World War Two, particularly in the reconstruction of West German cities.[14] By the mid 1960s, there were around 60 pedestrian malls in Germany, which received plaudits from planners internationally for its innovative approach.[15] As the country's first suburban shopping centres were developed, the creation of pedestrian malls with clusters of specialty shops, entertainment areas and restaurants was further encouraged in an effort to stave off the problems facing downtown America.[16] Robertson notes that Americans, in turn, copied the Europeans, arguing that the latter's vibrant street life and prosperous urban retail precincts had long been a point of envy amongst city officials in the United States.[17] Around 150 pedestrian malls were established in America in the 1960s and 1970s.[18] Victor Gruen was again a key player, believing that pedestrianisation could revitalise urban cores that had suffered so acutely from the suburban wave that his shopping centres had contributed to. A film about one of his pedestrian malls, *Fresno: A City Reborn*, was shown internationally and was "instrumental in the acceptance of the concept in Australia."[19]

During the 1970s, a number of pedestrian malls were created in Australia's state capitals and regional cities. The concept also spread beyond urban centres. Early examples include the inner Melbourne suburb of Footscray as well as Stawell, a regional town some 230 kilometres north-west of Melbourne. Echoing earlier shopping centre marketing claims that Gruen repeated in *Fresno*, proponents of the Stawell mall declared that it would make shopping "a pleasure rather than a chore … [attracting] shoppers from as wide a region as possible."[20] By the late 1970s, pedestrian malls were a topical planning consideration in many Australian municipalities.[21] Around 60 were eventually built, closing off high streets in the heart of Australia's capital cities, suburbs and rural towns.

Most pedestrian malls were initially welcomed by retailers and residents, but by the mid 1990s serious questions were being raised about their viability. This echoed concerns that had been emanating from America, even when Australia was first embarking on pedestrianisation schemes.[22] When a pedestrian mall was proposed for Gosford, on the central coast north of Sydney in 1995, one retailer claimed that the concept had been a universal failure. A spokesperson for a small shopping centre adjoining the proposed mall site said that she had "yet to see a mall anywhere in this country that is thriving."[23] In 1996, the *Sydney Morning Herald* declared that, like their counterparts across the country and internationally, "Sydney's suburban malls appear to be dying."[24]

Pedestrian malls proved an underwhelming mechanism for revitalising local retailing in any sustained way. During the 1990s, a number of municipalities across the country reviewed their previous strategies and reopened their high streets to full or partial traffic. *Inside Retailing* argued that this was because "many malls were constructed in dead retail areas to begin with and no attempt was ever made by the municipalities to recruit new retailers or to develop promotions and events to encourage public use."[25] This analysis failed to recognise the active role that councils and retailing groups had played in marketing many local malls. It also glossed over deeper issues: the difficulties pedestrian malls faced were really a story about the competitive strengths of the shopping centre format.[26]

As they grew in size, shopping centres drew more retailers in from the street, including traffic-generating anchors like department stores and supermarkets. Other high street department stores, including local firms that had served communities before the big city stores decentralised, also closed down. Services such as banks, Medicare offices and even post offices moved from the street into shopping centres. The loss of these customer traffic generators undermined the viability of strip shopping precincts, which no longer carried comprehensive mixes of merchandise. Even in the early 1970s, research suggested that merchandise mix, quality of goods and accessibility played a bigger role in shaping shopping patterns than the price of goods.[27] The inclusion of anchor stores and the capacity of unified management to continuously and dynamically curate tenancy mixes to match the needs of the surrounding market were thus a crucial competitive advantage that shopping centres held over high street retail. At the same time, the spread of stand-alone supermarkets forced many grocers in high streets out of business, further eroding the appeal of these retail precincts to shoppers.[28]

In the high street, there was no one individual or group coordinating tenancy mixes to ensure a complementary and cohesive offer for customers, nor to determine the locations of retailers. There was rarely control exerted over the appearance or performance of individual shops, both of which impacted on the tone and drawing power of the precinct. This had been an important development within the retail property industry. Michael Lonie argues that landlord control over shop fit-outs imposed a degree of professionalism on retailers. In order to attract

> the person going through the common area, the retailer had to be forced to do the fit out that made people want to go into their store … [like] the old moth flying to the light. It forced retailers to really think about their merchandising.[29]

Setting parameters for shop fit-out formed part of the broader responsibility of management to create compelling retail environments. An industry training seminar in 1979 advised trainee managers that

> at all times [the centre] must be sold to the public as being vibrant, alive and popular, thereby reinforcing [the customer's] decision to shop there and make it a shopping habit … we must endeavor to empty her purse … and prevent leakage to local strip shopping areas.[30]

One attendee at the 1969 Ashburton meeting had likened high street shops to "a string of sausages – not very appetizing, all strung together, and wishing they could be separated." Others suggested that lessons needed to be taken from shopping centres themselves: creating compelling social environments, conducting market research to identify the strengths and weaknesses of the precinct, branding and marketing shopping strips to create an identity, ensuring sufficient parking, creating shared standards of presentation, and planning the range of merchandise available across the shopping strip. The managing director of Foodland Stores and one of the organisers of the meeting, H. E. Towers, declared that "the only way to beat a shopping centre is to become a shopping centre."[31] And therein lay the problem.

Even when cars were removed from high streets, ease of pedestrian movement was better in shopping centres because parking was integral to their design, shops could be positioned closer together and on either side of walkways, there were few vacant stores or unplanned gaps in the shopping fabric, and multiple levels could be utilised. As a consequence, there were rarely delays or obstacles for customers to negotiate during their shopping trip.[32] In addition, air-conditioning and protection from the weather made shopping easier and more pleasant, while owners had a strong financial incentive to invest in maintenance and refurbishment of the total retail environment.[33] The imperative to continually invest in rejuvenation was far less pressing amongst public authorities or individual landlords in high streets.

Shopping centres also felt safer. After nightfall, attractively landscaped, tree-lined pedestrian malls with playgrounds and public art became shadowy, unregulated and potentially dangerous thoroughfares, particularly for women.[34] Shopping centres, in contrast, were brightly lit, had few hidden pockets, and were patrolled by private security guards. Their toilets were cleaner and more highly frequented. There were no drug users, transgressive youths (for any extended period of time), public alcohol consumption, vandals or other undesirables. There were no "anti-anchors" or customer deterrents such as methadone clinics. This meant that shopping centres were also not true town centres, because the customers they serviced were a subset of the broader community, identified by marketing through their spending habits.[35] But it made them more comfortable places to shop for much of middle Australia.[36] Some high streets and pedestrian malls have survived and even thrived, particularly where they align with a market segment such as gentrifiers or immigrant communities to which local businesses can position. But the competitive advantages that shopping centres held in terms of convenience, comfort and merchandise mix proved resilient and highly successful foundations for attracting shoppers.

Retail leasing legislation

Retailers are more dependent on location for success than other types of businesses that lease offices or industrial land,[37] and by the 1980s shopping centre firms were fast controlling the supply of the best retail sites in suburban and regional Australia.

Their format worked well for shoppers, while redevelopment provided a mechanism for increasing retail space and market share in retail trade areas. The value firms could extract from this position underpinned their financial performance. Correspondingly, the cost of doing business within them became a critical issue for retailers.[38] Some small operators, and even national chains, began to view their relationship with landlords as adversarial. Quantifying the extent of this is difficult, but there was certainly considerable agitation by retail traders' organisations. Some claimed that the competitive advantages shopping centres held over traditional shopping strips, and the protection they received from planning legislation, had created geographic monopolies. Further, like retail itself, the retail property industry was concentrating through acquisitions and development. Industry and geographic concentration, retailers argued, allowed landlords to charge unaffordable rents and impose inappropriate costs on tenants.[39] Speaking on behalf of such tenants, the Retail Traders' Association of New South Wales claimed that "the balance of power between all but the very large tenants and the landlords has been very much to the detriment of the tenant."[40]

Both retailers and landlords acknowledged that the problems between them usually began with misunderstandings during lease negotiations. Many tenants claimed that they were given misleading information, particularly on matters such as turnover estimates of the centre, the types of businesses they would be competing with, and the potential profitability of their own operation.[41] A survey conducted by the West Australian Shopping Centre Retailers' Association in 1983 claimed that 95 per cent of tenants said they had been given false figures when they signed their leases.[42] Parliamentarians recounted harrowing stories provided by their constituents. In 1980, Victorian Labor MP Cyril Kennedy declared that "these shopping centres are spreading like the measles around Melbourne. People cannot possibly make a living and they eventually lose everything, including their house."[43]

The cost of rents and the scale of their increases was a principal point of contention: some retailers claimed that leases sought to maximise investment returns "without consideration for the viability of tenants."[44] Rents typically included a base-level rent and a percentage of a store's turnover. The industry saw the latter as a reward for the landlord's role in successfully developing and managing a centre, and an ongoing incentive to provide a thriving commercial environment.[45] Some retailers saw it as a tax on success, with one describing it as a "ball and chain" around the necks of small retailers.[46] Leases also included clauses for ongoing rent increases and reviews. These were initially introduced to keep rentals in line with inflation and the rising value of sites,[47] but tenants argued that they had become a means by which the highest possible rent could be extracted from retailers "short of sending them to the wall."[48]

Complaints over steep rent hikes were voiced sporadically in the 1970s,[49] but by the 1980s were widespread. In 1985, the Shopping Centre Tenants Association of Queensland claimed that annual rent increases over the previous four years had averaged close to 20 per cent,[50] and that in 1984 some rents had jumped by as much as 90 per cent.[51] A survey of four Victorian shopping centres in the same year suggested that rents had increased by between 24 per cent and 80 per cent in the preceding twelve months.[52] In Sydney, another survey of four regional shopping centres found that total occupancy costs had increased by between 16 and 26 per cent in twelve months. Almost a fifth claimed to have faced increases in excess of 40 percent.[53] This survey data was self-reported, can't be taken as representative and is difficult to quantify, but rents certainly did increase dramatically and consistently, and many small retailers experienced significant stress as a result. Bill Pratt, Managing Director of the Safeway super-market chain, argued in 1980 that:

> developers, in order to obtain the economics for a centre, find a major retailer and then just see how many small shops can be fitted into the adjacent area … I think it is criminal negligence that some of these small shops are allowed to open in shopping centres when often life-savings go in the first couple of weeks when sales don't even account for the rent …[54]

Entrepreneur Dick Smith declared that small retailers were "working their guts out" for developers.[55] Bob Mathers of the Mathers Shoe chain concurred, claiming that rental levels put small tenants in a situation where they were effectively working for their landlords.[56] A 1985 commercial real estate advertisement in the *Australian Financial Review* traded on this narrative: "Perhaps the nicest aspect of owning a shopping centre is the thought of all those shopkeepers coming to work everyday to make you lots of money."[57] Bob Jameson, executive secretary of the Hardware Retailers' Association of NSW, claimed in 1987 that a new breed of "hungry landlord" driven by short-term investment goals had emerged and was shaping the retail leasing market.[58] By 1990, the Retail Traders' Association of NSW was claiming that Australian rents were the highest of any OECD country,[59] and "substantially higher" than in North America,[60] although this was not surprising given America had far more retail floor space per head of population.

The industry argued that if things were so bad there would be high vacancy rates in shopping centres and difficulties leasing space. In fact, there was rarely a shortage of applicants for tenancies in any major regional shopping centre and vacancy rates across the country were low. Shopping centre consultant, Terry Wimberley, told a Victorian retailing seminar in 1984 that traders who had celebrated a government restriction on further shopping centre development, were now irrationally upset that rentals were climbing in a restricted market of retail space. Ray Powys, national director of BOMA, claimed that Bob Mathers, who was a vocal complainant about high rents, paid the highest rent in Queensland for one of his chain's footwear stores after outbidding other retailers to secure the position. Powys argued that: "You can't bid high to shut out retail competitors and complain at the same time about landlords."[61]

In addition to rent, tenants had to pay "outgoings": a standard industry practice to recover a proportion of operating costs from tenants. However, outgoings were often poorly defined, and some inexperienced retailers signed leases accepting verbal explanations of vague terms such as "all outgoings" without knowing what they really meant.[62] In the 1970s and early 1980s, there were frequent complaints about unexpectedly large outgoing bills with little or no explanation of the expenses they covered.[63] Tenants were said to face "ever-increasing operational expenses" without having "any control over such expenses."[64] There were claims that the estimates of outgoings could "be half or a third of what they actually turn out to be," placing well-planned businesses in financial jeopardy.[65] There were allegations of outgoings covering the cost of centre managers' family cars, public relations lunches, alcohol and entertainment. A department store manager from Central Queensland declared that:

> If I went to our management and asked it to approve expenses like that I'd be thrown out the door. We control expenses very carefully in our company but some centres don't seem to bother because they just pass them on to tenants.[66]

The Queensland Shopping Centre Tenants Association began to prosecute the argument that lease terms effectively indemnified landlords against risk.[67] Landlords, it pointed out, were insured against increases in expenses and running costs through rent reviews.[68] They could pass on maintenance expenses for escalators, lifts and even buildings to tenants, covering themselves for the cost of providing the infrastructure that tenants were leasing from them.[69] And in some centres, tenants paid contributions to sinking funds that were used to finance large, infrequent, future maintenance expenses.[70]

For many retailers, the power inequalities between tenant and landlord came into clearest focus when negotiating the renewal of a lease. Without a right of renewal, they claimed, a coercive lever was always available to the landlord who could refuse to renew a lease, prevent the sale of the business, or impose a steep rent increase on a tenant that wished to continue their occupancy.[71] Bargaining from this position was further constrained by rental clauses attached to turnover that gave landlords access to lessees' sales figures.[72] Retailer organisations claimed that this allowed landlords to set rental levels by the tenant's capacity to pay rather than by the value of the site. Tenants, they said, were thus trapped, forced to "pay the increase or just walk away from their business."[73] Hundreds of thousands of dollars could be invested in goodwill, fixtures, fittings and stock.[74] The initial fit-out or refurbishments required by landlords to standardise the quality of the shopping centre environment might not have been amortised, especially if leases were only three years in duration.[75] Goodwill with shoppers could be difficult to transfer beyond a centre's walls.[76] All this created a distinct power differential between small traders and landlords, especially with shopping centres having achieved relative dominance in many trade areas, and when there was a higher demand for tenancies in shopping centres than there was supply.[77]

Much of the contest over shopping centre leases involved a debate about the nature of the shopping centre itself and how this affected the rights and responsibilities of landlord and tenant. For example, in the late 1970s, Keith Foster, the group general manager of the Sussan fashion chain, argued that tenants should not pay for the advertising costs of shopping centres. The value of the landlord's asset, he pointed out, was directly related to the number of people who visited it. Promotion was therefore the landlord's responsibility because it increased shopper visits, which the landlord monetised by selling retail space to tenants.[78] In contrast, Donald Burnett, a former Director at Lend Lease, likened such outgoings to residential rates: just as the rate-payer contributed to the total operating costs of the municipality, including contributions to the management costs of council, so, too, the tenant contributed to the running costs of the shopping centre environment of which it was a part.[79]

These claims revolved around a "unique" commercial relationship. The Queensland Committee for Inquiry into Shopping Centre Leases noted in 1982 that "a successful shopping complex requires the funds and management expertise supplied by the owner, combined with the retailing expertise of each tenant."[80] Each benefited from the other's performance, with the tenants required to comply with the directives of management if they wished to profit from its expertise. BOMA argued that tenants who did not accept these "special circumstances of shopping centres should not seek tenancies in them."[81] For tenants it was probably less a matter of acceptance than a belief that they were owed a greater share of the collaboration.

The retail property industry blamed the flood of complaints on underperforming, amateur retailers facing difficulties in a sluggish economy. Ron Farrow, president of the National Council of Shopping Centres, said that there were simply "too many small, untrained shopkeepers."[82] The poor management of their business, lack of planning and ignorance of their lease agreements, it was argued, led to protests about unfair conditions.[83] Rents only became "outrageous" after poorly researched businesses found they could not pay the market value rent that they had agreed upon when signing their con-tract.[84] Figures in the industry argued that they did their best to provide infor-mation up front, and that complainants were invariably those "who failed to examine their lease obligations as thoroughly as they were advised".[85]

There was also an acknowledgement that the industry's rapid growth had resulted in some poor practice. There was simply not enough accumulated experience to appoint capable shopping centre managers in all locations. Nor had the industry professionalised sufficiently to offer accredited training schemes to improve the quality of candidates. Bill Humble, the president of the Queensland branch of BOMA, explained that:

> the industry expanded like a mushroom and managers came out of the woodwork and were chucked in to run centres without proper training. Well some of them haven't been good and some have been plain bad. We had to do some housekeeping, like everybody else.

Inexperience was also an issue among small retailers. Commentators noted in the 1980s that many people entered small business retailing as a means of employment, rather than as an entrepreneurial endeavour. This resulted in a heavy "concentration of inexperienced business people" in the sector.[86] The Trethowan Report, resulting from an investigation of shopping centres in Western Australia, suggested that many small tenants had "little or no background in either business or retailing."[87] Some tenants complaining about their leasing conditions had never thoroughly read their lease.[88] Others planned poorly, did not accurately project their expenses, were undercapitalised, or misjudged their capacity to recoup establishment costs within the term of their lease.[89] There was a tendency not to seek professional advice to clarify issues, and complaints were invariably made after leases had been signed.[90]

Retail trade associations in each state continued to air allegations of exploitation and press for change, causing considerable alarm as well as some reflection within the industry. In 1980, general manager of AMP, Alan Coates, claimed that

> too much attention has been paid to the development of propositions acceptable to the major retail groups, at the expense of the smaller specialty shops, where high rents have been imposed in an endeavour to bring the developments to an acceptable level of overall return.

This, he suggested, had created a hostile and active small business lobby, that had caught the ear of politicians who were likely to overreact with restrictive legislation.[91] Other figures lamented the industry's handling of public relations.[92] Even retailers themselves tended to be philosophically opposed to legislative intervention.[93] But the issues being aired coincided with a developing governmental interest in the protection and promotion of small business, and from the late 1970s onwards, government inquiries into retail leasing were held in all the mainland states.[94]

These inquiries all reported significant issues but noted the complexity of regulating a market relationship in which tenants chose to enter into contracts. Most inquiries initially endorsed voluntary industry codes of conduct. These were universally unsuccessful in stemming complaints and legislation was introduced in all states, beginning with Queensland in 1984. Western Australia followed in 1985, South Australia and Victoria in 1986. New South Wales introduced its Retail Tenancy Act in 1994.[95] The Acts varied and have been amended over time, but their initial intent was to moderate the power differentials between landlords and tenants. The Retail Leases Act (NSW) of 1994 was a culmination of the first wave of state legislation, and its provisions give an indication of the general tenor of legislation elsewhere.[96]

The NSW Act required lessees to be advised in writing of all pertinent facts via a disclosure statement prior to signing a lease.[97] Disclosure statements included details about all outgoings, which if not listed, could not be recovered.[98] A simplified standard lease was devised to aid clarity. The Act also outlawed key-money payments and ratchet rents that could only ever scale upwards. Leases were set to a minimum of five years to allow businesses the chance to recoup their investments and to provide some security of tenure. Outgoings had to be substantiated with audited reports or receipts.[99] Retailers operating within shopping centres were given safeguards ensuring privacy of turnover information, disclosure of promotional spending and some protection regarding changes to core trading hours. A Registrar of Retail Tenancy Disputes was created to provide a cost-effective forum for mediation and dispute resolution.[100] This proved highly successful in resolving disputes relatively cheaply and efficiently.[101]

These significant protections slowed but did not end complaints about retail tenancies in Australian shopping centres. In 1997, an inquiry by the Federal Government's Standing Committee on Industry, Science and Resources suggested there was a pervasive sense that "a 'war' [was] going on in shopping centres around Australia."[102] Later inquiries were less damning, but noted ongoing issues, as well as continued misperceptions about the nature of trading in a shopping centre. In 2007, a report by the Australian Government's Productivity Commission noted that:

> Many of the perceptions of shopping centres' 'misuse' of negotiating power stem from a lack of understanding or acceptance that the business model of a retail shopping centre is fundamentally different from traditional retail strips. Retailers who sign a lease in a large managed shopping centre without realising that the 'rules of the game' are very different, are at a disadvantage and can be seriously disappointed, if not financially devastated. Retailers who do understand the shopping centre model, and work within it, can prosper. Well managed shopping centres can unify a large and divergent group of tenants and help centre trade. In return, tenants in centres generally pay higher rents and outgoing expenses than similar tenants in a shopping strip and forego some independence in operating their business.[103]

Inquiries into shopping centre leasing generally acknowledged this context. Resulting legislation sought to establish more equitable bargaining positions for small retail tenants, to place constraints on the ways in which landlords could leverage power differentials to their advantage, and to introduce "machinery to minimise and resolve conflict."[104] Legislation has been continually reviewed and amended since the early 1980s – by 2007 there were around 700 pages of highly prescriptive, increasingly diverse legislation across state jurisdictions.[105] Some legislation overturned previous legislation to return to conditions that had been imposed by legislation before that.[106] All this served to demonstrate the difficulty of balancing power differentials in a market with deeply invested stakeholders, with entwined but competing interests, operating on a vast range of scales. Legislation and supportive infrastructure such as tenancy tribunals helped to mitigate conflict, as did the increasing professionalisation of the retail and retail property sectors. As the focus of the Commission's inquiry indicated, however conflict (and conflicting interests) remained a constant presence as shopping centres continued to evolve, grow and spread in the first decade of the twenty-first century.

Notes

1 *IR*, 22 July 1974, 5.
2 *IR*, 29 July 1974, 1.
3 Australian Institute of Urban Studies, "Perth Metropolitan Region," 7.
4 *IR*, 12 August 1974, 5.
5 Westfield Holdings Ltd, *Westfield Story*, 52, 56; Sammartino and Van Ruth, "Westfield Group," 312–13.
6 *GSJWA*, 20 January 1960, 14.
7 Kiel, "Retailing and Shopping Centre Development in Queensland," 1.
8 *IR*, 9 July 1984, 1.
9 Stimson, "Summary of Policy Issues," 1.
10 Author interview with Tony Dimasi.
11 Powys, "Economic Impact Statements," 71. For examples of arguments about the inevitably of change in the United States, see, Howard, *From Main Street to Mall*, 7.
12 *GSJWA*, January 1966, 16.
13 Town & Country Planning Board, "Pedestrian Malls," 3.
14 Orski, "Practical Experience," 42; Roberts, *Pedestrian Precincts*, 16.
15 Monheim, "Pedestrianization in German Towns," 30.
16 Rubenstein, *Pedestrian Malls,* 15–17; Orski, "Practical Experience," 42.
17 Robertson, "Status of the Pedestrian Mall," 250–1.
18 Carr, Francis, Rivlin and Stone, *Public Space*, 72. See also Schuyler, *City Transformed*, 35–58.
19 Flannigan, "Life for Traditional Shopping Streets," 283.
20 Howells, "Stawell's Pedestrian Mall."
21 Town & Country Planning Board, "Pedestrian Malls"; Burrows, "Practical Design."
22 Flannigan, "Life for Traditional Shopping Streets," 283.
23 *IR*, 1 May 1995, 5.
24 *SMH*, 6 August 1996, 8.
25 *IR*, 2 February 1998.
26 *SMH*, 6 August 1996, 8.
27 Dawson and Murray, "Karrinyup Shopping Centre," 59.
28 *IR*, 2 July 1973, 3.
29 Author interview with Michael Lonie.
30 Haselhurst, "Leasing Newtown Mall."
31 *GSJWA*, January 1966, 16.
32 Flannigan, "Life for Traditional Shopping Streets," 287.
33 Author interview with John Schroder, 4 March 2015.
34 Carr, Francis, Rivlin and Stone, *Public Space*, 102; Antoniou "Planning for Pedestrians," 237.
35 Cohen, "From Town Center to Shopping Center," 1059; Sandercock, "From Main Street to Fortress," 28; Whyte, *City*, 208; Webb, *City Square*, 206.
36 White and Sutton, "Social Planning," 67–68; Voyce, "Privatisation of Public Property," 251.
37 *RT*, March 1958, 44; Australian Government Productivity Commission, "Market for Retail Tenancy Leases," 89.
38 CMA, Box 340, Critical issues: Specialty store retailing, February 1981, 37.
39 Crosby, "Evaluation of Policy Implications," 8–9.

40 Coote, "President's Report."
41 *IR*, 21 April 1980, 11; *IR*, 13 October 1980, 13; *IR*, 22 August 1983, 3.
42 *IR*, 22 August 1983, 3.
43 *IR*, 20 October 1980, 7.
44 *RT*, October/ November/December 1984, 1.
45 Burnett, *Shopping Centre Management*, 5; *IR*, 29 June 1981, 3; *VSCAN*, September 1981, 3.
46 *IR*, 22 September 1980, 7.
47 Burnett, *Shopping Centre Management*, 5–8.
48 *IR*, 9 September 1985, 5.
49 *IR*, 27 January 1975, 4.
50 *IR*, 16 September 1985, 7.
51 *IR*, 27 May 1985, 7.
52 *IR*, 7 October 1985, 1.
53 *IR*, 21 October 1985, 1.
54 *IR*, 24 March 1980, 17.
55 *IR*, 7 April 1980, 6.
56 *IR*, 21 April 1980, 11.
57 *RT*, July 1985, 3.
58 *IR*, 23 March 1987, 3.
59 *RT*, March 1991, 1.
60 Coote, "President's Report."
61 *IR*, 12 November 1984, 3.
62 *IR*, 22 June 1981, 16.
63 *IR*, 21 April 1980, 11; *IR*, 25 July 1983, 12.
64 *IR*, 13 October 1980, 14.
65 *IR*, 25 July 1983, 12.
66 *IR*, 16 December 1985, 6.
67 *IR*, 7 July 1986, 7.
68 Paine and Dennler, "Review of Lease," 63.
69 *IR*, 14 April 1980, 4; *IR*, 21 April 1980, 7.
70 *IR*, 7 July 1986, 7. The Queensland Committee of Inquiry into Shopping Complex Leasing Practices in 1981 recommended against outgoings being used to pay for centre management, structural repairs and major renovations.
71 *IR*, 1 March 1982, 6; *The West Coast Retailer*, August 1986, 9.
72 *RT*, January 1989, 1; author interview with Mark Paterson, 9 June 2017.
73 *IR*, 28 April 1986, 9.
74 *IR*, 21 May 1984, 12.
75 *IR*, 11 August 1986, 8–9; *IR*, 31 August 1987, 12.
76 *IR*, 11 August 1986, 8–9.
77 Carkagis, *Law of Retail Leasing*, 4.
78 *IR*, 17 April 1978, 8.
79 Burnett, *Shopping Centre Management*, 11.
80 *Independent Retailer of W.A.*, Jan/ Feb 1982, 13–15; BOMA, Submission to the Clarke Inquiry into Commercial Tenancy Agreements (Western Australia), 7 October 1983, 9–10.
81 BOMA, Submission to the Clarke Inquiry, 12.
82 *IR*, 29 September 1980, 12.
83 *IR*, 16 August 1982, 3; *IR*, 24 March 1980, 17.

84 *IR*, 16 August 1982, 4.
85 *IR*, 13 September 1982, 11.
86 Watson, "Commercial Tenancies Legislation."
87 Cited in BOMA, Submission to the Clarke Inquiry, 15.
88 *RT*, July 1989, 4.
89 *IR*, 5 May 1980, 15; *IR*, 1 March 1982, 10.
90 *IR*, 5 May 1980, 15.
91 *IR*, 15 September 1980, 10.
92 *IR*, 21 April 1980, 11.
93 Tarlo, "The Great Shop Lease Controversy," 26; Taylor, "Introductory Lecture – Sydney," 40.
94 Williams, *What Is the Problem*, 6.
95 Bradbrook and Croft, *Commercial Tenancy Law* (1st edn), 351, 370–1; Bradbrook and Croft, *Commercial Tenancy Law in Australia* (2nd edn), 519–20, 557–8, 575–6.
96 Author interview with Lexia Wilson and Mark Paterson, 9 June 2017.
97 Eakin, "New Retail Leases Regime," 63.
98 Rawlinson, *Commercial Tenancy Disputes in New South Wales*, 15, 19; Cameron, "Pitfalls for Purchasers," 62.
99 Eakin, "New Retail Leases Regime," 63.
100 J. H. Murray (Member for Drummoyne), Retail Leases Bill 2nd Reading, NSW Parliamentary Debates, Legislative Assembly, 13 May 1994, 2641.
101 Author interview with Lexia Wilson, 9 June 2017.
102 Australian Parliament House of Representatives Standing Committee on Industry, Science and Technology , "Finding a Balance," 15.
103 Australian Government Productivity Commission, "Market for Retail Tenancy Leases," xxii.
104 Clarke, An Inquiry into Commercial Tenancy Agreements," 8.
105 Australian Government Productivity Commission, "Market for Retail Tenancy Leases," xvi.
106 Author interview with Lexia Wilson and Mark Paterson.

Epilogue

In the nineteenth century, the rise of the department store aggregated the fashion-related aspects of buying and selling and then extended the scale and scope of their activities to become one-stop-shops for general merchandise. Everyday food and household shopping were left to markets and specialty shops, which also delivered daily supplies to individual households. As cities expanded and suburbs grew in size, high streets evolved, providing simple services and daily shopping within walking distance of houses and public transport. In the city centre, the department stores maintained a focus on style, fashion and big-ticket items. The private motorcar fundamentally disrupted this arrangement. With mobile consumers and retail formats designed for their convenience, it became possible to reunite the two forms of consumption – food and fashion – in a new type of modern marketplace.[1]

Shopping centres in Australia followed quickly on the heels of post-war developments in the United States, and echoed its tripartite neighbourhood, community and regional hierarchy. With customer-attracting anchor stores, weather protection, air-conditioning and parking stations, they offered a more convenient, efficient and comfortable shopping environment than the alternatives available at the time. Regional shopping centres matched the range of goods previously only available in the city; neighbourhood centres traded on the strength of supermarkets, providing everyday goods for nearby residents. In doing so, they met the needs of communities as well as the interests of the country's biggest retailers that used shopping centres as vehicles for national expansion. As the market matured and new retail formats were introduced, shopping centres proliferated and the larger complexes expanded their function. Discount department stores, specialty retail chains, franchise operations, multiplex cinemas and food courts all enhanced the shopping centre offer.

The location and growth of shopping centres were framed by local planning regimes. The Australian balance gave more freedom to private enterprise than was generally the case in European retail development, but placed more constraints on it than the laissez-faire American approach. This is reflected in retail floor space per capita. Australia has more than Europe and less than America.[2] Tighter planning also resulted in Australian retail geographies being more concentrated than in the United States. Big retailers and developers complained about the difficulties of acquiring sites and the onerous approval processes required to get them rezoned. But once built, large shopping centres were offered a considerable degree of protection from new, rival developments. By providing barriers to entry, planning regimes made retail property investment more secure than in America where there was no guarantee a new mall would not be built nearby at any time in the future. It also encouraged the redevelopment of existing sites. Australian sub-regional and regional shopping centres have been steadily growing in size for 40 years.

Australian shopping centres were also highly efficient and productive. Developers learned early to get the most out of space, because they were building in established suburban areas where land was more expensive than the greenfield sites used in America.[3] This was one of the competitive advantages Westfield and Lend Lease took with them to other countries.[4] In Australia, too, the decline of department stores has been offset by the presence of supermarkets and DDSs in regional shopping centres. Their integration into tenancy mixes meant that Australian regional and sub-regional shopping centres offered both non-discretionary everyday shopping and "leisurely" consumer experiences. This was a key Australian innovation and a pillar of the industry's success:[5]

> Australians have got a very good formula, because shopping centres are all-encompassing. You have got cinemas, you have got DDSs, you have got Myer [department stores], you have got supermarkets. It is all encompassed in shopping centres. You know … cinemas, restaurant precincts, libraries. Over in America, it is quite a bit different. Supermarkets are always free-standing. DDSs are always free-standing. The [American shopping] centres are basically just fashion houses and do not encompass [a comprehensive offer]. The recipe in Australia is the best recipe in the world.[6]

This recipe resulted in shopping centres with broad, cross-class appeal, continuing a long tradition in Australian retailing. In the nineteenth and early twentieth century, Australia produced few truly upmarket stores of any size. Georges in Melbourne and David Jones in Sydney were exceptions, but most department stores catered to a middle market. These still employed theatrical elements to provoke engagement and stimulate desire, but many stores mixed this with fairly basic open-selling display techniques (Figure 1.3). Competition on price had been a feature of the city stores' advertising campaigns since at least the 1930s. In Melbourne, Myer told female shoppers that "shopping could be sophisticated without being extravagant."[7] Similar positioning was continued in post-war shopping centres, to which department store firms like Myer, Boans and Grace Bros. were significant contributors. Marketers from these firms entreated shoppers to "step into tomorrow," in casual clothes, to a new type of social space.[8] This spoke to shifting cultural mores in post-war Australia, as "middle-class aspirations such as the car, the house, the club and the credit card swamped the old working-class ones of rent, beer, the union and the races."[9] The changing sensibilities of the Australian middle class have subsequently been reflected in shopping centre refurbishments and tenancy mixes across their history. As Tony Dimasi notes:

> the recurring theme is the flexibility and adaptability of Australian shopping centres … Every step of the way, they might have come across a bit of a rough patch but they adapt and they change. This is exactly what has happened and what continues to happen to this day … they're going to look ever-better and have ever-more options, integrate the open-air ever-increasingly with the enclosed mall.[10]

In recent years, the introduction of international retailers to shopping centres again demonstrated a capacity to adapt and to leverage emerging opportunities. As with the Australian chains before them, shopping centres offered global brands like fashion giants Zara, Uniqlo and H&M, and German supermarket chain Aldi, sites in any desired municipality across the country. In doing so, they reduced barriers to entry in Australia. The fashion chains have located in city centres and major regional shopping centres. Aldi, as a daily food provider, is far more widely spread. Like the DDS chains in the 1970s, it initially pursued stand-alone development before adapting and taking shopping centre tenancies to accelerate expansion.

Their flexibility, and the importance of location in retailing, have made shopping centres less vulnerable to disruption than retailers, including the big department stores. The latter's past decisions to sell their substantial shopping centre portfolios mark a momentous fork in their respective roads. Suburban shopping centres funnelled car-driving customers to tenants, but these traders could be remixed as new retail innovations emerged, as services and entertainment operators sought access to customers and as consumer tastes and spending power shifted. At every step, retailers had to respond to competition, while shopping centres absorbed the improved performance this produced. Global fashion chains hold competitive advantages over national retailers and department stores on scale, branding, supply chain management, analytics and vertical integration. They use highly efficient in-house design and manufacturing processes and global supply chains to deliver compelling and constantly changing product ranges to customers.[11] Shopping centres provided sites for them in Australia, gaining new traffic-driving anchors, rental income and marketing cache.[12] Local traders, in contrast, faced sales leakage to new competitors – including to those operating within the same centre.

The shopping centre even proved flexible enough to function without the car. Growing inner-urban populations brought a reinvestment in inner-city retail in the early twenty-first century. Shopping centres resembling larger, more streamlined, less ornate nineteenth-century arcades were introduced to urban environments. Customers mostly arrived by foot and public transport. When the Emporium – a "seven-level shopping utopia" with 225 stores – launched in the heart of Melbourne in 2014, press coverage reported that glamour had returned to the former Myer department store site.[13] Like other centres built in Australia's capital cities, it catered to international brands seeking CBD sites as well as Australian designers and chain retailers.[14] The press suggested that urban shopping centres like these "breathed new life" into cities, raising "the calibre of retail."[15] They also marked another step in the privatisation of the city proper and, as McDonald's had found with suburban food courts, showed that the inner logics of the shopping centre format were transferable competitive advantages. Curated collections of retailers in a single site, under unified management, with air-conditioning and protection from the weather, were effective in urban cores as well as the suburbs.

Shopping centres have also managed to integrate online retailing, which was initially touted as a major drain on bricks-and-mortar retailing. E-commerce was more accessible, potentially more convenient, and had an unlimited product range. Monolithic physical structures were immovable and had to draw customers in. Online reached out, found customers in their homes, during their commutes, and even in their workplaces. In sharp contrast to the battle physical stores had faced extending trading hours, online never closed. Virtual retailers targeted niche market segments and produced deep analytic data that enabled them to do so. Where the financial model of the shopping centre relied on retailers paying high fixed costs in rents, online retail had low occupancy costs and could therefore offer cheaper prices.[16]

E-commerce produced a brief period of high anxiety in the retail industry, especially as it arrived in force in Australia during the global financial crisis. But it also encouraged reflection and incentivised innovation. Physical retailers incorporated online into their existing operations more effectively, creating multi-channel formats that offered the benefits of both worlds. Regional shopping centres also adapted, extending their entertainment and leisure offerings to create more experiential environments. Sophisticated restaurant food mixes, improved ambience and openness to the street were notable examples of this trend. By 2018, 10 per cent of all retail sales in Australia were made online, but this included sales to the online channels of traditional retailers, many of which still held locations in shopping centres.[17] Online retailing thus helped to clarify the identity of physical stores and shopping environments, bringing a reassertion of shopping's social dimension: the experience of interacting with other people; the thrill and excitement of engaging with products displayed to entice and tempt; the hedonistic combination of food, entertainment, shopping and leisure.[18]

However, a corollary of Gruen and Smith's observation that marketplaces are shaped by the historical contexts within which they arise, is that they are also all transient. As a former Woolworths executive noted in 1996:

> All forms of retail have a circle, a shelf-life and they get to the point where they have got to change or call it quits. You get a format and it works and you might have it for a decade, you might have it for two decades, but something will change which is outside your control … you just have to change.[19]

The department store is currently under siege from sophisticated, large-scale operators in every product category that define its remaining individual departments. The shopping centre has surpassed it as a one-stop shop. In Australia, the three DDS chains have never all been successful at the same time,[20] and together with the remaining traditional department stores, face consolidation in the near future.[21] Shopping centres, too, face ongoing challenges. The extraordinary expansion in physical scale and rental income achieved across the industry over the past 60 years may not continue. Increasing populations and urban density suggest the ongoing viability of shopping centres for some time, but growth might be more incremental than exponential in the future.

The fortunes of retailers are directly linked to a country's economy and the employment prospects of its people: retail sales depend on spending power and confidence. During the global financial crisis, discretionary spending materially slowed. People decided that they didn't need so much stuff, or didn't need to replace it so quickly. The two post-war booms produced cultures of abundance in Australia. But this is not how the world necessarily operates. In most places, in most times, things are much harder. As many young people in Australia can testify today, each generation does not automatically grow richer and more prosperous than their parents.[22] How much will these Australians be spending in middle age? Shut out of the property market. Working in precarious casual employment. Forced to save more for an ever-receding retirement during which they will be still be paying rent. The future of work in Australia has deep implications for the value of multi-billion-dollar, inter-generational retail property investments. As does the country's health. The COVID-19 pandemic challenged the security and profitability of shopping centres like no other disruption in their history. The pandemic will provide a new impetus for online innovation that is likely to overturn many established practices and customs, including in retailing.

Consumer choices are also conditioned by values. It is becoming clearer to more people, that in a climate-changing world, the cost of what we buy extends far beyond the price tag. This may be an elite preoccupation at the moment, but the discussion has started and the problems that sparked it are not going away. In 2017, a television series on the publicly funded Australian Broadcasting Corporation, *War on Waste*, attracted more than 3.8 million viewers. A further 3.3 million tuned in for its second series in 2018. One report claimed that the show caused changes in the consumption practices of around 20 per cent of Australian adults, as well as sustainability initiatives in hundreds of businesses.[23] Shifts like these carry across to shopping behaviour. In recent years, farmers' markets have seen a revival in Australian cities. Like traditional markets, they link buyers, sellers and producers far more simply than rationalised supermarket systems. Other types of direct selling where buyers have a sense of the producer, their processes and ethics, are also becoming more popular, whether online or through local markets. Shopping centres seek to incorporate these kinds of "authentic" experiences through pop-up food fairs, weekend markets and children's garden projects. They are also becoming greener in their operation.[24]

Again this shows a capacity to adapt, but there may be other retail forms that arise with more organic connections to sustainability principles.

In the mid 1990s, when asked what the future held for retailing in Australia, former Managing Director of Woolworths, Theo Kelly, reflected:

> I wouldn't like to say what is going to happen. But fifty years ago, who would have thought of shopping centres? The idea of plonking a piece of [developed] land out of the city on its own, people thought you were mad. Heaven knows what it will be when you are my age.[25]

Future Australian shoppers might find themselves in ever-larger, self-contained, replicable, privatised cities in which all units of space are measured for productivity. Alternatively, they might find something a little more traditional in which retailing is less standardised, shoppers less surveilled, time slower, and some spaces left unproductive.[26] In what may well be a socially fractured, less democratic, more densely populated future under greater stress from the weather, the first scenario would extend current retail property logics with additional levels of security and interiority. The second responds to these rising external forces with spaces built from the ground up by communities around ethics of sustainability, small-scale production and local cultural expression. These are not mass-distribution formats and are appealing for that reason. Shopping cities, in contrast, house a great variety of mass-market retailers, but are enormously expensive to build and run. Investors require returns. Shoppers have to be willing to pay for the product. In Australia, shopping centres diversified in response to the internet threat, improving ambience and adding additional layers of services, food and entertainment. This improved their appeal but may dilute their productivity. Their own history shows that not all leisure activities can be monetised. It's probable, too, that people do not want them to be. This all creates space for innovation and the potential for new shopping formats that meet the needs of an ever-changing market. It is a challenge that has animated retailers for centuries.

Notes

1 My thanks to Beverley Kingston for these points.
2 Shopping Centre Council of Australia, www.scca.org.au/industry-information/key-facts.
3 Sammartino and Van Ruth, "Westfield Group," 313.
4 Author interview with Jack Rich.
5 Author interview with Brian Hynes; Michael Lloyd; John Schroder.
6 Author interview with Graham Terry.
7 Kingston, *Basket, Bag and Trolley*, 54, 66.
8 *Torch*, 20 October 1965, n.p.
9 McGregor, *Class in Australia*, 156.
10 Author interview with Tony Dimasi.
11 Sammartino, "Shopkeepers of the World Unite."

12 Author interview with Brian Hynes, 2 March 2015.
13 *HS*, 28 March 2014, 57; *HS*, 16 April 2014, 5.
14 *AFR*, 17 April 2014, 44.
15 *SMH*, 20 February 2010, 20; *SMH*, 26 June 2010, 20.
16 On the competitive advantages of online shopping, see Stobart, *Spend, Spend, Spend*, 232–5.
17 Australia Post, "Inside Australian Online Shopping," 7.
18 Author interview with Brian Hynes.
19 SLNSW, MLOH 451, Nos. 28 and 29, Jenny Hudson interview with Bill Dean, 26 August 1996, transcript, 6, 14.
20 Bailey, "Absorptive Capacity."
21 *SMH*, 2–3 November 2019, Business Section, 4.
22 Rayner, *Generation Less*.
23 Downes, Williams, Calder and Dominish, "Impact of the ABC's *War on Waste*," 5.
24 Author interview with Mark Fookes, 6 November 2014.
25 SLNSW, MLOH 451, No. 61, Jenny Hudson interview with Sir Theo Kelly, ca. 1996, transcript, 17.
26 For a discussion on consumerism, sustainability and the future, see Trentmann, *Empire of Things*, 682–90.

Bibliography

Oral history interviewees

Helen Bakewell, Alan Briggs, Greg Chubb, Richard Clarke, Milton Cockburn, Tony Dimasi, Mort Dowling, Mark Fookes, Steve Gosper, Peter Holland, Bryan Hynes, Neil Ingham, Reg Jebb, Craig Kimberley, Michael Lloyd, Michael Lonie, Graeme Maher, Bruce McIntosh, Ian Newton, Mark Paterson, Jack Ritch, Simon Rumbold, Guy Russo, John Schroder, Carol Schwartz, Andrew Scott, Graham Terry, Peter Wilkinson, Lexia Wilson, Craig Woolford

Newspapers and periodicals

Advertiser
Age
Australian
Australian Business (AB)
Australian Financial Review (AFR)
Australian Retailing (AR)
Australian Women's Weekly (AWW)
Bankstown Observer (BO)
BOMA Bulletin
BOMA (NSW) News
Building, Lighting, Engineering (BLE)
Business Review Weekly (BRW)
Canberra Times (CT)
Courier-Mail (CM)
Daily Telegraph (DT)
Discount Store News
Foodweek
Grocers and Storekeepers' Journal of WA (GSJWA)
Guardian
Herald
Independent Retailer of W.A.
Inside Retailing (IR)
Journal of the Retailers' Association of NSW (JRTANSW)
Manly Daily (MD)

North-East Leader
North Shore Times
North West Telegraph
Northern District Times (NDT)
Property
Retail Merchandiser (RM)
Retail Trader (RT)
Retail World (RW)
Reuters News
Shopping Centre News (SCN)
St. George and Sutherland Shire Leader (SGSSL)
Standard (Warrnambool)
Sun
Sun-Herald (SH)
Sunday Telegraph (ST)
Sydney Morning Herald (SMH)
Torch
Victorian Shopping Centres Association News (VSCAN)
West Australian (WA)
West Coast Retailer

Books, articles and chapters

ACIL Australia. "Trading Hours in the Australian Capital Territory." Canberra, 1991.

Alexander, Andrew, Dawn Nell, Adrian R. Bailey and Gareth Shaw. "The Co-Creation of a Retail Innovation: Shoppers and the Early Supermarket in Britain." *Enterprise & Society* 10, no. 3 (2009): 529–58.

Alexander, Andrew, and Simon Phillips. "Retail Innovation and Shopping Practices: Consumers' Reactions to Self-Service Retailing." *Environment and Planning A* 40, no. 9 (2008): 2204–21.

Alexander, David. *Retailing in England during the Industrial Revolution.* London: Athlone Press, 1970.

Allan, Andrew. "Marion: A Study of a Super-Regional Centre and Its Impact on Adelaide." *Urban Policy and Research* 16, no. 2 (1998): 117–30.

Altman, Dennis. *Rehearsals for Change: Politics and Culture in Australia.* Perth: Australian Research Institute, 2004.

Anon. "Cato, Frederick John (1858–1935)." *Australian Dictionary of Biography.* Melbourne: Melbourne University Publishing, 1979.

Anon. "Hammerson PLC." In *International Directory of Company Histories.* Detroit: St. James Press, 2012.

Anon. "The Supermarket Diet." *Nation*, 16 January 1960: 17–19.

Antoniou, James. "Planning for Pedestrians." In *Urban Transportation: Perspectives and Prospects*, edited by Herbert S. Levinson and Robert A. Weant, 231–40. Westport, CT: Eno Foundation for Transportation, 1982.

Architectural Record. *Design for Modern Merchandising: Stores, Shopping Centers, Showrooms.* New York: F.W. Dodge, 1954.

Armstrong, R.W., and C. Ong. "Deregulation of Trading Hours: Evidence from Western Australia." *International Business Journal* 8, no. 1 (1989): 51–60.

Arrow, Michelle. *Friday on Our Minds: Popular Culture in Australia since 1945*. Sydney: University of New South Wales Press, 2009.

Ashton, Paul. "Suburban Sydney." *Sydney Journal* 1, no. 3 (2008): 36–50.

Ashton, Paul, Jennifer Cornwall and Annette Salt. *Sutherland Shire: A History*. Sydney: University of New South Wales Press, 2006.

Athique, Adrian Mabbott, and Douglas Hill. "Multiplex Cinemas and Urban Redevelopment in India." *Media International Australia* 124 (2007): 108–18.

Atkinson, Bruce. "Business Improvement in Traditional Shopping Centres: A Component of Townscape Improvement Programs." Melbourne: Townscape Advisory Service, Ministry for Planning and Environment, 1985.

Australia Post. "Inside Australian Online Shopping: 2019 Ecommerce Industry Report." Melbourne: Australia Post, 2019. https://auspost.com.au/content/dam/auspost_corp/media/documents/inside-australian-online-shopping-ecommerce-report.pdf.

Australian Government Productivity Commission. "The Market for Retail Tenancy Leases in Australia." Belconnen, ACT.: Productivity Commission, 2007.

Australian Institute of Urban Studies. "Perth Metropolitan Region Retail Shopping Survey." Perth: Australian Institute of Urban Studies, 1974.

Australian Parliament House of Representatives Standing Committee on Industry, Science and Technology. "Finding a Balance: Towards Fair Trading in Australia." Canberra: The Committee, 1997.

Australian Stock Exchange. "Property Trusts, Equity Investors and Trustee Companies." Sydney: Australian Stock Exchange, 1989.

Bailey, Matthew. "Absorptive Capacity, International Business Knowledge Transfer and Local Adaptation: Establishing Discount Department Stores in Australia." *Australian Economic History Review* 57, no. 2 (2017): 194–216.

———. "'Ill-Natured Cartels of Anonymous Spite and Abuse': The Rise and Decline of Valentine's Day in Nineteenth-century Australia." In *The Popular Culture of Romantic Love in Australia*, edited by Hsu-Ming Teo, 65–90. North Melbourne: Australian Scholarly Publishing, 2017.

———. "Inside Suburban 'Persian Bazaars': The Reception of Regional Shopping Centres in Sydney during the 1960s." In *Consumer Australia: Historical and Contemporary Perspectives*, edited by Robert Crawford, Kim Humphery and Judy Smart, 119–33. Newcastle-upon-Tyne: Cambridge Scholars Press, 2010.

———. "Marketing to the Big Middle: Establishing Australian Discount Department Stores." *Journal of Historical Research in Marketing* 8, no. 3 (2016): 416–33.

———. "Power, Politics and Payments in Pot Plants: Shopping Centre Development in Bankstown 1955 – 2005." *Melbourne Historical Journal* 33, no. 1 (2005): 13–24.

———. "Retailing and the Home in 1960s Sydney." *History Australia* 11, no. 1 (2014): 59–81.

———. "Shopping for Entertainment: Malls and Multiplexes in Sydney, Australia." *Urban History* 42, no. 2 (2015): 309–29.

———. "Urban Disruption, Suburbanization and Retail Innovation: Establishing Shopping Centres in Australia." *Urban History* (forthcoming).

Baker, E., N. Coffee and G. Hugo. "Australia: State of the Environment." In *Second Technical Paper Series (Human Settlements), Series 2*. Canberra: Department of the Environment and Heritage, 2000.

Baker, Geoffrey, and Bruno Funaro. *Shopping Centers: Design and Operation*. New York: Reinhold, 1951.

Baker, Robert G. V. ""What Hours Should We Trade, 'Mr Superstore'?": A Review of the 1994 Australian Experience." *Urban Policy and Research* 13, no. 2 (1995): 97–105.

Barber, Stella M. *Your Store Myer: The Story of Australia's Leading Department Store.* Woolloomooloo, NSW: Focus, 2008.

Barrett, Lindsay. "Roselands or Everything under One Roof." *UTS Review* 4, no. 2 (1998): 123–37.

Beech, Amy, Rosetta Dollman, Richard Finlay and Gianni La Cava. "The Distribution of Household Spending in Australia." Bulletin (Reserve Bank of Australia), March 2014, 13–22.

Beed, Terrence W. "The Growth of Suburban Retailing in Sydney: A Preliminary Study of Some Factors Affecting the Form and Function of Suburban Shopping Centres." PhD, University of Sydney, 1964.

Benjamin, Walter. "The Arcades Project." In *The Blackwell City Reader*, edited by Gary Bridge and Sophie Watson, 119–25. Chichester, West Sussex: Wiley-Blackwell, 2010.

Betts, G. J. *The Birth of Target Australia: A Memoir.* North Geelong, Vic.: Geoff Betts, 2010.

Blackwell, R. D., and W. Talarzyk. "Life-style Retailing: Competitive Strategies for the 1980s." *Journal of Retailing* 59, no. 4 (1983): 7–27.

Bloch, Peter H., Nancy M. Ridgway and Scott A. Dawson. "The Shopping Mall as Consumer Habitat." *Journal of Retailing* 70, no. 1 (1994): 23–42.

BOMA National Council of Shopping Centres. *Directory of Australian Shopping Centres.* Armadale Vic.: Brian Zouch, 1980.

BOMA, NSW Division. *Shopping Centre Directory NSW & ACT.* Sydney: BOMA, 1995.

BOMA, Queensland Division. *Directory of Shopping Centres, Queensland.* Brisbane: BOMA, 1995.

BOMA, South Australian Division. *Directory of Shopping Centres, South Australia.* Adelaide: BOMA, 1995.

BOMA, Victorian Division. *Directory of Shopping Centres, Victoria.* Melbourne: BOMA, 1995.

BOMA, Western Australian Division. *Directory of Shopping Centres, Western Australia.* Perth: BOMA, 1995.

Bosisto, Brian. "Marion Shopping Centre." State Library of South Australia, PRG 1418/ F-26, 1966.

Bowlby, S. R. "Planning for Women to Shop in Postwar Britain." *Environment and Planning D* 2, no. 2 (1984): 179–99.

Bradbrook, Adrian J., and Clyde E. Croft. *Commercial Tenancy Law in Australia.* 1st edn. North Ryde, NSW: Butterworths, 1990.

———. *Commercial Tenancy Law in Australia.* 2nd edn. North Ryde, NSW: Butterworths, 1997.

Brash, Nicholas. *The Model Store 1885 – 1985.* Adelaide: Griffin Press, 1985.

Brill, Michael. "Transformation, Nostalgia and Illusion in Public Life and Public Space." In *Public Places and Spaces*, edited by Irwin Altman and Erwin H. Zube, 7–30. New York: Plenham Press, 1989.

Brown-May, Andrew. *Melbourne Street Life: The Itinerary of Our Days.* Kew, Vic.: Australian Scholarly Publishing, 1998.

Bryan, Harvey, and Susan Stuebing. "Natural Light and the Urban Environment." In *Public Streets for Public Use*, edited by Anne Vernez Moudon, 299–309. New York: Columbia University Press, 1991.

Burnett, D.W. *Shopping Centre Management: The Shopping Centre Lease.* Sydney: Building Owners & Managers Association of Australia, 1981.

Burns, Wilfred. *British Shopping Centres: New Trends in Layout and Distribution.* London: Hill, 1959.

Burrows, C. Geoffrey. "The Practical Design and Construction of the Quadrant Mall, Launceston." *Memo* 35 (August 1979): 29.

Cameron, Neil. "Pitfalls for Purchasers under the New Retail Leases Act." *Law Society Journal* 33, no. 5 (1995): 62–3.

Cardew, Richard. "Retailing and Office Development in Sydney." In *Why Cities Change Updated: Urban Development and Economic Change in the Late 1980s,* edited by J. V. Langdale, D. C. Rich and R. V. Cardew, 34–55. Gladesville, NSW: Geographical Society of New South Wales, 1989.

Cardew, Richard V., and Peter L. Simons. "Retailing in Sydney." In *Why Cities Change: Urban Development and Economic Change in Sydney,* edited by R.V. Cardew, J. V. Langdale and D. C. Rich, 151–79. Sydney: George Allen & Unwin, 1982.

Carkagis, Peter. *The Law of Retail Leasing in New South Wales.* St Leonards, NSW: Prospect, 1997.

Carr, Stephen, Mark Francis, Leanne G. Rivlin and Andrew M. Stone. *Public Space.* Cambridge: Cambridge University Press, 1992.

Cassady, Ralph Jr, and W. K. Bowden. "Shifting Retail Trade within the Los Angeles Metropolitan Market." *Journal of Marketing* 8, no. 4 (1944): 398–404.

Chandler, A. D. *Scale and Scope: The Dynamics of Industrial Capitalism.* Cambridge, MA: Belknap Press, 1990.

Christensen, C. M., and R. S. Tedlow. "Patterns of Disruption in Retailing." *Harvard Business Review* 78, no. 1 (2000): 42–5.

Clarke, Nigel. "An Inquiry into Commercial Tenancy Agreements: Report to the Minister for Economic Development and Technology, the Honourable M. J. Bryce." Perth: Government Printer, 1984.

Clausen, Meredith L. "Northgate Regional Shopping Center – Paradigm from the Provinces." *Journal of the Society of Architectural Historians* 43, no. 2 (May 1984): 153–61.

Cohen, Lizabeth. *A Consumers' Republic: The Politics of Mass Consumption in Postwar America.* New York: Vintage, 2003.

———. "From Town Center to Shopping Center: The Reconfiguration of Community Marketplaces in Postwar America." *American Historical Review* 101, no. 4 (1996): 1050–81.

Cohen, Yehoshua S. *Diffusion of an Innovation in an Urban System: The Spread of Planned Regional Shopping Centers in the United States 1949–1968.* Chicago: Department of Geography, University of Chicago, 1972.

Collins, Alan, Chris Hand and Andrew Ryder. "The Lure of the Multiplex? The Interplay of Time, Distance, and Cinema Attendance." *Environment and Planning A* 37, no. 3 (2005): 483–501.

Collins, Diane. *Hollywood Down Under: Australians at the Movies: 1896 to the Present Day.* North Ryde, NSW: Angus & Robertson, 1987.

Connell, R.W., and T. H. Irving. *Class Structure in Australian History: Poverty and Progress.* Melbourne: Longman Cheshire, 1992.

Coote, Antony. "President's Report for the Year 1988–1989." Sydney: Retail Traders' Association of New South Wales, 1989.

Crawford, Margaret. "The World in a Shopping Mall." In *Variations on a Theme Park: The New American City and the End of Public Space*, edited by Michael Sorkin, 3–30. New York: Hill & Wang, 1992.

Crosby, Neil. "An Evaluation of the Policy Implications for the UK of the Approach to Small Business Tenant Legislation in Australia." Reading: University of Reading, 2006.

Cumberland County Council. "The Effects of Urban Decentralisation on the City & Suburban Business Centres." Sydney: Cumberland County Council, 1958.

Cunningham, John. *Hungarian Cinema: From Coffee House to Multiplex.* London and New York: Wallflower, 2004.

Cupers, Kenny. "Shopping à l'américaine." In *Shopping Towns Europe: Commercial Collectivity and the Architecture of the Shopping Centre, 1945–1975*, edited by Janina Gosseye and Tom Avermaete, 25–37. London and New York: Bloomsbury Academic, 2017.

Daly, Maurice T. "Finance, the Capital Market and Sydney's Development." In *Why Cities Change Updated: Urban Development and Economic Change in Sydney*, edited by J. V. Langdale, D. C. Rich and R. V. Cardew, 48–53. Sydney: George Allen & Unwin, 1982.

Davidson, Jim, and Peter Spearritt. *Holiday Business: Tourism in Australia since 1870.* Carlton South, Vic.: Melbourne University Press, 2000.

Davis, Dorothy. *A History of Shopping.* London: Routledge & Kegan Paul, 1966.

Davison, Graeme. *Car Wars: How the Car Won Our Hearts and Conquered Our Cities.* Crows Nest, NSW: Allen & Unwin, 2004.

———. "From the Market to the Mall: A Short History of Shopping in Melbourne: Background Report, Victorian Retail Policy Review." Melbourne: Department of Planning and Community Development, 2006.

———. "The Great Australian Sprawl." *Historic Environment* 13, no. 1 (1997): 10–17.

———. *The Rise and Fall of Marvellous Melbourne.* Carlton, Vic.: Melbourne University Press, 1978.

Dawson, John A. *Shopping Centre Development.* London and New York: Longman, 1983.

Dawson, J. A., and I. David Murray. "Aspects of the Impact of Karrinyup Shopping Centre, Western Australia." Perth: Department of Geography, University of Western Australia, 1973.

De Grazia, Victoria. *Irresistible Empire: America's Advance through Twentieth-century Europe.* Cambridge, MA: Belknap Press, 2005.

Dingle, Tony. "'Gloria Soame': The Spread of Suburbia in Post-war Australia." In *Changing Suburbs: Foundation, Form and Function*, edited by Richard Harris and Peter J. Larkham, 187–201. London: E. & F.N. Spon, 1999.

Downes, J., L. Williams, T. Calder and E. Dominish. "The Impact of the ABC's *War on Waste*." Sydney: Institute for Sustainable Futures, University of Technology Sydney, 2019.

Doyle, Barry. "Return of the Super Cinema." *History Today* 48, no. 2 (1998): 2–5.

Drew-Bear, Robert. *Mass Merchandising: Revolution & Evolution.* New York: Fairchild, 1970.

Eakin, Tim. "New Retail Leases Regime." *Law Society Journal* 32, no. 6 (1994): 63–66.

Ebury, Sue. *The Many Lives of Kenneth Myer.* Carlton, Vic.: Miegunyah Press, 2008.

Edwards, Paul. "Reimagining the Shopping Mall: European Invention of the 'American' Consumer Space." *US Studies Online*, 7 (2005): n.p.

Ellmoos, Laila. "Queen Victoria Building." *Dictionary of Sydney.* Sydney: Dictionary of Sydney Trust, 2008.

Elvins, Sarah. "History of the Department Store." In *The Routledge Companion to the History of Retailing*, edited by Jon Stobart and Vicki Howard, 136–53. London and New York: Routledge, 2019.

Ewing, John S. "Marketing in Australia." *Journal of Marketing* 26, no. 2 (April 1962): 54–8.

Farrell, J. J. *One Nation under Goods: Malls and the Seduction of American Shopping.* Washington, DC: Smithsonian Institution, 2003.

Fisher, P. M. J. "Assessing Economic Impact in the Australian Retail Industry: Some Extra Spatial Considerations, an Examination of the Institutional Setting for the Introduction of New Technology." In *Assessing the Economic Impact of Retail Centres: Issues, Methods and Implications for Government Policy*, edited by R. Stimson and R. Sanderson, 45–70. Canberra: Australian Institute of Urban Studies, 1985.

Fitzgerald, Tony. "Report of a Commission of Inquiry Pursuant to Orders in Council." Brisbane: Government Printer, 1989.

Flannigan, Nigel. "Life for Traditional Shopping Streets: Avoiding the 'Quick-Fix' Solution." *Landscape Australia* 11, no. 3 (1989): 283–94.

Fleming, Grant, David Merrett and Simon Ville. *The Big End of Town: Big Business and Corporate Leadership in Twentieth-century Australia.* Cambridge: Cambridge University Press, 2004.

Forster, Clive. *Australian Cities: Continuity and Change.* 3rd edn. Melbourne: Oxford University Press, 2004.

Friedberg, Anne. "Les flâneurs du Mall (1): Cinema and the Postmodern Condition." *PMLA* 106, no. 3 (1991): 419–31.

Frost, Lionel, and Tony Dingle. "Sustaining Suburbia: An Historical Perspective on Australia's Growth." In *Australian Cities: Issues, Strategies and Policies for Urban Australia in the 1990s*, edited by Patrick Troy, 20–38. Cambridge: Cambridge University Press, 1995.

Frost, Lionel, and Seamus O'Hanlon. "Urban History and the Future of Australian Cities." *Australian Economic History Review* 49, no. 1 (March 2009): 1–18.

Game, Ann, and Rosemary Pringle. *Gender at Work.* Sydney: George Allen & Unwin, 1983.

Gare, Shelley. "The Fast Food Phenomenon: Let Them Eat Hamburgers." *Cleo*, March 1977: 19–21.

Geist, Johann Friedrich. *Arcades: The History of a Building Type.* Cambridge, MA: MIT Press, 1983.

Gilbert, Alan D. "Cities and Suburbs." In *Australians from 1939*, edited by Ann Curthoys, A. W. Martin and Tim Rowse, 77–98. Sydney: Fairfax, Syme & Weldon Associates, 1987.

Gosseye, Janina. "The Janus-Faced Shopping Center: The Low Countries in Search of a Fitting Shopping Paradigm." *Journal of Urban History* 44, no. 5 (2018): 862–86.

Gosseye, Janina, and Tom Avermaete. "Shopping Towns Europe, 1945–1975." In *Shopping Towns Europe: Commercial Collectivity and the Architecture of the Shopping Centre, 1945–1975*, edited by Janina Gosseye and Tom Cupers, 1–24. London and New York: Bloomsbury Academic, 2017.

Gosseye, Janina, and Peter Vernon. "Shopping Towns Australia, 1957–67: From Reformist Figure of Collectivity to Profit-Driven Box of Gold." Paper presented at the Society of Architectural Historians, Australia and New Zealand, Melbourne, 2016.

Gruen, Victor. "The Sad Story of Shopping Centres." *Town and Country Planning* 46 (1978): 350–2.

Gruen, Victor, and Larry Smith. *Shopping Towns USA: The Planning of Shopping Centers.* New York: Reinhold, 1960.

Guàrdia, Manel, José Luis Oyón and Sergi Garriga. "Markets and Market Halls." In *The Routledge Companion to the History of Retailing*, edited by Jon Stobart and Vicki Howard, 101–18. London and New York: Routledge, 2019.

Guernsey, John. "Suburban Branches." *Department Store Economist* (1951): 42-42, 78, 111.

Guy, Clifford. *The Retail Development Process: Location, Property and Planning.* London and New York: Routledge, 1994.

———. "Whatever Happened to Regional Shopping Centres?" *Geography* 79, no. 4 (1994): 293–312.

Hall, Alicia. "Trends in Home Ownership in Australia: A Quick Guide." Parliamentary Library Research Paper. Canberra: Parliament of Australia, 2017.

Hardwick, M. Jeffrey. *Mall Maker: Victor Gruen, Architect of an American Dream.* Philadelphia: University of Pennsylvania Press, 2004.

Hargreaves, Kaye. *Women at Work.* Ringwood, Vic.: Penguin, 1982.

Harris, D. D., and B. Y. Harper. *Urbs and Suburbs.* Melbourne: Cheshire, 1971.

Harrison, Molly. *People and Shopping: A Social Background.* London: E. Benn; Totowa, NJ: Rowman & Littlefield, 1975.

Haselhurst, Howard. "Leasing Newtown Mall." In *BOMA National Council of Shopping Centers, Proceedings of Shopping Centre Management Workshop: Managing for a Profit*, 9–10 March 1979.

Hayden, Delores. *Building Suburbia: Green Fields and Urban Growth, 1820–2000.* New York: Vintage, 2003.

Heino, Brett. "Trading Hours Deregulation in Tasmania and Western Australia: Large Retailer Dominance and Changing Models of Development." *Labour & Industry* 27, no. 2 (2017): 95–112.

Henderson-Smith, Barbara. "From Booth to Shop to Shopping Mall: Continuities in Consumer Spaces from 1650 to 2000." PhD, Griffith University, 2000.

Hough, David John. *Boans for Service: The Story of a Department Store 1895–1986.* Claremont, WA: Estate of F. T. Boan, 2009.

———. "From Clogs to Clogs in Three Generations: The Rise and Fall of Boans Ltd 1895–1986." PhD, University of Western Australia, 2012.

Howard, Vicki. *From Main Street to Mall: The Rise and Fall of the American Department Store.* Philadelphia: University of Pennsylvania Press, 2015.

Howard, Vicki, and Jon Stobart. "Arcades, Shopping Centres, and Shopping Malls." In *The Routledge Companion to the History of Retailing*, edited by Jon Stobart and Vicki Howard, 197–215. London and New York: Routledge, 2019.

Howells, A. "Stawell's Pedestrian Mall." *Memo* 31 (August/October 1978): 32–34.

Hoyt, Homer. "The Current Trend in New Shopping Centres: Four Different Types." *Urban Land* 12 (April 1953): 1–15.

———. *One Hundred Years of Land Values in Chicago: The Relationship of the Growth of Chicago to the Rise in Its Land Values, 1830–1933.* Chicago: University of Chicago Press, 1933.

Hubbard, Phil. "Fear and Loathing at the Multiplex: Everyday Anxiety in the Post-Industrial City." *Capital & Class* 27, no. 2 (2003): 51–75.

Hudson, W. J. "1951–72." In *A New History of Australia*, edited by F. K. Crowley, 504–51. Melbourne: William Heinemann, 1977.

Humphery, Kim. *Shelf Life: Supermarkets and the Changing Cultures of Consumption.* Cambridge and Melbourne: Cambridge University Press, 1998.

Hutchings, Alan, and Christine Garnaut. "The Private Development Company and the Building of Planned Communities in Post-War South Australia: Reid Murray Developments, Realty Development Corporation and Their Successors." *Journal of the Historical Society of South Australia* 40 (2012): 96–116.

Hutchings, Karen. "The Battle for Consumer Power: Post-War Women and Advertising." *Journal of Australian Studies* 20, nos. 50–1 (1996): 66–77.

Hutson, Andrew. "'I Dream of Jeannie?' The American Origins of the Chadstone Shopping Centre." *Fabrications* 9, no. 1 (1999): 17–33.

Industrial Commission of New South Wales. "Management, Control and Operations of Chain Stores in New South Wales: Report of the Industrial Commission of New South Wales on the Reference from the Honourable the Minister for Labour and Industry, 7th July 1939." Sydney: Industrial Commission of New South Wales, 1939.

Jackson, Kenneth T. "All the World's a Mall: Reflections on the Social and Economic Consequences of the American Shopping Center." *American Historical Review* 101, no. 4 (1996): 1111–21.

Jackson, Peter. "Consumption and Identity: The Cultural Politics of Shopping." *European Planning Studies* 7, no. 1 (1999): 25–39.

JLW Research and Consultancy. "Examining Investment in Community Shopping Centres." Property Research Paper. Sydney: JLW Research and Consultancy, 1993.

Kemeny, Jim. "The South Australian Housing Trust: A Socioeconomic Case Study in Public Housing." *Australian Journal of Social Issues* 15, no. 2 (1980): 108–22.

Kiel, Geoffrey. "Retailing and Shopping Centre Development in Queensland – a Reassessment of the Issues." Business Paper no. 15. Brisbane: Department of Management, University of Queensland, 1979.

Kingston, Beverley. *Basket, Bag and Trolley: A History of Shopping in Australia.* Melbourne: Oxford University Press, 1994.

Kowinski, William Severini. *The Malling of America: An Inside Look at the Great Consumer Paradise.* New York: W. Morrow, 1985.

Kune, Gabriel A. *Nothing Is Impossible: The John Saunders Story.* Carlton North, Vic.: Scribe, 1999.

Lambert, Sue, and Ray Petridis. "Slow Progress: The Integration of Women into the Australian Labour Market." Working Paper no. 117. Perth: Economics Programme, Murdoch University, 1995.

Lancaster, William. *The Department Store: A Social History.* London: Leicester University Press, 1995.

Larcombe, Frederick Arthur. *Change and Challenge: A History of the Municipality of Canterbury, N.S.W.* Canterbury, NSW: Canterbury Municipal Council, 1979.

Lawrence, Joan, Brian Madden and Lesley Muir. *A Pictorial History of Canterbury Bankstown.* Alexandria, NSW: Kingsclear, 1999.

Liebs, Chester H. *Main Street to Miracle Mile: American Roadside Architecture.* 2nd edn. Baltimore, MD: Johns Hopkins University Press, 1995.

Longstreth, Richard. *City Center to Regional Mall Architecture, the Automobile, and Retailing in Los Angeles, 1920–1950.* Cambridge, MA: MIT Press, 1997.

Mackay, Hugh. *Reinventing Australia: The Mind and Mood of Australia in the 90s.* Pymble, NSW: Angus & Robertson, 1993.

MacPherson, Kerrie L. "Introduction: Asia's Universal Providers." In *Asian Department Stores,* edited by Kerrie L. MacPherson, 1–32. Richmond: Curzon Press, 1998.

Magretta, J. "Why Business Models Matter." *Harvard Business Review* 80, no. 5 (2002): 86–92.

Malherek, Joseph. "Victor Gruen's Retail Therapy: Exiled Jewish Communities and the Invention of the American Shopping Mall as a Postwar Ideal." *Leo Baeck Institute Year Book* 61, no. 1 (2016): 219–32.

Maltby, Richard. *Hollywood Cinema.* Malden, MA: Blackwell, 2003.

Margetts, Dee. "National Competition Policy and the Retail Sector." *Journal of Australian Political Economy* 67 (2011): 68–94.

Margo, Jill. *Frank Lowy: Pushing the Limits.* Pymble, NSW: HarperCollins, 2001.

Marsden, Susan. "The South Australian Housing Trust, Elizabeth and Twentieth Century Heritage." *Journal of the Historical Society of South Australia* 28 (2000): 49–61.

McCalman, Janet. "Private Life in the Garden Suburbs between the Wars or 'What Will People Say?'" In *The Cream Brick Frontier: Histories of Australian Suburbia*, edited by Graeme Davison, Tony Dingle and Seamus O'Hanlon, 51–61. Clayton, Vic.: Monash Publications in History, 1995.

McGregor, Craig. *Class in Australia.* Ringwood, Vic.: Penguin Australia, 1997.

McIntosh, Angus. *Towns and Cities: Competing for Survival.* London and New York: E. & F. N. Spon, 1997.

McKeever, J. Ross. "Technical Bulletin No. 20, Shopping Centers: Planning Principles and Tested Policies Based on Experience from the Community Builders Council." In *Design for Modern Merchandising: Stores, Shopping Centers, Showrooms*, 145–67. New York: Architectural Record, 1954.

McKeever, J. Ross, Frank H. Spink, Nathaniel M. Griffin and Urban Land Institute (US), Commercial and Office Development Council, Executive Group. *Shopping Center Development Handbook.* Washington, DC: Urban Land Institute, 1977.

McLaughlin, Judith. *Nothing over Half a Crown: A Personal History of the Founder of the G. J. Coles Stores.* Main Ridge, Vic.: Loch Haven, 1991.

McLeod, Amanda. *Abundance: Buying and Selling in Postwar Australia.* North Melbourne, Vic.: Australian Scholarly Publishing, 2007.

Mennel, Timothy. "Victor Gruen and the Construction of Cold War Utopias." *Journal of Planning History* 3, no. 2 (2004): 116–50.

Merrett, David T. "The Making of Australia's Supermarket Duopoly, 1958–2000." *Australian Economic History Review* (2020, forthcoming).

Miller, Dale. "Retailing in Australia and New Zealand." In *The Routledge Companion to the History of Retailing*, edited by Jon Stobart and Vicki Howard, 413–28. London and New York: Routledge, 2019.

Miller, Michael. *The Bon Marché: Bourgeois Culture and the Department Store, 1869–1920.* Princeton: Princeton University Press, 1981.

Milliken, Robert. "The Lost Picture Show." *National Times*, 6–12 January 1984, 35.

Modern Merchandising Methods. *Australian Shopping Centres.* Australia: Modern Merchandising Methods, 1965.

———. *Australian Shopping Centres.* Australia: Modern Merchandising Methods, 1971.

Monheim, Rolf. "Pedestrianization in German Towns: A Process of Continual Development." *Built Environment* 12, nos. 1–2 (1986): 30–43.

Moore, Keith. "Bodgies, Widgies and Moral Panic in Australia 1955–1959." In *Social Change in the 21st Century*, edited by C. Bailey, D. Cabrera and L. Buys. Brisbane: Centre for Social Change Research, Queensland University of Technology, 2004.

Moss, Alan. "Report of the 2006/07 Review of the Shop Trading Act 1977, South Australia." Keswick, SA: SafeWork SA: 2006.

Murphy, Mary. *Challenges of Change: The Lend Lease Story.* Sydney: Lend Lease Group of Companies, 1984.

Murray, Andrew. "A Faster Taste: Red Rooster and the Architecture of Australian Fast Food." *Historic Environment* 30, no. 2 (2018): 100–11.

Murray, James. *The Woolworths Way: A Great Australian Success Story 1924–1999.* Edgecliff, NSW: Woolworths, 1999.

Naftaly, Gerald E. *Northland Mall.* Charleston, SC: Arcadia, 2016.

O'Hanlon, Seamus. "Cities, Suburbs and Communities." In *Australia's History: Themes and Debates,* edited by Martyn Lyons and Penny Russell, 172–89. Sydney: University of New South Wales Press, 2005.

———. "Modernism and Prefabrication in Postwar Melbourne." *Journal of Australian Studies* 22, no. 57 (1998): 108–18.

O'Neill, Sally. "Gibson, William (1842–1918)." *Australian Dictionary of Biography.* Melbourne: Melbourne University Press, 1981.

Orski, C. Kenneth. "Practical Experience." In *Streets for People,* 41–48. Paris: OECD, 1974.

Ostrow, Ruth. *The New Boy Network: Taking over Corporate Australia.* Richmond, Vic.: Heinemann, 1987.

Paine, Campbell, and Glenda Dennler. "Review of Lease for Commercial Premises Highlighting Important Features & Problem Areas & Reviewing the Law." In *Commercial Leases: Papers Delivered at a Masterclass, Business Law Education Centre.* Melbourne: Business Law Education Centre, 1989.

Panelas, Tom. "Adolescents and Video Games: Consumption of Leisure and the Social Construction of the Peer Group." *Youth & Society,* 15 (1983): 51–65.

Pasdermadjian, Hrant. *The Department Store: Its Origins, Evolution, and Economics.* London: Newman, 1954.

Patterson, Carla Maree, and Judi A. Porter. "Are We Contributing to the Development of a Generation Who Cannot Prepare Food?" *Journal of the Home Economics Institute of Australia* 1, no. 4 (1994): 37–42.

Patterson, Patrick Hyder. "The Supermarket as a Global Historical Development." In *The Routledge Companion to the History of Retailing,* edited by Jon Stobart and Vicki Howard, 154–79. London and New York: Routledge, 2019.

Paul, William. "The K-Mart Audience at the Movies." Film History 6, no. 4 (1994), 487–501.

Peel, Mark. *Good Times, Hard Times: The Past and the Future in Elizabeth.* Carlton, Vic.: Melbourne University Press, 1995.

———. "Planning the Good City in Australia: Elizabeth as a New Town." *Urban Research Program Working Papers* 30 (1992): 1–60.

Phillips, Charles F. "The Chain Store in the United States and Canada." *American Economic Review* 27, no. 1 (1937): 87–95.

Powys, R. O. "Economic Impact Statements: A Market View." In *Assessing the Economic Impact of Retail Centres: Issues, Methods and Implications for Government Policy,* edited by R. Stimson and R. Sanderson, 71–6. Canberra: Australian Institute of Urban Studies, 1985.

Pratt, Bill. *My Safeway Story: Making It Happen.* Melbourne: Brolga, 2006.

Prerost, Sandra. "Technological Change and Women's Employment." In *Worth Her Salt: Women at Work in Australia,* edited by Margaret Bevege, Margaret James and Carmel Shute, 134–47. Sydney: Hale & Iremonger, 1982.

Price, Robin. "Extending Trading Hours – More Retail Jobs?" *International Journal of Employment* 13, no. 1 (2005): 133–56.

Probert, Belinda. *Working Life: Arguments about Work in Australian Society.* Melbourne, Vic.: McPhee Gribble, 1989.

Queensland Committee of Inquiry into Shopping Complex Leasing Practices. "Report of the Committee of Inquiry into Shopping Complex Leasing Practices." Brisbane: Department of Commerce and Industry, 1981.

Rayner, Jennifer. *Generation Less: How Australia Is Cheating the Young.* Carlton, Vic: Redback Quarterly, 2016.

Redstone, Louis G. *New Dimensions in Shopping Centers and Stores.* New York: McGraw-Hill, 1973.

Reekie, Gail. "Market Research and the Post-war Housewife." *Australian Feminist Studies* 14 (1991): 15–27.

———. *Temptations: Sex, Selling, and the Department Store.* St Leonards, NSW: Allen & Unwin, 1993.

Rivkin and Company. *Westfield Limited: A Company Review.* Sydney: Rivkin and Company, 1972.

Roberts, John. *Pedestrian Precincts in Britain.* London: Transport and Environment Studies, 1981.

Robertson, Kent A. "The Status of the Pedestrian Mall in American Downtowns." *Urban Affairs Quarterly* 6, no. 2 (1990): 250–73.

Rosewarne, S. "The Political Economy of Retailing into the Eighties: Part I." *Journal of Australian Political Economy* 15 (1983): 18–38.

Rowley, Laura. *On Target: How the World's Hottest Retailer Hit a Bull's-Eye.* New York and Chichester: Wiley, 2003.

Rubenstein, Harvey M. *Pedestrian Malls, Streetscapes, and Urban Spaces.* New York: Wiley, 1992.

Sammartino, André. "Retail." In *The Internationalisation Strategies of Small-Country Firms: The Australian Experience of Globalisation*, edited by Howard Dick and David Merrett, 175–94. Cheltenham: Edward Elgar, 2007.

Sammartino, André. "Shopkeepers of the World Unite: Uniqlo Heading to Australia." *The Conversation*, 10 October 2013.

Sammartino, André, and Frances Van Ruth. "The Westfield Group." In *The Internationalisation Strategies of Small-Country Firms: The Australian Experience of Globalisation*, edited by Howard Dick and David Merrett, 308–18. Cheltenham: Edward Elgar, 2007.

Sandercock, Leonie. "From Main Street to Fortress: The Future of Malls as Public Spaces – or – 'Shut up and Shop.'" *Just Policy* 9 (1997): 27–34.

Sax, David. "If You Build It…." *Canadian Business* 78, no. 8 (2005): 23–4.

Schmiechen, James, and Kenneth Carls. *The British Market Hall: A Social and Architectural History.* New Haven, CT: Yale University Press, 1999.

Schuyler, David. *A City Transformed: Redevelopment, Race, and Suburbanization in Lancaster, Pennsylvania, 1940–1980.* University Park: Pennsylvania State University Press, 2003.

Scott, N. Keith. *Shopping Centre Design.* London: Van Nostrand Rheinhold (International), 1989.

Scott, Peter. *The Property Masters: A History of the British Commercial Property Sector* London: Routledge, 1996.

Shaw, Gareth. "Evolution and Impact of Large-Scale Retailing in Britain." In *The Evolution of Retail Systems, c. 1800–1914*, edited by John Benson and Gareth Shaw, 135–65. London and New York: Leicester University Press, 1992.

———. "Large-Scale Retailing in Germany and the Development of New Retail Organisations." In *The Evolution of Retail Systems, c. 1800–1914*, edited by John

Benson and Gareth Shaw, 166–85. London and New York: Leicester University Press, 1992.

Simpson, William, and Charles O'Connell. "The Chatswood Town Centre." Sydney: Department of Environment and Planning, 1981.

Sloan, A. G. "Marion – a 'One-Stop' Shopping Centre." *Journal of Industry* 36, no. 4 (1968): 25–9.

Small Business Development Corporation. "Investigation into the Issue of Extended Retail Trading Hours." Brisbane: Queensland Small Business Development Corporation, 1981.

Smith, H. P. "Town Planning in Elizabeth, South Australia." *Architecture Today* January 1959: 16–23.

Smith, Paul E. *Shopping Centers: Planning and Management.* New York: National Retail Dry Goods Association, 1956.

Spearritt, Peter. "Cars for the People." In *Australians from 1939*, edited by Ann Curthoys, A. W. Martin and Tim Rowse, 119–32. Sydney: Fairfax, Syme & Weldon Associates, 1987.

———. "I Shop Therefore I Am." In *Suburban Dreaming: An Interdisciplinary Approach to Australian Cities*, edited by Louise C. Johnson, 129–40. Geelong, Vic.: Deakin University Press, 1994.

———. "Suburban Cathedrals: The Rise of the Drive-in Shopping Centre." In *The Cream Brick Frontier: Histories of Australian Suburbia*, edited by Graeme Davison, Tony Dingle and Seamus O'Hanlon, 88–107. Clayton, Vic.: Monash Publications in History, 1995.

———. *Sydney's Century: A History.* Sydney: University of New South Wales Press, 1999.

Spector, Robert. *Category Killers: The Retail Revolution and Its Impact on Consumer Culture.* Boston, MA: Harvard Business School Press, 2005.

Stimson, R. J. "Summary of Policy Issues." In *Assessing the Economic Impact of Retail Centres: Issues, Methods and Implications for Government Policy*, edited by R. Stimson and R. Sanderson, 1–6. Canberra: Australian Institute of Urban Studies, 1985.

Stobart, Jon. "Cathedrals of Consumption? Provincial Department Stores in England, c.1880–1930." *Enterprise & Society* 18, no. 4 (2017): 810–45.

———. *Spend, Spend, Spend: A History of Shopping.* Stroud: Tempus, 2008.

Strahan, Frank. "Watts, Ernest Alfred (1893–1979)." *Australian Dictionary of Biography.* Melbourne: Melbourne University Press, 2002.

Sullivan, Rodney. "Kern, Ronald Gerald (Ron) (1922–1976)." *Australian Dictionary of Biography.* Melbourne: Melbourne University Press, 2000.

Taksa, Lucy. "The Cultural Diffusion of Scientific Management: The United States and New South Wales." *Journal of Industrial Relations* 37, no. 3 (1995): 427–61.

Tarlo, H. "The Great Shop Lease Controversy." *University of Queensland Law Journal* 13 (1983–4): 7–27.

Taylor, Mary-Lynne. "Introductory Lecture – Sydney." In *Commercial Leases: Papers Delivered at a Masterclass, Business Law Education Centre.* Melbourne: Business Law Education Centre, 1989.

Tedlow, Richard S. "The Fourth Phase of Marketing: Marketing History and the Business World Today." In *The Rise and Fall of Mass Marketing*, edited by Richard S. Tedlow and Geoffrey G. Jones, 8–35. London and New York: Routledge, 1993.

Thomas, Mark. "The Service Sector." In *The Cambridge Economic History of Modern Britain, Volume II: Economic Maturity, 1860–1939*, edited by Roderick Floud and Paul Johnson, 99–132. Cambridge: Cambridge University Press, 2004.

Town & Country Planning Board. "Pedestrian Malls: A Discussion Paper." Melbourne: Town & Country Planning Board, 1977.

Trentmann, Frank. *Empire of Things: How We Became a World of Consumers, from the Fifteenth Century to the Twenty-First* New York: HarperCollins, 2017.

Troy, Patrick. "Introduction." In *Australian Cities: Issues, Strategies and Policies for Urban Australia in the 1990s*, edited by Patrick Troy, 1–18. Cambridge and Melbourne: Cambridge University Press, 1995.

Tulloh, J. K. "Australia's First Fully Air-conditioned Shopping Centre." *Journal of Industry* 31, no. 10 (1963): 77–82.

Vernon, Peter. "Shopping Towns Australia." *Fabrications: The Journal of the Society of Architectural Historians* 22, no. 1 (2012): 102–21.

Voyce, Malcolm. "The Privatisation of Public Property: The Development of a Shopping Mall in Sydney and Its Implications for Governance through Spatial Practices." *Urban Policy and Research* 21, no. 3 (2003): 249–62.

Walker, Robin, and Dave Roberts. *From Scarcity to Surfeit: A History of Food and Nutrition in New South Wales.* Kensington: New South Wales University Press, 1988.

Warner, Leigh. "The Evolution of Brisbane Retailing." Brisbane: Jones Lang LaSalle, 2013.

Watson, Peter. "Commercial Tenancies Legislation – the Practical Implications for Small Business." In *Law Society of Western Australia Leases and Tenancies Seminar.* Perth: Law Society of Western Australia, 1985.

Webb, Michael. *The City Square: A Historical Evolution.* London: Thames & Hudson, 1990.

Welch, Kenneth C. "Regional Shopping Centres." In *Design for Modern Merchandising: Stores, Shopping Centers, Showrooms*, 169–72. New York: Architectural Record, 1954.

Westfield Holdings Ltd. *The Westfield Story: The First 40 Years.* Sydney: Westfield Holdings, 2000.

White, G. S. "The Changing Nature of Planned Regional Shopping Centres in Sydney in the 1980s." Master Geoscience Thesis, Macquarie University, 1989.

White, Richard. *Inventing Australia: Images and Identity 1688–1980.* Sydney: Allen & Unwin, 1981.

———. *On Holidays: A History of Getting Away in Australia.* North Melbourne, Vic.: Pluto Press, 2005.

White, Rob, and Adam Sutton. "Social Planning for Mall Redevelopment: An Australian Case-Study." *Local Environment* 6, no. 1 (2001): 65–80.

Whitwell, Greg. *Making the Market: The Rise of Consumer Society.* Fitzroy, Vic.: McPhee Gribble, 1989.

Whyte, William H. *City.* New York: Doubleday, 1988.

Williams, Philip L. *What Is the Problem of Small Business?* Melbourne: Committee for Economic Development of Australia, 1984.

Wolfers, Howard. "The Big Stores between the Wars." In *Twentieth Century Sydney: Studies in Urban and Social History*, edited by Jill Roe, 18–33. Sydney: Hale & Iremonger, 1980.

Wotherspoon, Gary. *City of the Plain: History of a Gay Sub-Culture.* Sydney: Hale & Iremonger, 1991.

Zukin, Sharon. *Landscapes of Power: From Detroit to Disney World.* Berkeley: University of California Press, 1991.

———. "Urban Lifestyles: Diversity and Standardisation in Spaces of Consumption." *Urban Studies* 35, nos. 5–6 (1998): 825–39.

Index

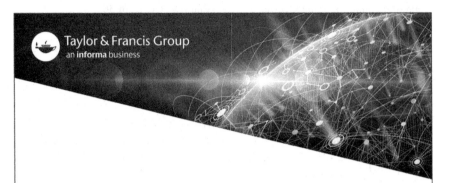

Printed in the United States
by Baker & Taylor Publisher Services